IMAGES
of America

HARTSVILLE AND TROUSDALE COUNTY

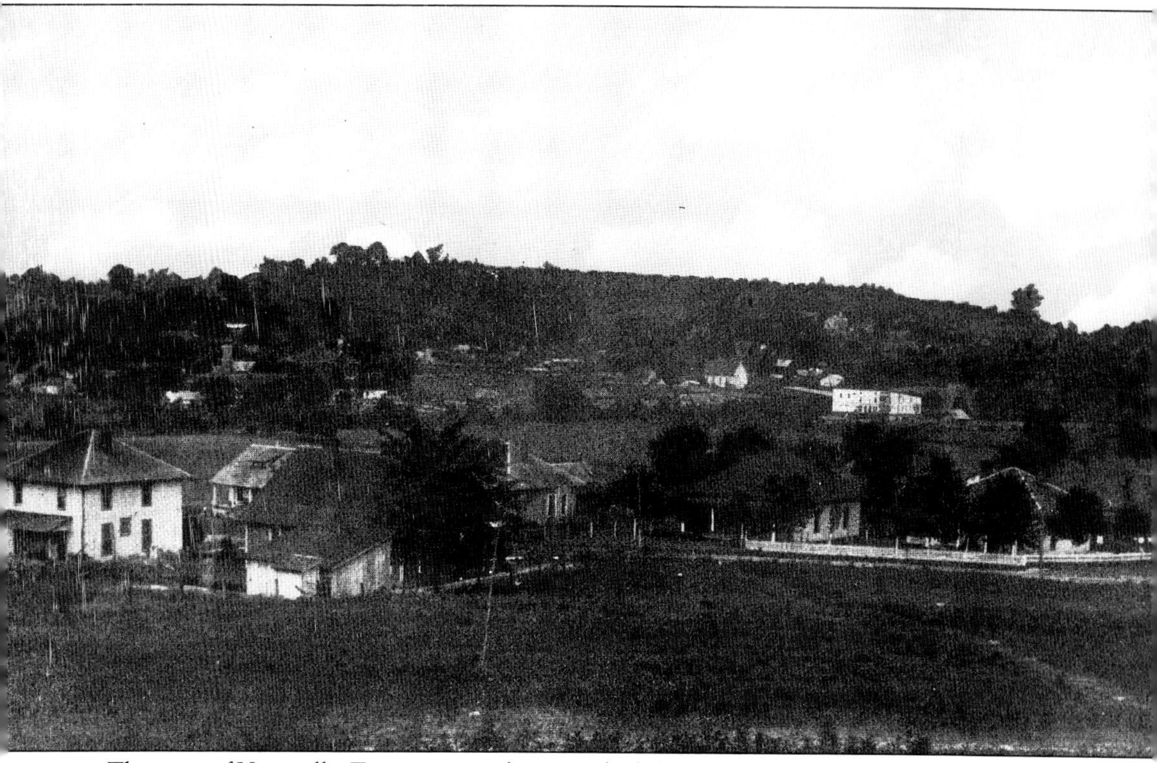

This view of Hartsville, Tennessee, made across the hill where the high school stands, shows how small and rural the town is. Although this view was made around 1910, it is still representative of the little-changed area of today.

IMAGES
of America

HARTSVILLE AND TROUSDALE COUNTY

John L. Oliver Jr. and the
Trousdale County Historical Society

ARCADIA
PUBLISHING

ISBN 978-0-7385-5418-1

Published by Arcadia Publishing
Charleston, South Carolina

Printed in the United States of America

Library of Congress Catalog Card Number: Applied for

For all general information contact Arcadia Publishing at:
Telephone 843-853-2070
Fax 843-853-0044
E-mail sales@arcadiapublishing.com
For customer service and orders:
Toll-Free 1-888-313-2665

Visit us on the Internet at www.arcadiapublishing.com

On the front cover: Tobacco workers pause while working on the Providence community farm of Hubert Ward.

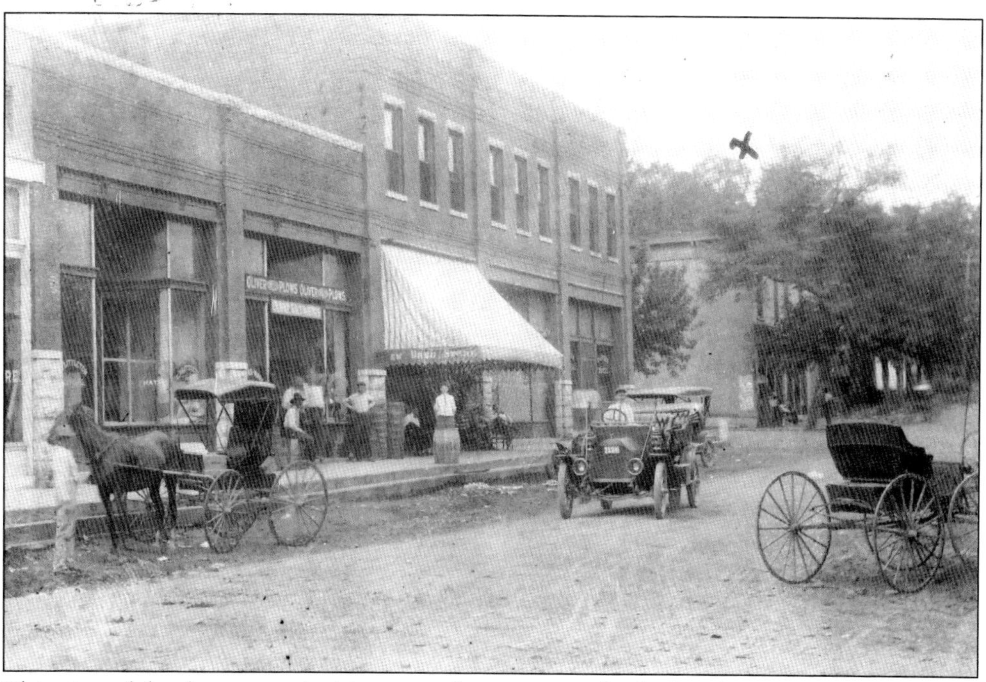

This view of the downtown, looking west, shows a two-cylinder Brush, one of Hartsville's first cars. Buggies are still very much in evidence. When automobiles entered town, the people standing around would make bets on whether or not the vehicles could make it over Jail Hill, to the rear of the photograph.

Contents

Introduction 7

1. Hartsville 9

2. The Community 27

3. Travel 37

4. The River 49

5. Churches and Schools 65

6. Homes 85

7. People 99

8. Farming and Tobacco 115

Acknowledgments 128

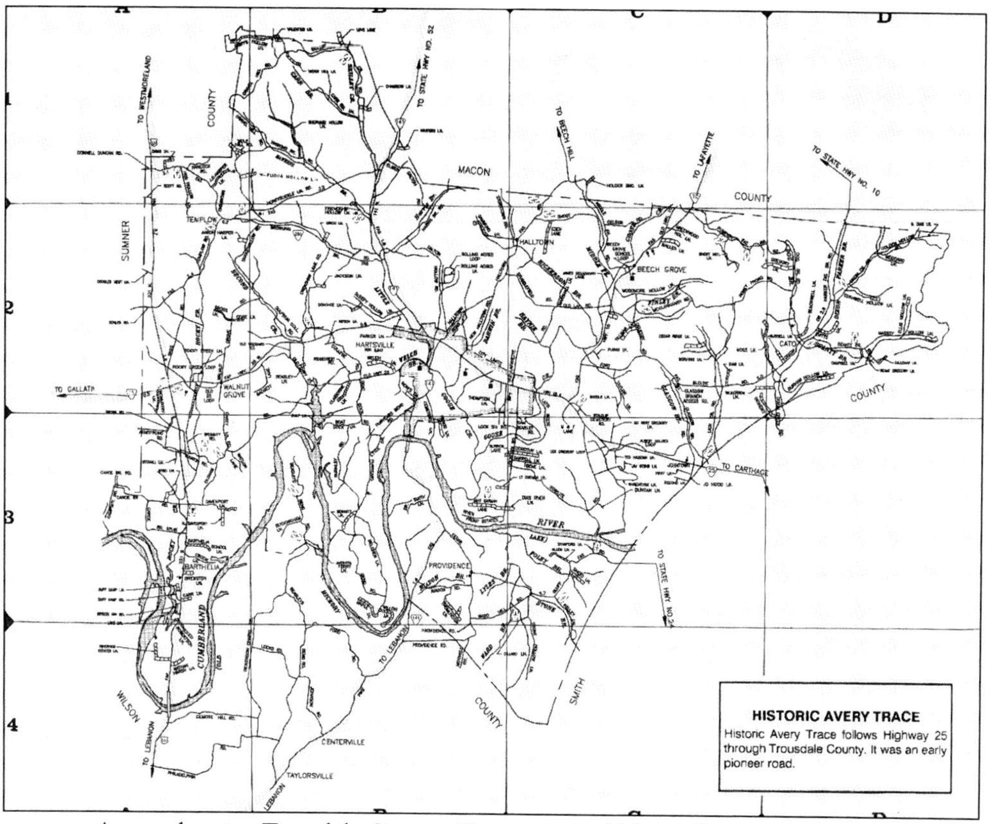

A map showing Trousdale County, Tennessee; and Hartsville, its county seat.

INTRODUCTION

Weighing in at a mere 106 square miles, Trousdale County is the smallest of Tennessee's ninety-five counties. Despite its small size, it has managed to make a dent in the state's history and has achieved a fair share of superlatives. Rolling hills, fertile bottom land, spring fed "hollers," and the flowing Cumberland River make the area one of the most scenic in the state. The human element is no less distinguished, with the county contributing to the state's political, social, and business arenas. It has been said, "If you once wear out a pair of shoes in Trousdale County, you will stay forever." The statement only hints at the area's charm and allure from the past to the present.

The first humans to visit the forested hills of Trousdale County were Native Americans attracted by plentiful game. One group of these, the mound builders, fished the waters of the Cumberland River, and traveled trails established over millennia by elk, deer, and woodland buffalo.

After the mound builders' arrival, the area became a hunting ground shared by the Shawnee and Cherokee tribes. Later, the Cherokee and Creek Indians resisted the white man's invasion. Those early white explorers, called "long hunters," ranged the hills and valleys and realized their potential as farmland. The long hunters soon brought their families and began to fell trees. Cabins were built, made of centuries-old yellow poplar, cedar, and even walnut and cherry. The Avery Trace, also called the "Immigrant Trail," passed through the county. Some of these early settlers were title holders to land grants given for service in the War for American Independence. At the time, the area was considered to be part of North Carolina. This changed when Tennessee became the sixteenth state in 1796. By then, despite the occasional threat of Indian raids, this area was homesteaded by a great many families, some of whose descendants are residents of the county even today.

The county did not exist as a separate entity in 1796. The areas encompassed by its boundaries today were then parts of Sumner County, and later Wilson, Macon, and Smith Counties. While Trousdale was not officially created until 1870, Hartsville had its start well before that. First known as "Donoho's Mill" in 1797 and later called "Damascus," it became "Hartsville" when the James Hart family donated several plots of land to the community for a cemetery, a school, and a church. Previous settlement had largely been on the east side of Little Goose Creek. The Harts owned land on the west side. Their generous gifts and the subsequent selling of lots for houses and businesses led to the town shifting to the west side and taking on the name of the Harts. Thus it was that in 1807, "Hartsville" was assigned a post office.

The Hart family operated a ferry on the Cumberland River, and closer to town they had a race track. Harts' Race Track attracted crowds from across the new state, one of whom was Andrew Jackson. Jackson raced his own horses there and was a frequent visitor to several homes. In 1828 a ball was held there in his honor, at Capt. Duffy's. By 1830 Hartsville had thirty families, four stores, two taverns, and several blacksmith shops. A Masonic Lodge was organized in 1845. In

1851 the Enon Baptist Association established a college between Hartsville and Gallatin in the Payne's Store area. It would operate until 1882.

The growing town began to press for the creation of a new county as early as 1840. The surrounding communities were using Hartsville as a trade town. Its central location made it more convenient than the county seats in Gallatin, Lafayette, Carthage, and Lebanon. The Civil War put a halt to these plans as first Confederate troops, and later Union forces entered the town. While under Union occupation, Confederate Colonel John Hunt Morgan surprised the Union Garrison with an early morning attack on December 7, 1862. The resulting battle has been called the most successful cavalry raid of the war, as Morgan quickly maneuvered the Union forces into surrender. The battle made front page news across the nation.

The war and its aftermath were a blow to the area's cotton economy. Within a few years, however, it began to revive. Farmers turned to other crops, among them tobacco. With time, efforts began again to create a new county and in 1870 the state legislature pulled together parts of Sumner, Macon, Smith, and Wilson Counties to create Trousdale County, named for former governor William Trousdale. Voters quickly chose Hartsville as the county seat. By 1877 a county jail and courthouse had been built.

By 1886, six dry goods stores, three groceries, a drug store, a bank, a hardware store, a livery stable, a newspaper, two saddle and harness makers, an undertaker, a grist mill, and a saw mill all were flourishing and a rail line was planned. By the turn of the century, the town had suffered several disastrous fires. The present courthouse, built in 1905, is the fourth one, the previous three burning in fires. Floods in 1847 and 1883 had also been devastating to crops and businesses. Later floods in 1926 and 1946 would cause greater damage.

After the turn of the century, tobacco became a major influence in the county when a tobacco auction house was built and a loose leaf market established. Two tobacco companies went into business.

In the next few years, the county survived the rigors of World War I and the deprivations of the Great Depression. Farming continued to be the chief means of livelihood and life moved at a leisurely pace until the Second World War brought the upheaval of sons, brothers, and neighbors going off to war. When the war began middle Tennessee found itself the site of vast U.S. Army maneuvers, Trousdale County included.

After the war, and the return of the country's native sons, the county saw a facelift with the construction of new bridges, the paving of roads, new schools, a hospital, industry, a new jail, and a new community center. Hartsville became host to the Tobacco Bowl, one of the state's first high school bowl games. Even so, the population of the county stayed between five and six thousand for the next two decades.

The biggest event in the county came in the 1970s when the Tennessee Valley Authority chose the county as its site for a four-reactor nuclear plant—planned to be the world's largest. Though partly built, changes in national energy needs forced cancellation of the plant. The county recovered from the experience and the next decade saw slow, steady growth. Subdivisions were developed and a number of small factories built. Tobacco was still the major cash crop of the county. The downtown retail area of Hartsville lost out to the lure of shopping malls in other towns, yet the county and the town have a strong chamber of commerce that has begun to tap into the well of tourism with an eye to the future.

One

Hartsville

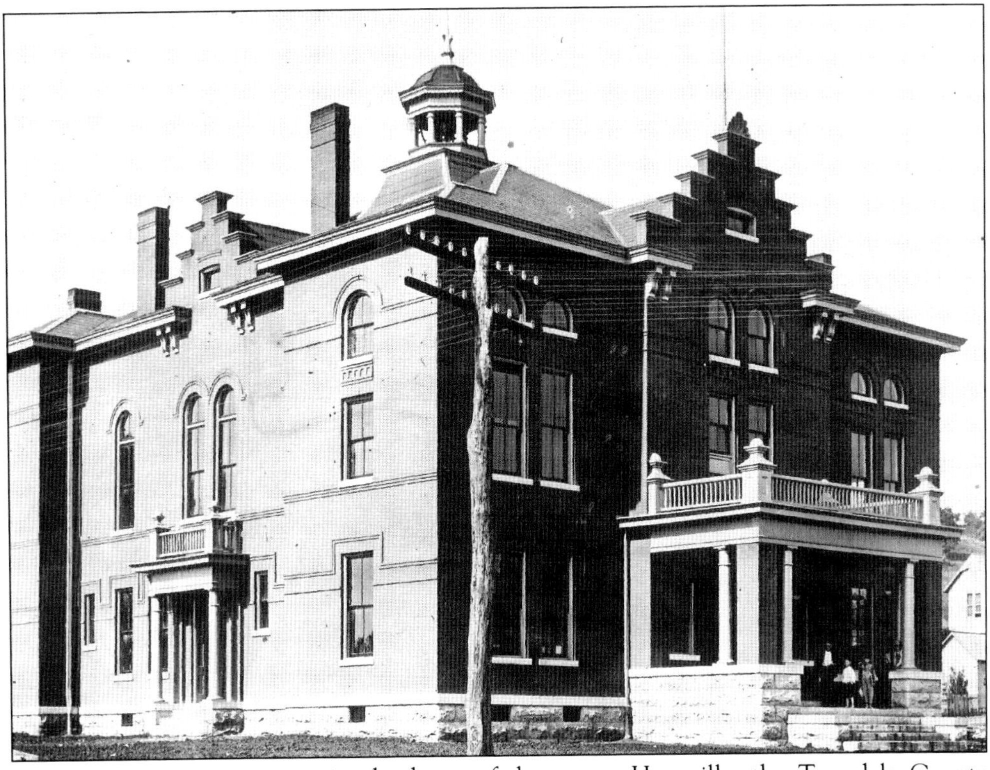

From its prominent position in the heart of downtown Hartsville, the Trousdale County Courthouse has presided over close to a century of history. Constructed in 1905, it was brand new when this photograph was made. It was built by F. M. Winn of Hartsville to replace an earlier one that stood across the street. That courthouse was destroyed in a fire.

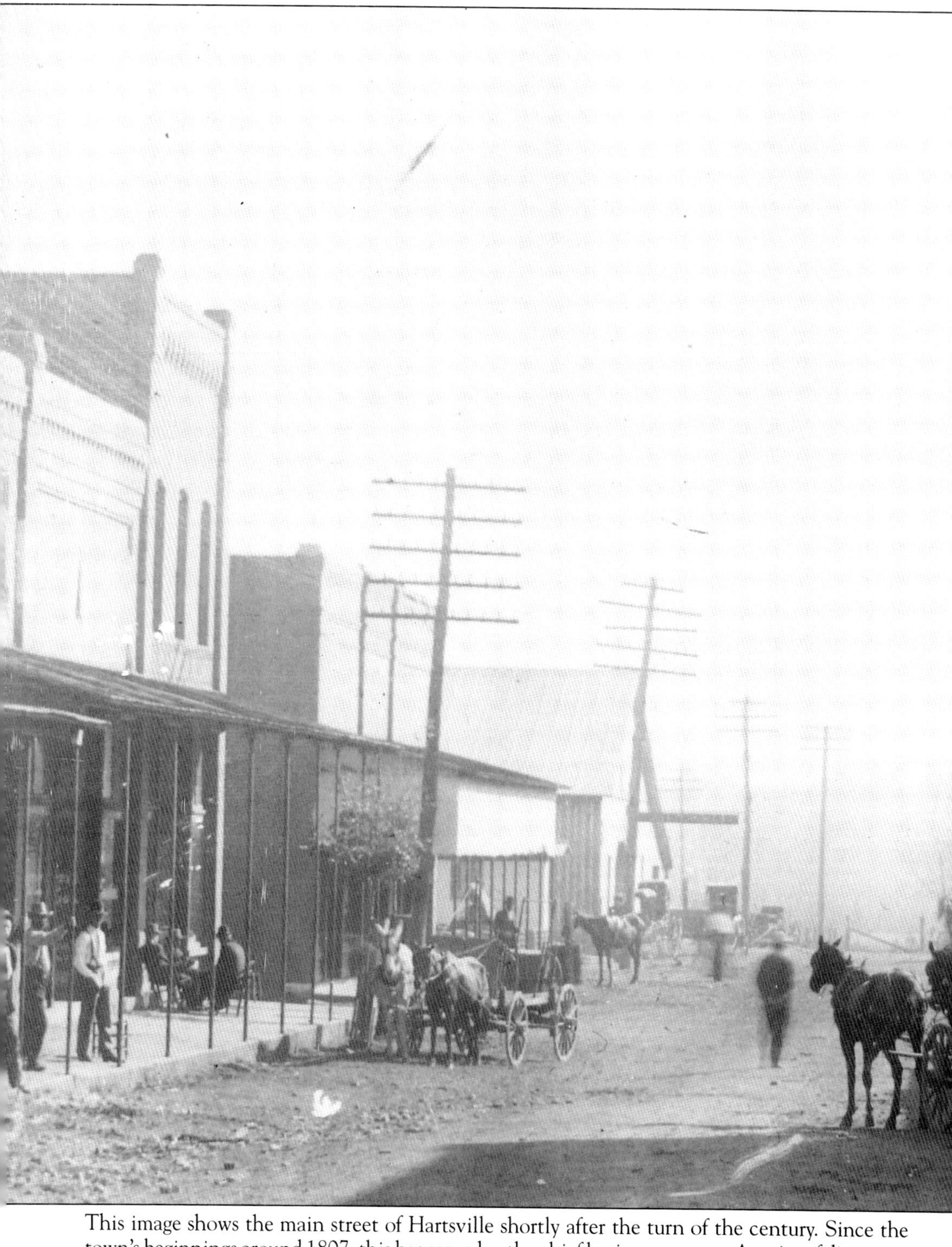

This image shows the main street of Hartsville shortly after the turn of the century. Since the town's beginnings around 1807, this has served as the chief business avenue. A series of disastrous

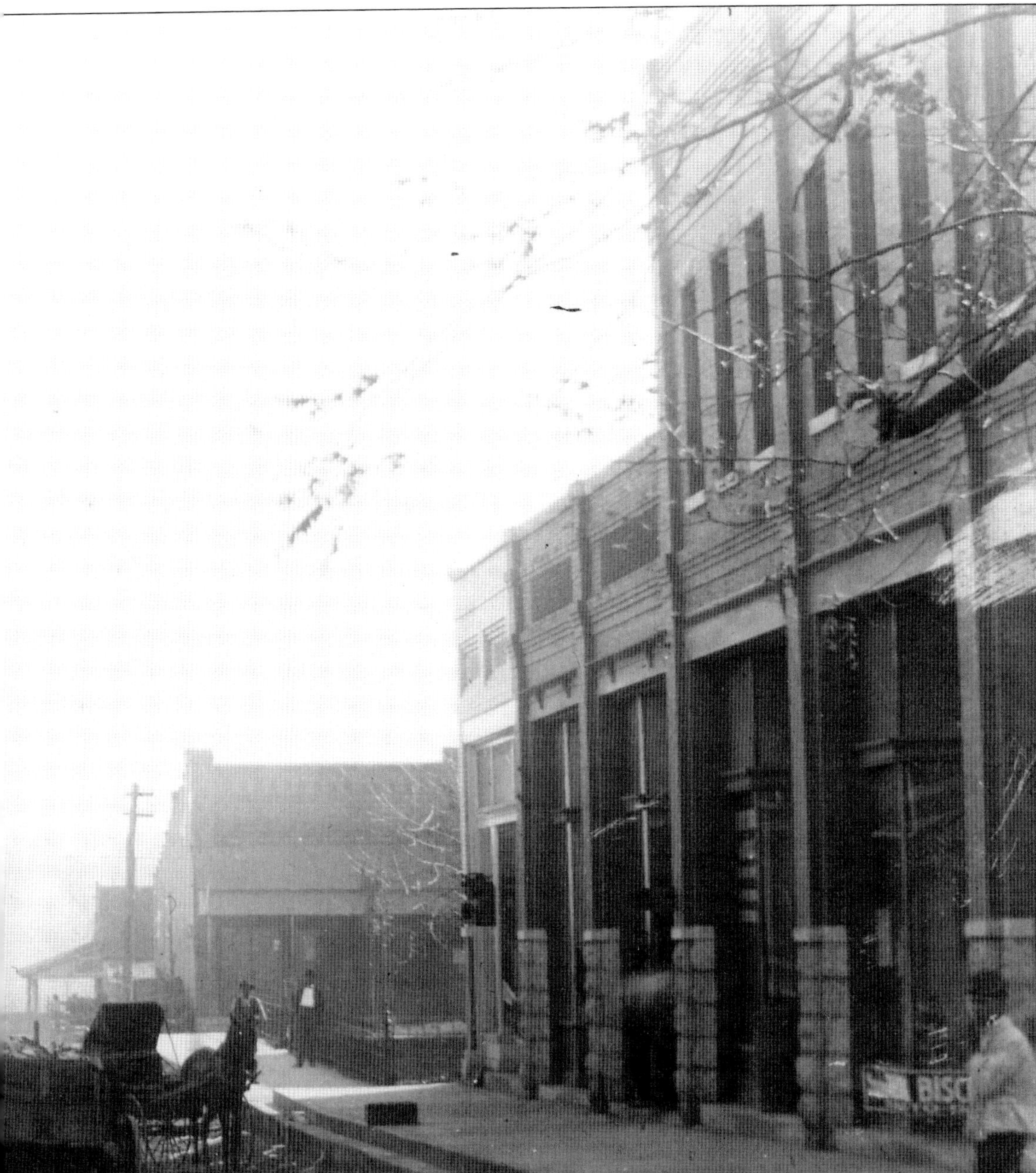

fires forced merchants here to build with brick rather than board. They were successful in their efforts—all of these brick buildings are still standing today.

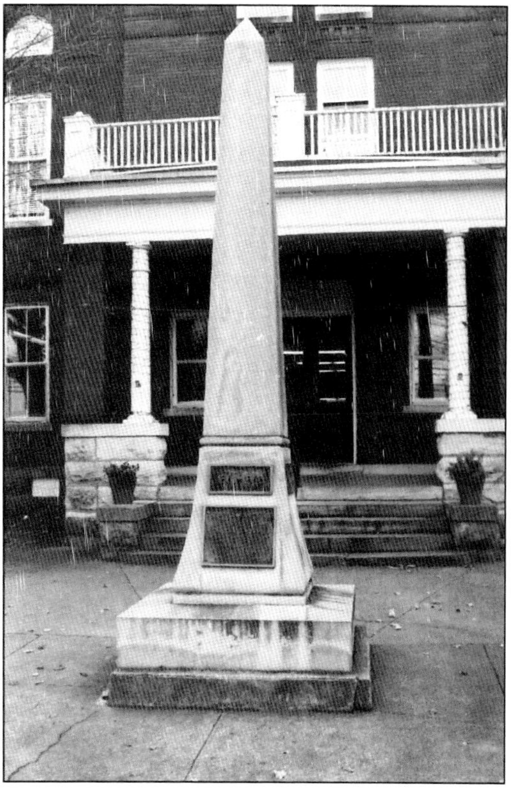

The Memorial to Soldiers of Past Wars is one of Trousdale County's most recognized structures. It was dedicated after World War I to honor those soldiers in particular. At the dedication ceremony, Col. Luke Lea was the featured speaker. Lea was the owner of the *Nashville Tennessean*, a former U.S. Senator, and a war hero. Later, a plaque in recognition of the Civil War Battle of Hartsville was moved here and attached to the monument base.

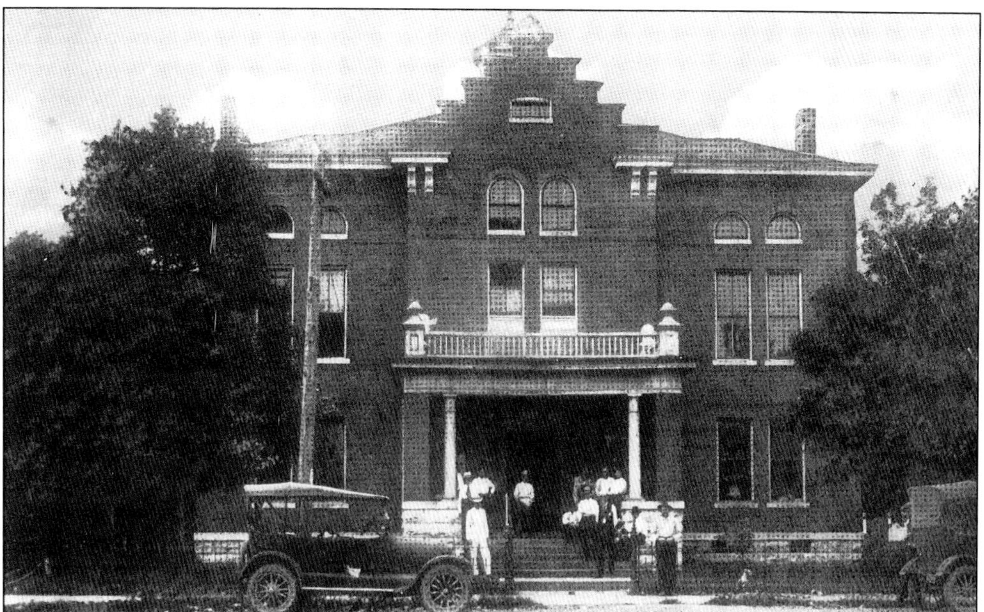

This image shows the Trousdale County Courthouse several years after its construction, but before the monument was placed in front. The iron fence around the courthouse yard was removed before the Second World War.

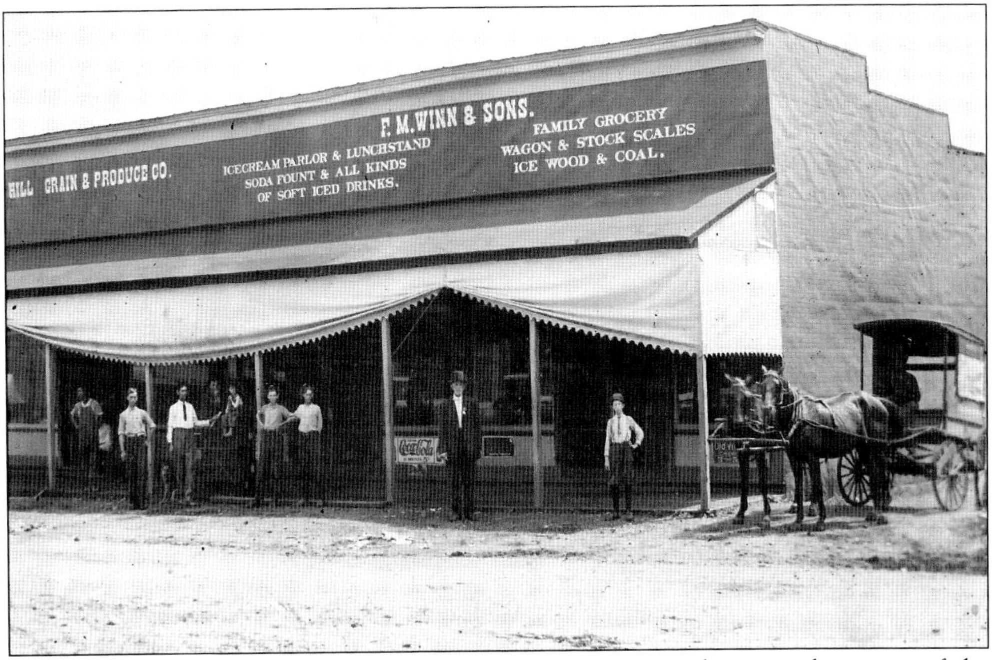

F. M. Winn and Son's store was on River Street. Mr. Winn is shown in the center of the photograph; the others are employees. The wagon on the right was used to deliver ice. This business featured an ice cream parlor and soda fountain. The sign on the front advertises Coca-Cola for a nickel. The building, now gone, once stood where the River Street Deli is today.

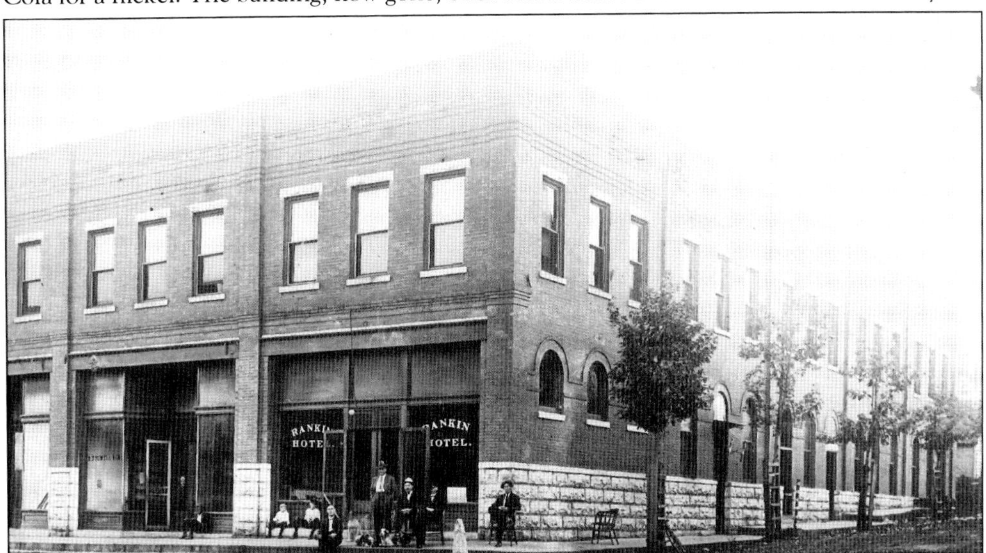

Built at a cost of thirty-thousand dollars, the Rankin Hotel opened in December of 1907. The hotel featured a restaurant and a ballroom. In later years, the building was gutted to create the old Eveska Theatre, now the Hartsville Christian Fellowship Church. In the 1913 flood, a steamboat rode into town and tied up on the steps of the hotel, allowing citizens to attend a dance held aboard the boat.

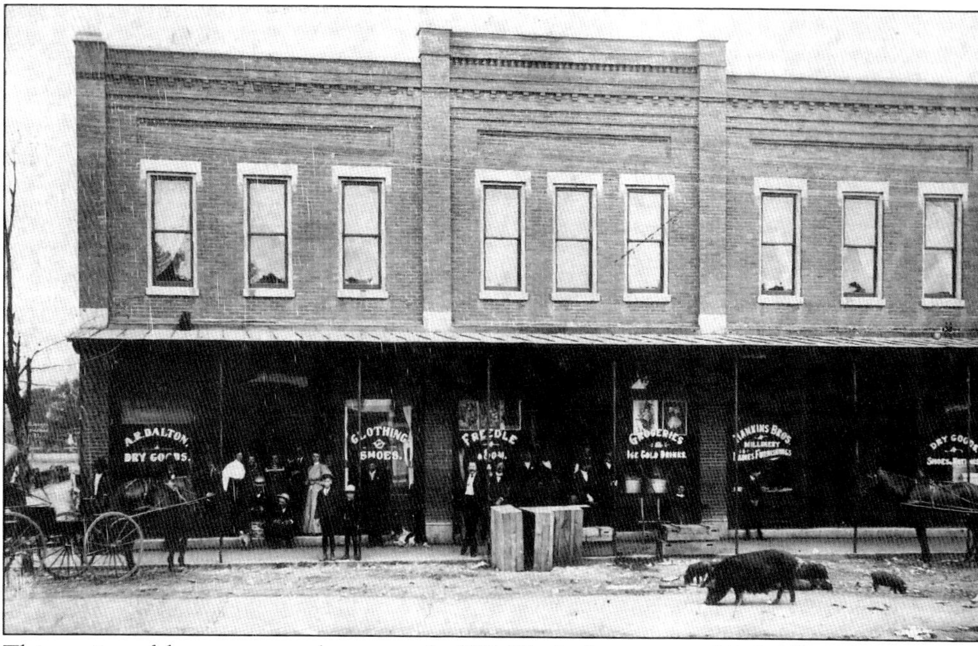

This section of downtown was known as the Ellis Block, for its owner H. C. Ellis, who was also a founder of the Bank of Hartsville. The stores shown are A. R. Dalton's Dry Goods, Freedle and Son Groceries, and Hankins Brothers Dry Goods. The free-ranging pigs are a clue to the rural nature of the community. These buildings burned in 1998.

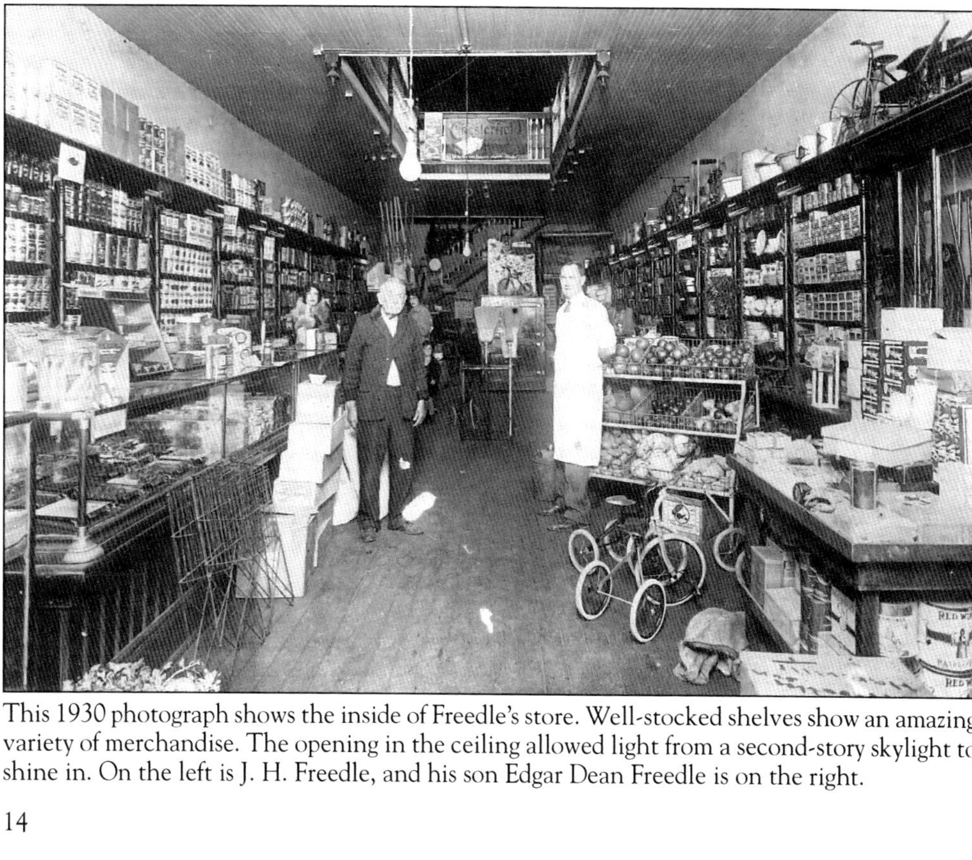

This 1930 photograph shows the inside of Freedle's store. Well-stocked shelves show an amazing variety of merchandise. The opening in the ceiling allowed light from a second-story skylight to shine in. On the left is J. H. Freedle, and his son Edgar Dean Freedle is on the right.

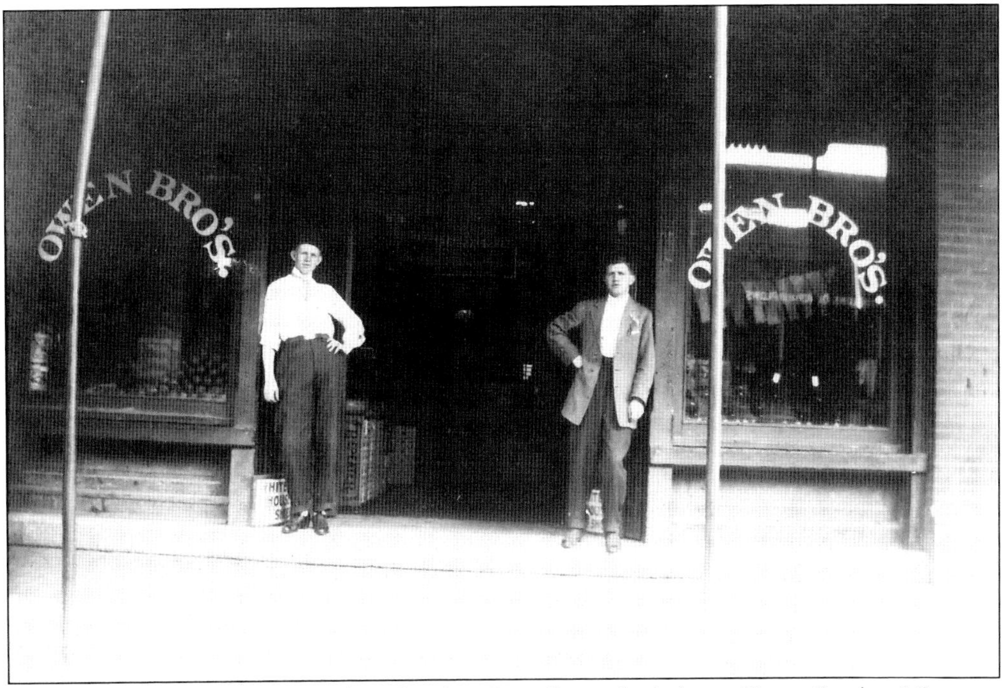

"Cotton" Dick Owen (left) and his brother Sam Owen (right) ran Owen Brothers' Store, a general store on Main Street. In this 1906 photograph the two appear ready for customers.

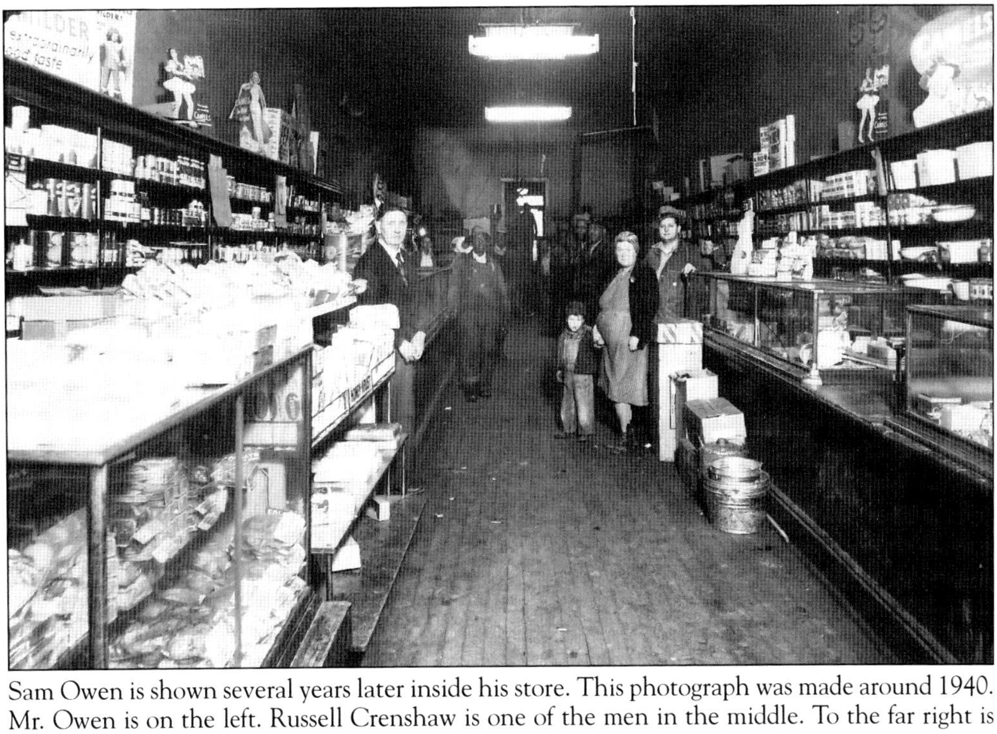

Sam Owen is shown several years later inside his store. This photograph was made around 1940. Mr. Owen is on the left. Russell Crenshaw is one of the men in the middle. To the far right is Sam Owen's son, James, who practiced law in Hartsville for many years.

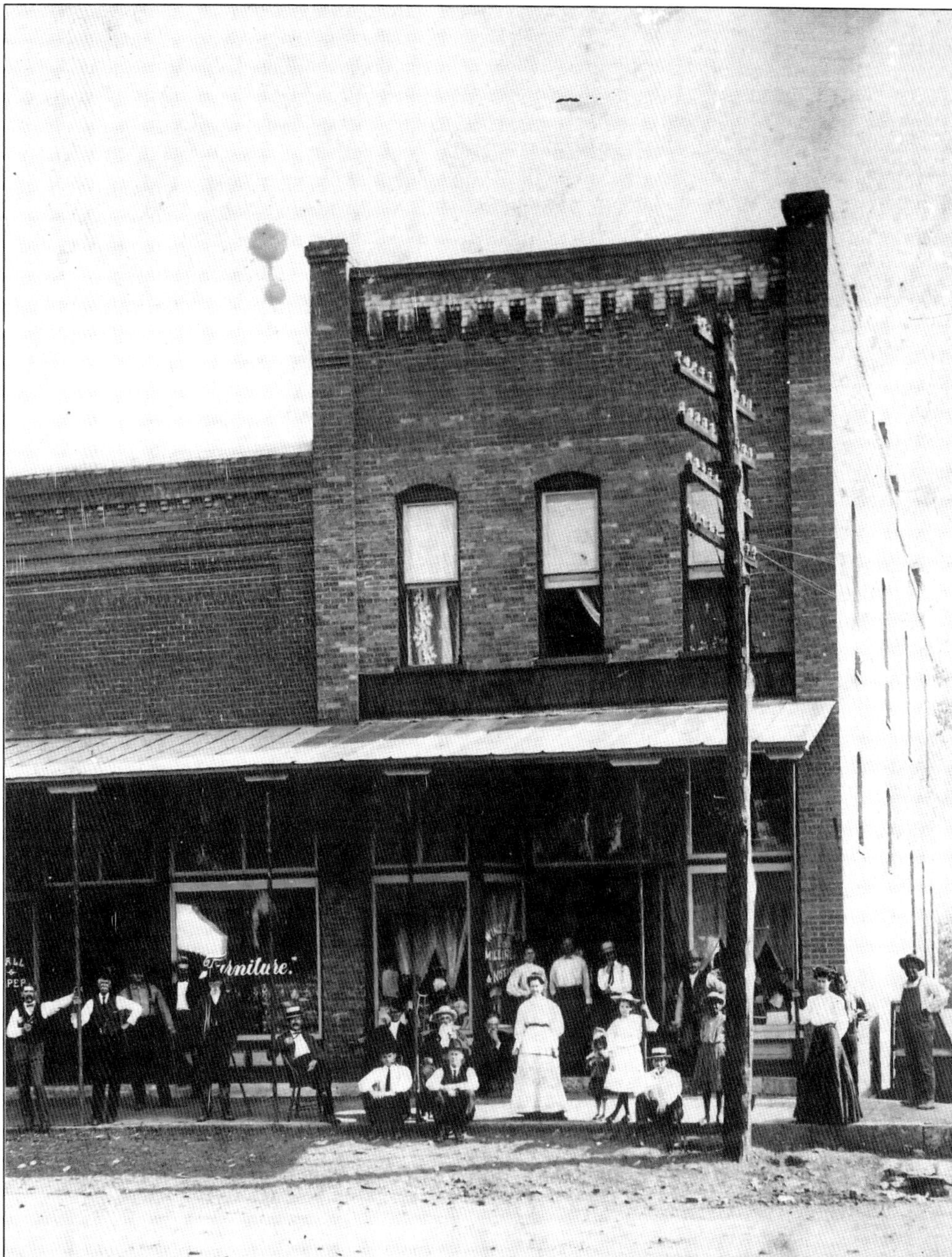

Winston's Millinery and Notions Store on Main Street was run by Miss Nannie Winston. The store featured ladies' hats and sewing goods. In the upstairs of the store were living quarters. The building was damaged by fire in the 1960s and the roof line changed considerably. To the left was Col. W. J. Hale's furniture business.

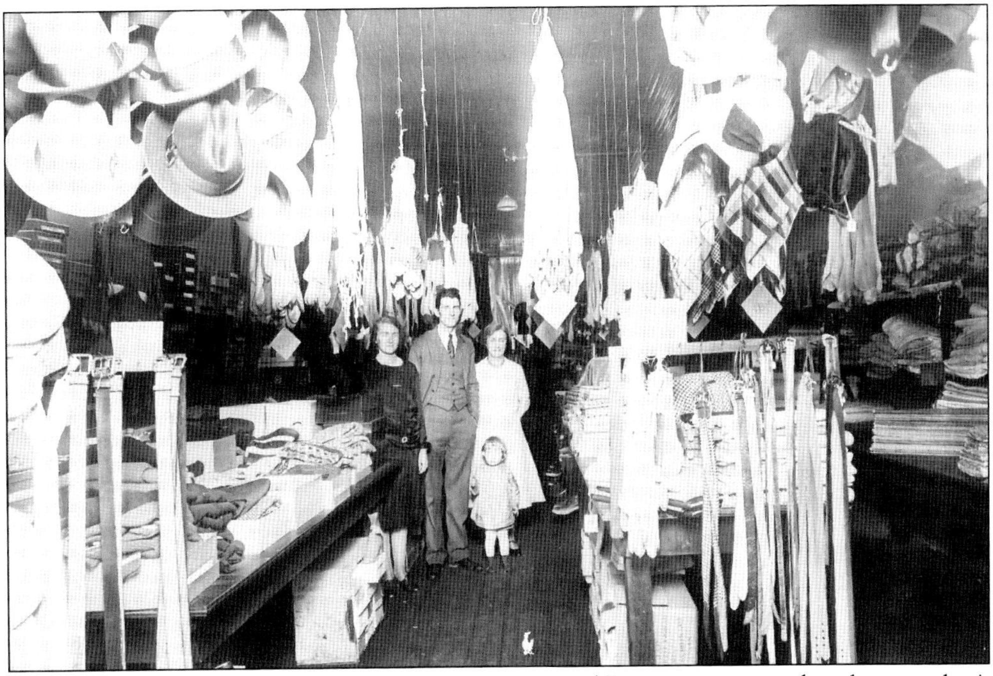

By 1930, Winston's Millinery was replaced by Draper and Darwin as seen in this photograph. A clothing and dry goods store, it appears to have used every available space to display merchandise. The gentleman is the store manager Squire Julius Herod. On the left is store clerk Mrs. Will Gwin. On the right is Julius' wife, Sammye, and daughter, Julia Irene. The Herods lived in the upstairs of the store. In later years that space was used as an office by Dr. Rhea Garrett.

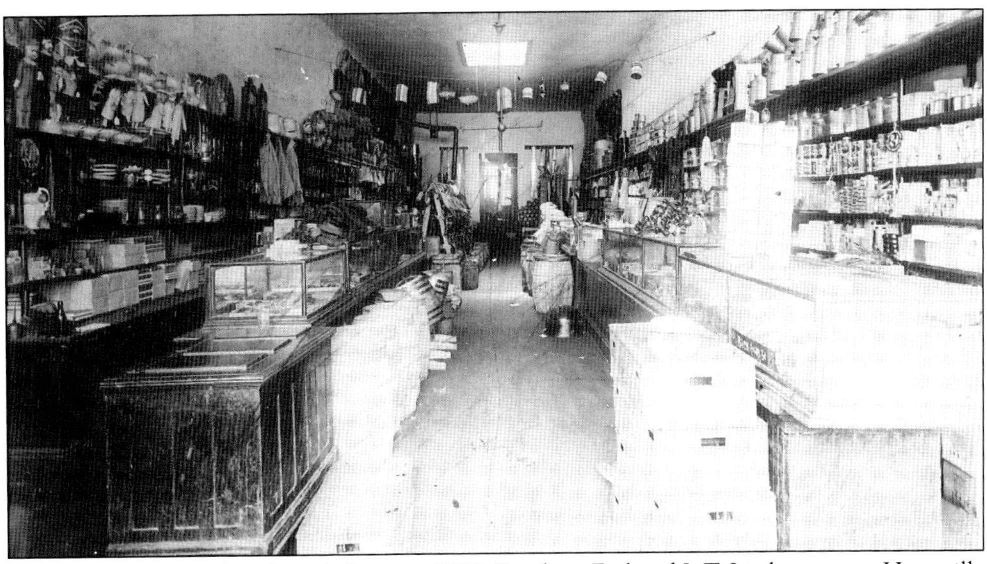

This is the interior of Littleton's Store in 1910. Brothers Earl and I. T. Littleton were Hartsville institutions from the early 1900s to the 1970s. Their store originally stood on the south side of main street. Notice the skylight in the photograph. The store sold groceries and hardware but introduced furniture in the 1930s. In 1947, after I. T.'s death, Earl moved the store to Church Street and sold furniture exclusively. Today that building is Hartsville Electronics.

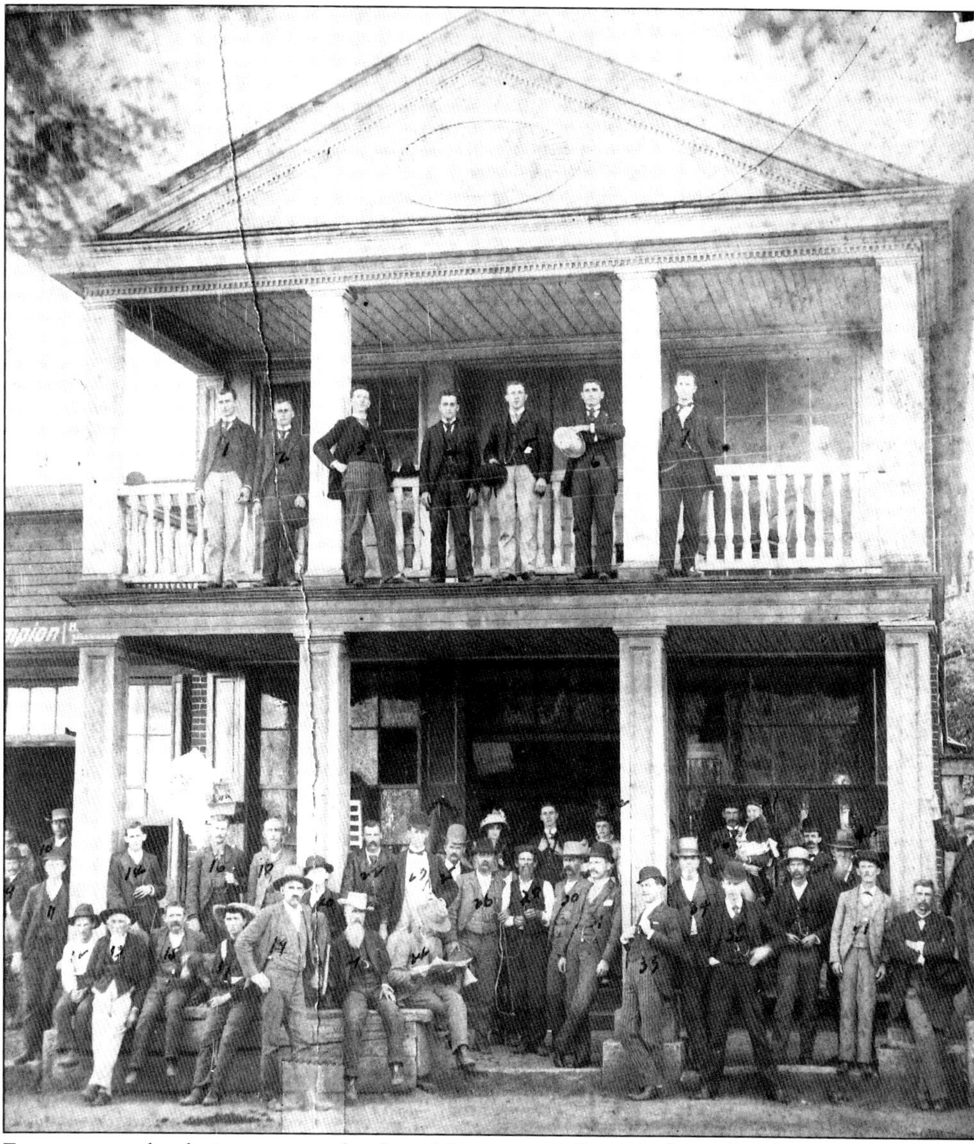

Every young dandy in town, and a few old ones as well, turned out for the photographer on September 27, 1892, when this photograph was made. The building was the old Allen Hotel. It stood where the courthouse now stands. The structure burned in the same fire that destroyed the old courthouse. The child in the man's arms is Mamie Hammoch, who was the president of the Bank of Hartsville from 1947 to 1972.

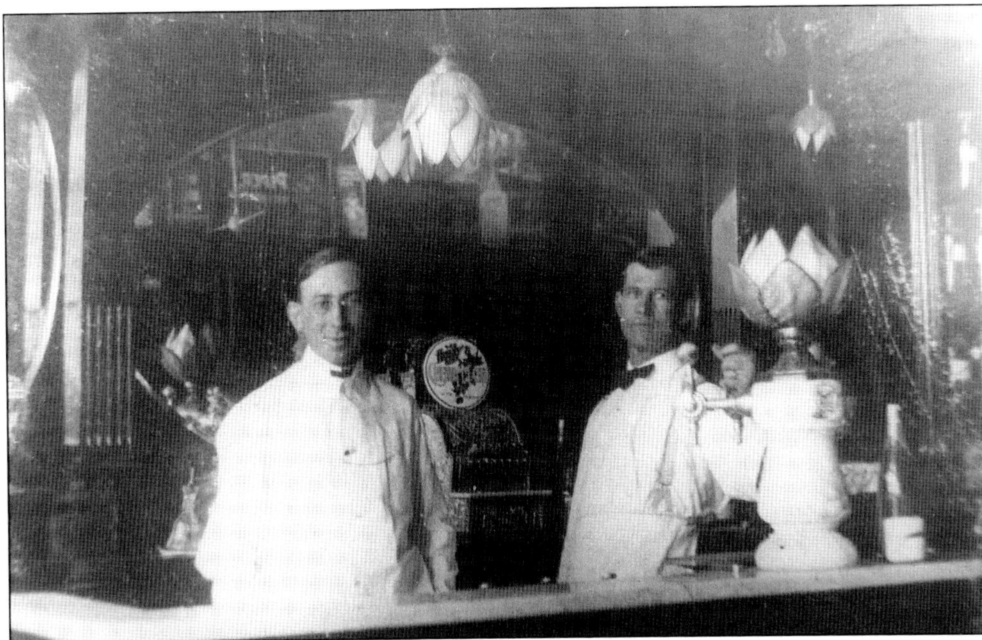

In the early 1900s, Williams' Drug Store was the place to go for aches and pains or a refreshing soda. Druggist Luther Williams is on the left. The other gentleman is unidentified. The drug store was on Main Street. It was followed in the same location by Perkins and Sweeny Druggists, and later by Vaught's Drugs.

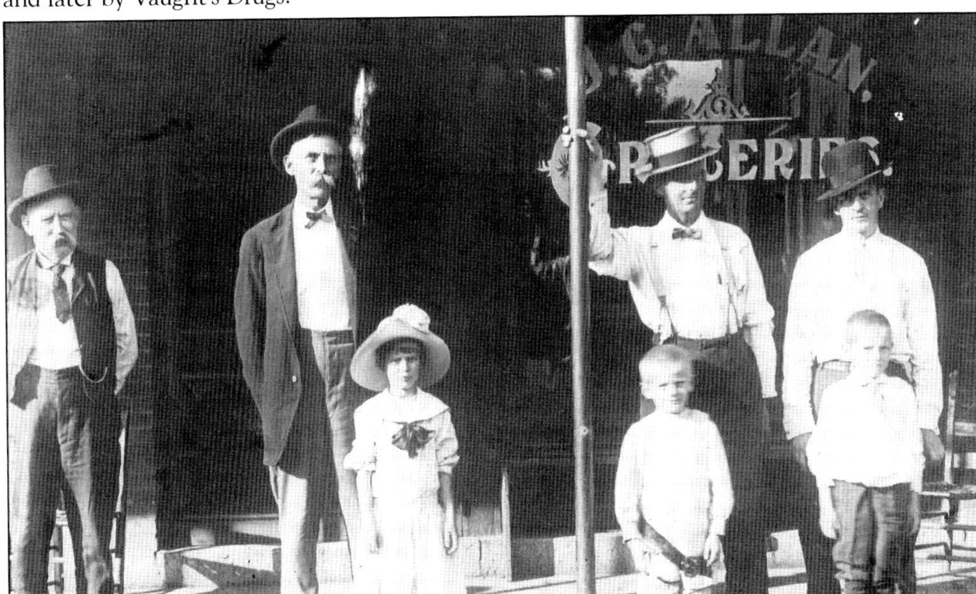

There was a time when no self-respecting gentleman would be seen in public without a hat. These men are standing in front of J. C. Allen's Grocery Store. The store stood opposite the courthouse, where Citizen's Bank stood for many years and now is the law office of Sharon Linville. Pictured, from left to right, are: John Throp, Bailey Lipscomb, J. C. Affen, and R. C. Owen. The children are Kitty Haynie, Robert Owen, and Carter Owen. The photograph was made around 1910.

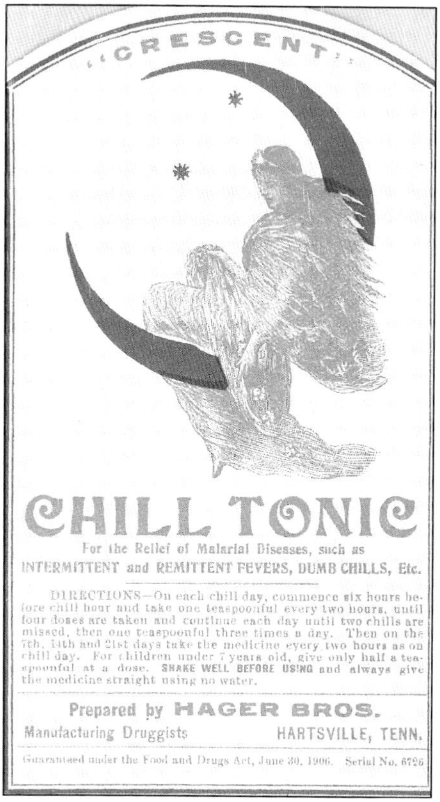

Hager Brothers Drug Store was a fixture in the town of Hartsville from the 1870s to the 1950s. The Hagers manufactured many of their own drugs, among them was Chill Tonic, as seen in this label. Other popular medicines included Hager's All-O.K. Prophylos, Propho-Donto, Tasteless Castor Oil, and Bed Bug Poison.

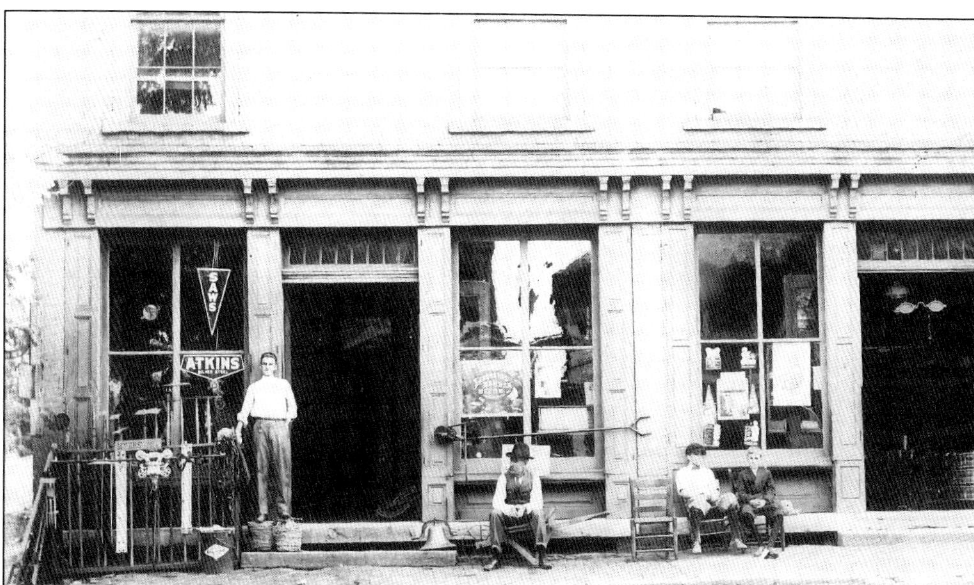

The Hager Brothers' stores on Main Street. These adjoining brick structures are the oldest business buildings in Hartsville, built before the Civil War. In the aftermath of the Battle of Hartsville, the upstairs of both buildings was used as a hospital for the wounded, both Confederate and Union. The store to the left was the hardware store; to the right was the drug store. Will Hager is the man seated in the middle of the photograph.

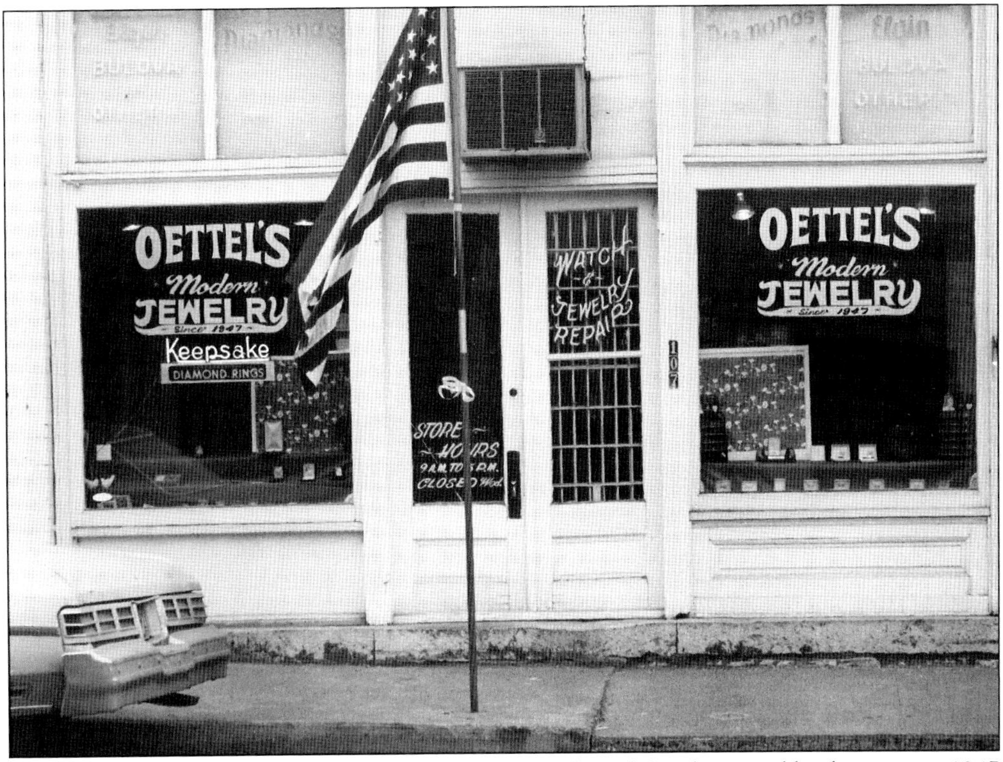

Oettle's Jewelry stood behind the old Bank of Hartsville. Al Oettle started his business in 1947 and began using this building in 1957. The building burned in 1984 in a fire that also destroyed Dillehay's Cafe. Both businesses relocated and are still in business today.

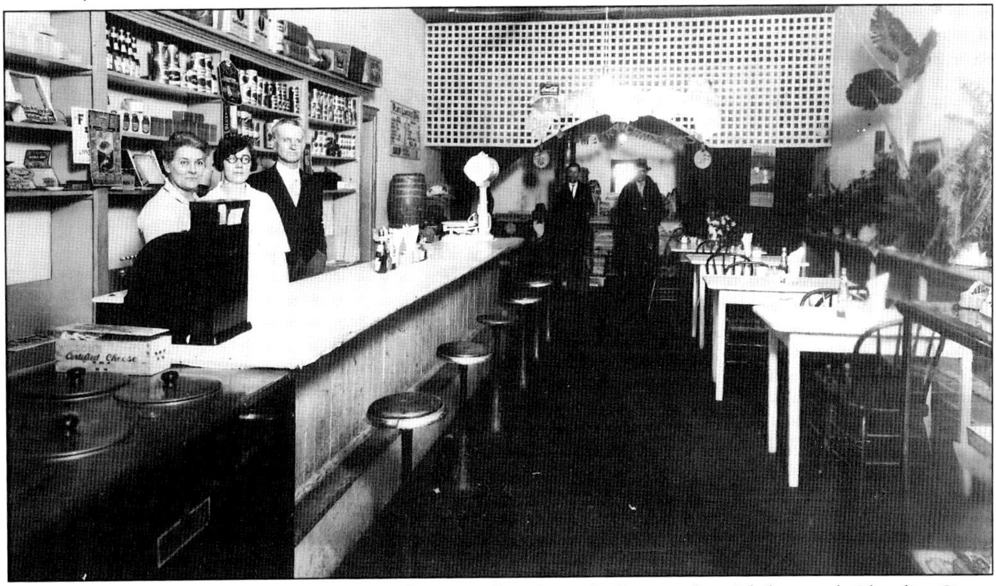

Also behind the old Bank of Hartsville was the City Cafe, run by Alpha and Charlie Cato, shown in 1926 behind the counter with an unidentified waitress between them. Later Mrs. Jordan Vance ran a restaurant here and still later Mrs. Neoma Dillehay ran her restaurant here. The building burned when Oettle's burned.

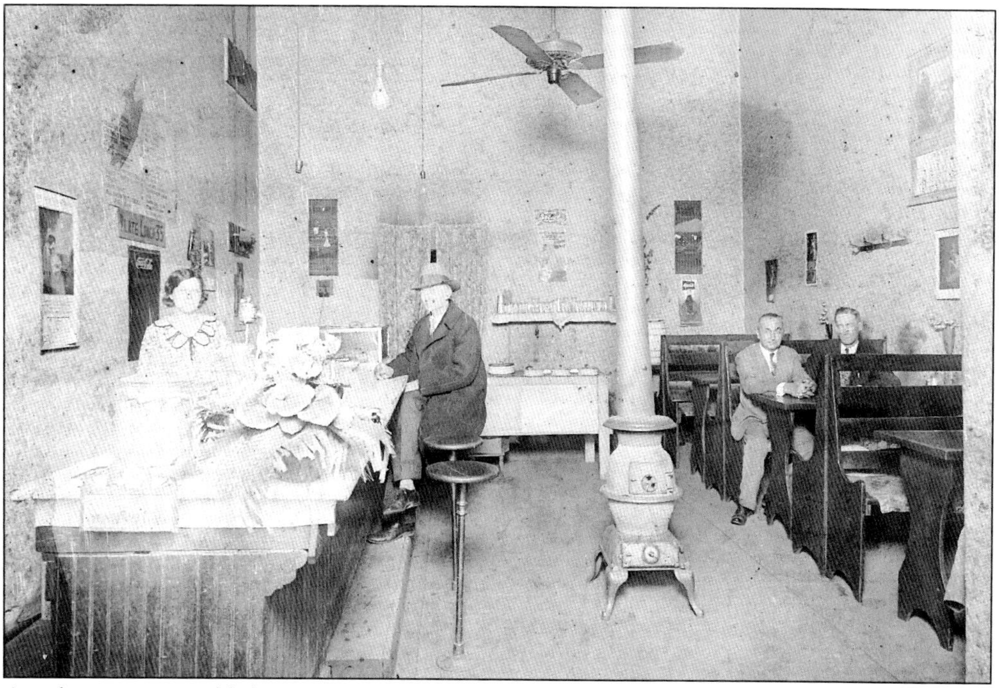

Another eating establishment in town was Oakley's Tea Room, on Main Street next to the hotel. In this 1925 photograph, a sign advertises a plate lunch for 35¢. Edna Throp Oakley is standing behind the counter. At the counter is Mr. McCormack, who ran the hotel.

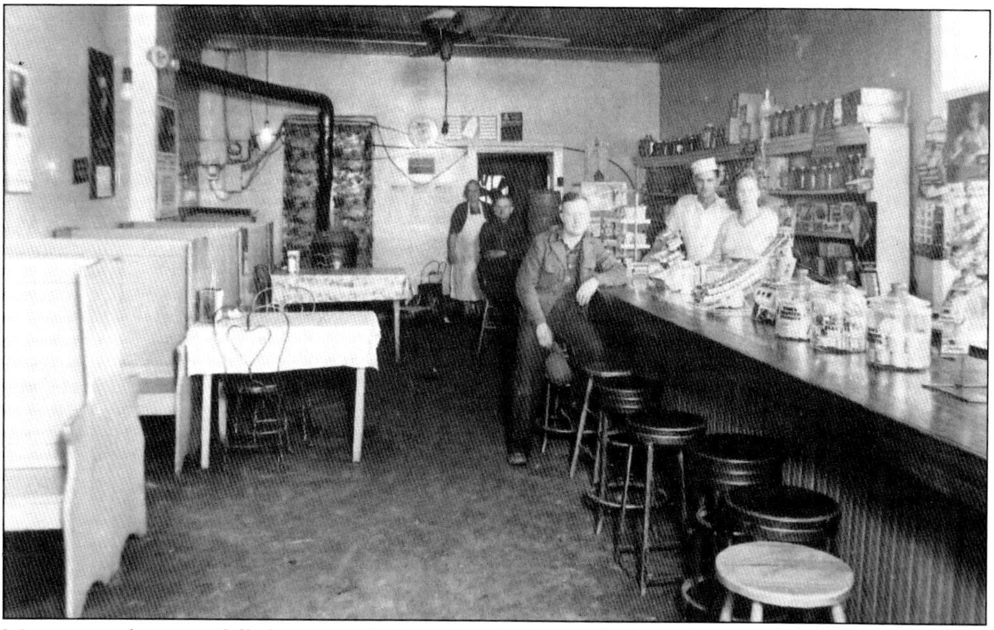

More recently, townsfolk frequented this cafe, which stood where the present VFW hall stands, across the street from the courthouse. Donley's Cafe was operated by Lloyd and Anna Donley for over twenty-five years. They opened for business in 1945. In this 1953 photograph Mr. and Mrs. Donley stand behind the counter. For 75¢ you could get a meat, vegetables, bread, a drink, and a piece of pie.

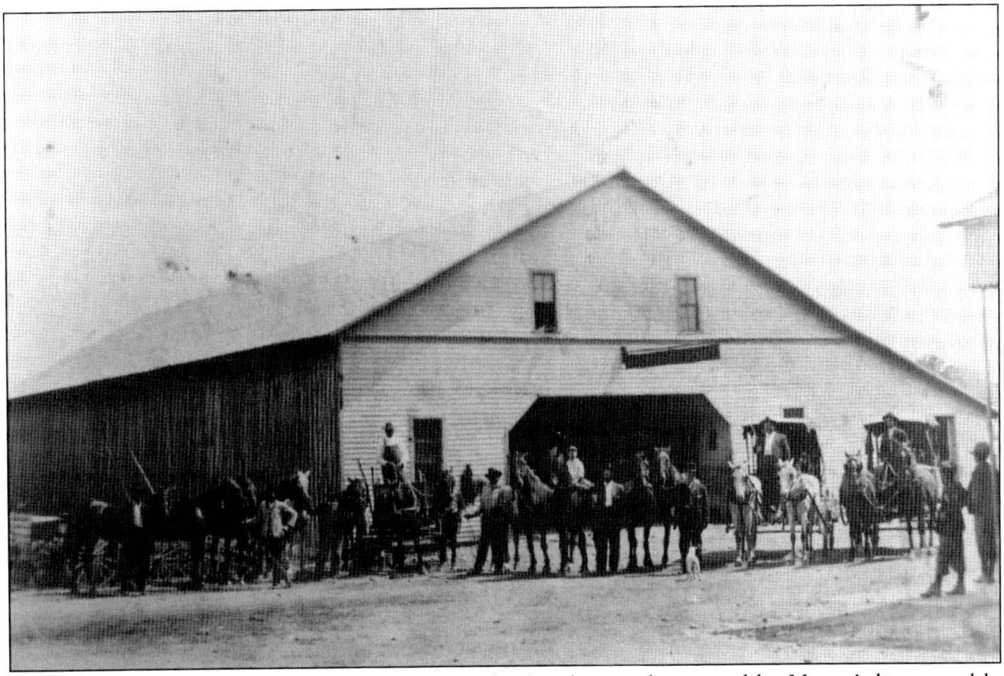

In the days of horses and buggies every town had to have a livery stable. Vance's livery stable stood about where the gazebo is today, on Main Street. There, you could leave your horse for the day while you tended to business, or rent a horse and buggy to ride out of town. Mr. Vance is the man with the dog at his feet in this photograph from the early 1900s.

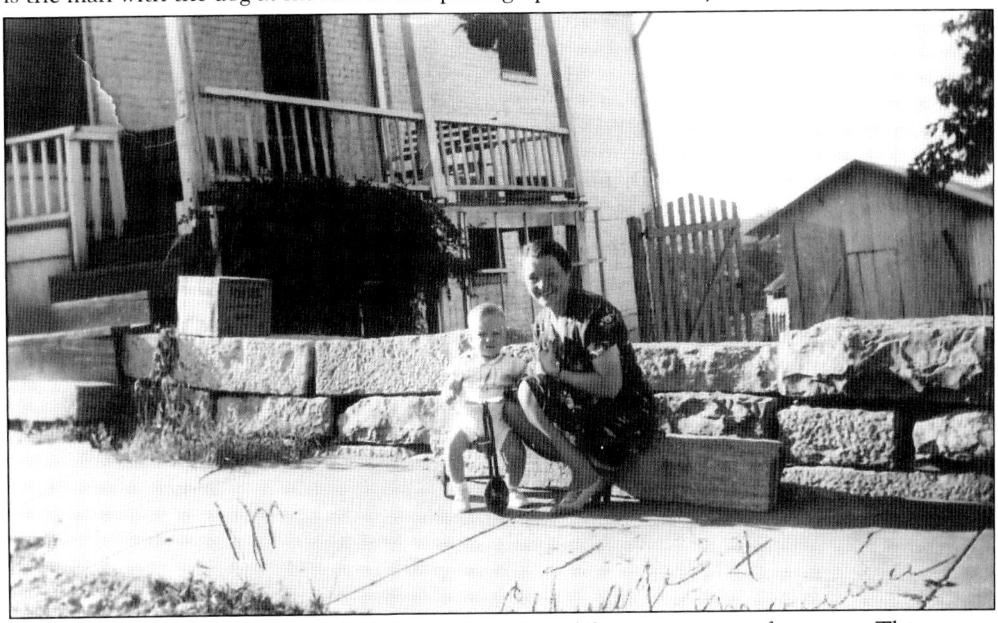

The Trousdale County Jail was built by 1877 and used for over seventy-five years. This corner of the building shows the steps to the sheriff's quarters with the lock up area behind. The child is Etherage Parker Jr., who was born while his father was sheriff. With him is his mother Annie Lee Davis Parker. The jail building was torn down after the new jail was built. No known photograph exists that shows the entire building.

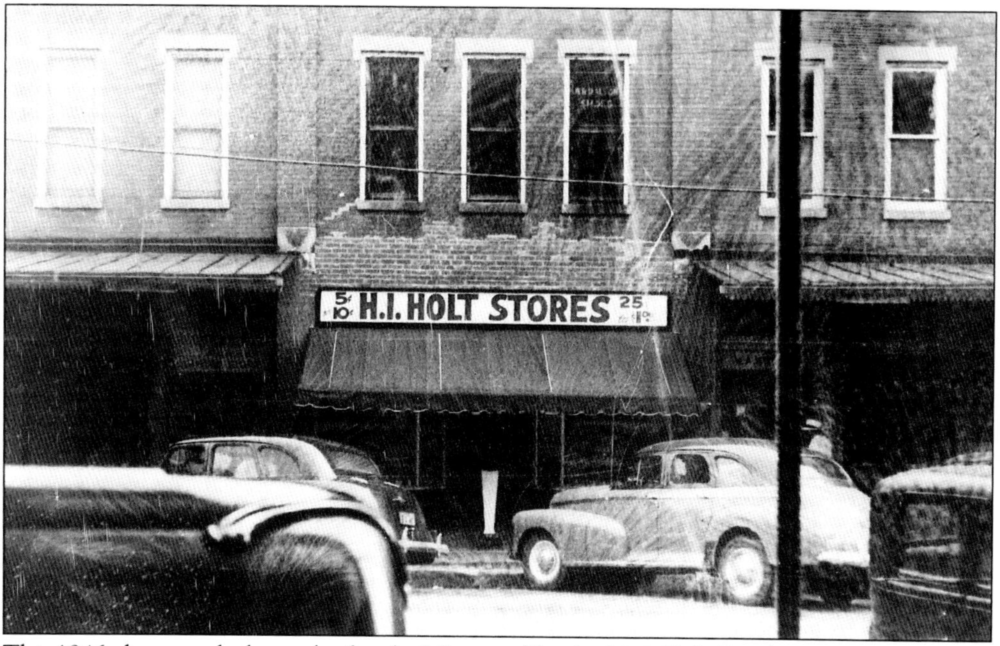

This 1946 photograph shows the first building used by the H. I. Holt 5 and 10 store. It occupied the center of the Ellis Block but later moved across the street. Holt was in business in downtown Hartsville for over forty years. It was a tradition for Holt's to sell live chicks, rabbits, and ducks every Easter.

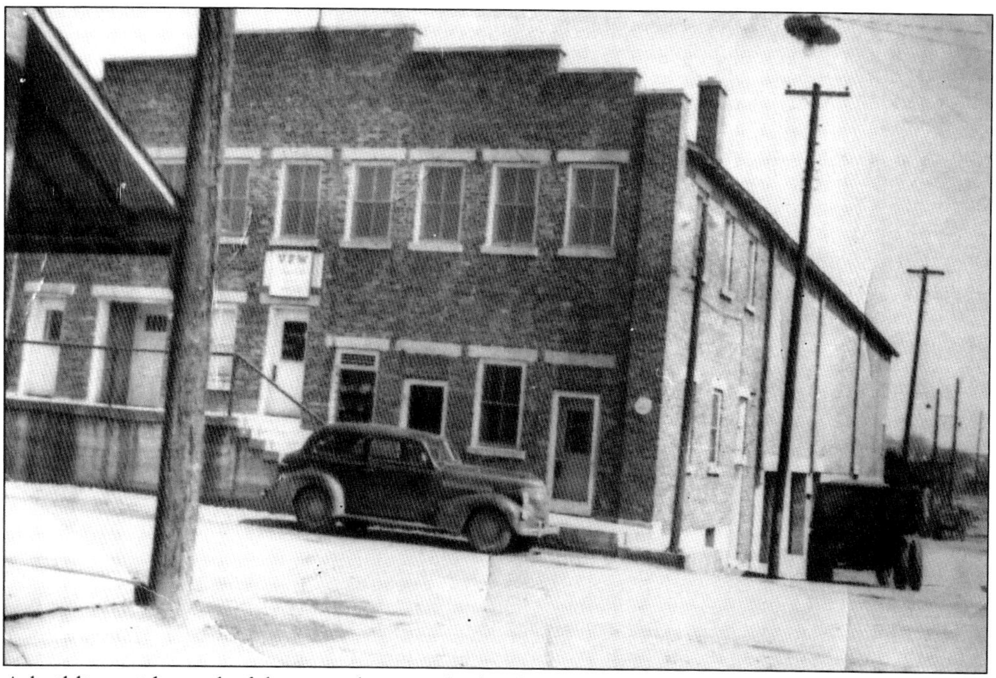

A building with a colorful past is this one, built after World War II as a community center. For years it offered the town and county dances and roller skating. The city had offices here and the downstairs housed the fire department. It later was used by the VFW. More recently it has been used as a pool hall and is the scene of weekly wrestling matches.

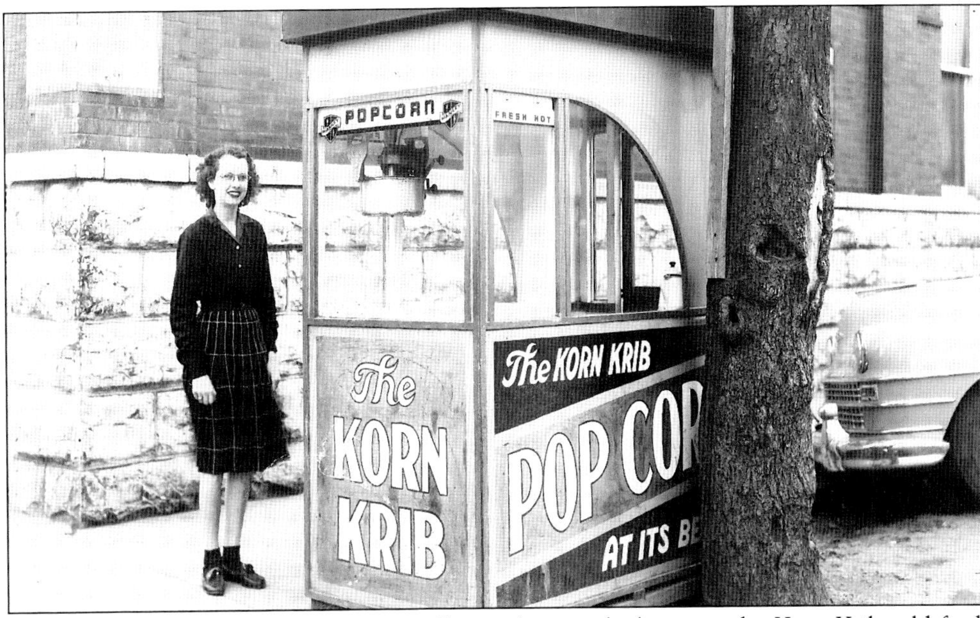

Every Saturday, when downtown Hartsville was busy with shoppers, the Korn Krib sold fresh hot popcorn. Beginning in the 1930s "the Kernel," Johnny Russell, sold popcorn from this stand on the corner of Church and Main Streets. He sold popcorn at local events and in neighboring towns as well. Today his son James Russell still pops corn, retailing it to schools and major grocery chains. James and his wife Annie Bell pop 15 to 20 50-pound bags a week. This photograph was made in 1943. Shown is Mildred Dies Gammon.

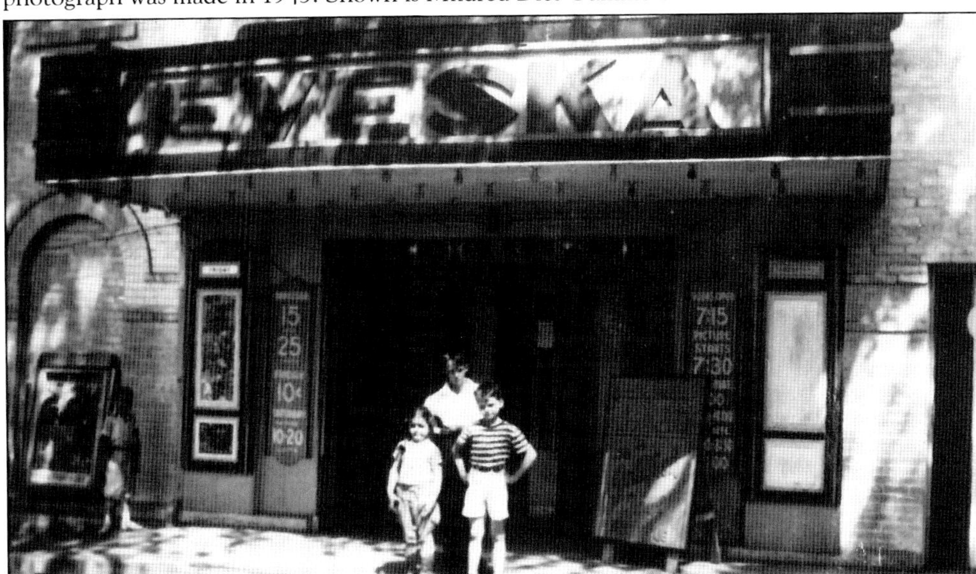

The Eveska Theatre was a popular hangout with young and old from the late 1930s to the 70s. It stood in the corner of the Rankin Hotel, made from the hotel's dining room and the upstairs ballroom. The name was created from the first letters of the three owner's wives' names, Eva, Estelle, and Kathleen. The theater changed hands and name when Johnny Russell and his family purchased it and called it the Gay Theater. Today the, building houses the Hartsville Christian Fellowship Church.

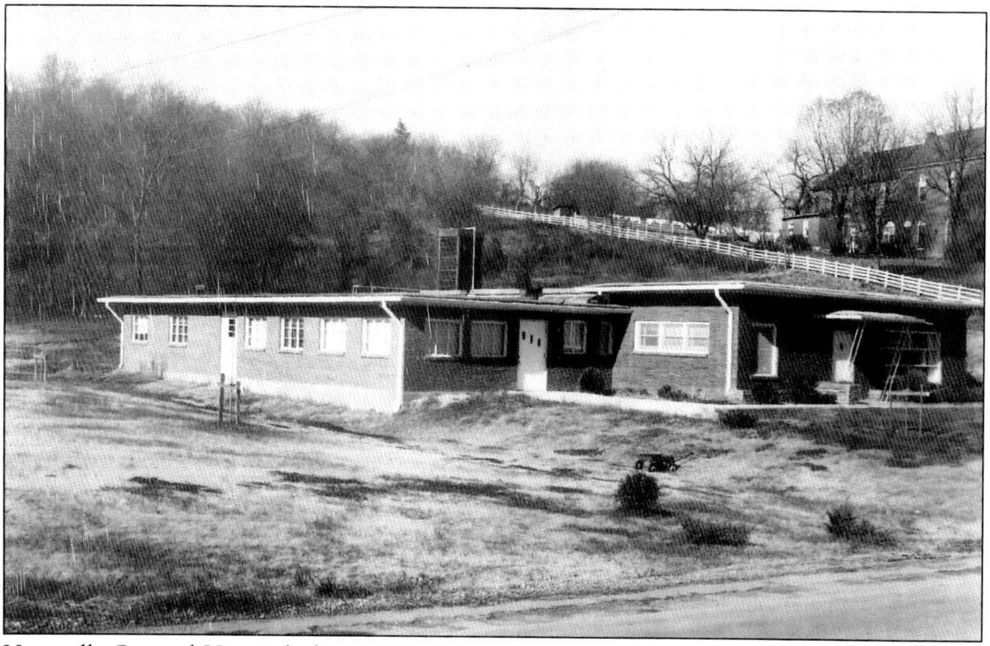

Hartsville General Hospital, the town's first, was built in 1952 by Dr. E. K. Bratton and Dr. C. S. Morrow. This photograph shows the hospital soon after construction. It was built on a vacant lot that had long been used by the town kids for baseball games. In the background the old Hartsville Academy building can be seen.

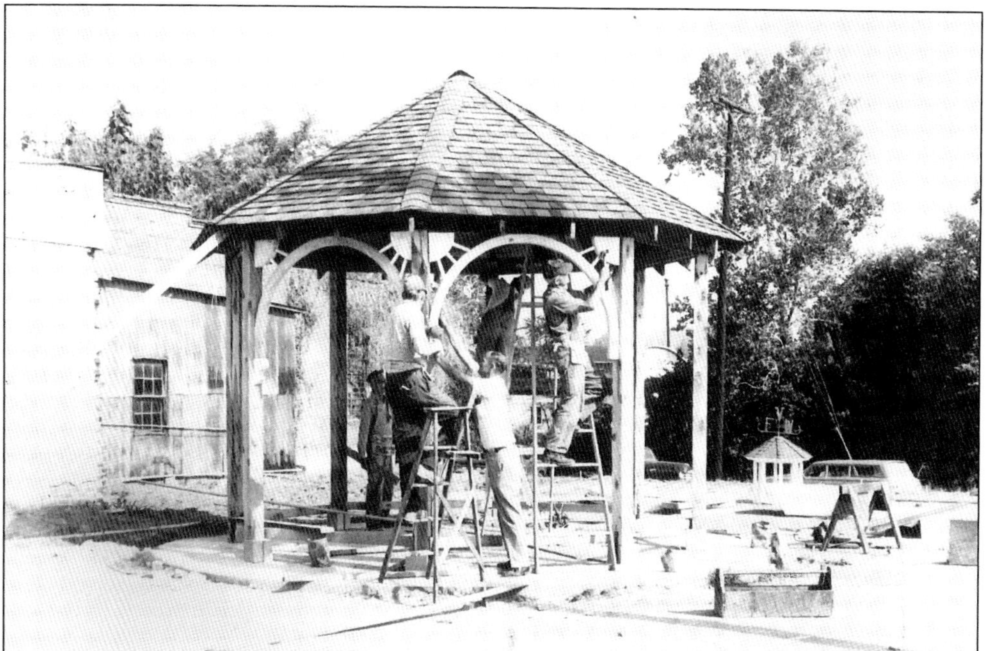

A landmark in recent years has been the VFW gazebo across the street from the courthouse. This photograph shows the gazebo during construction. It was designed and built by Dean Ford. Local carpenters were invited to help assemble it during a "gazebo raising." Two of the men shown, besides Ford, are Bill Davis and William Patterson.

Two

The Community

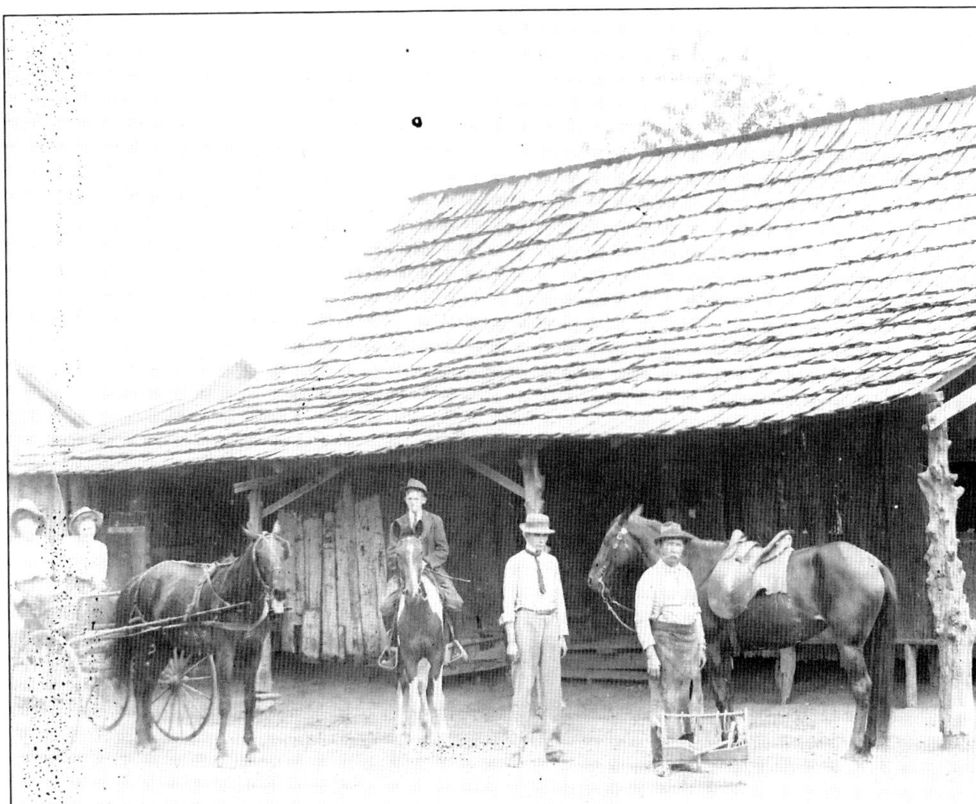

Out of town, other merchants did business with the public. One of these was John P. Hall, a blacksmith. His shop stood in the area of the present-day Highway 25 and Highway 141 intersection. Hall is shown wearing his heavy leather apron, standing by his box of tools. The young man beside him is Dee Bass. The girls in the buggy were the Bass sisters. On the horse is Irby Dalton.

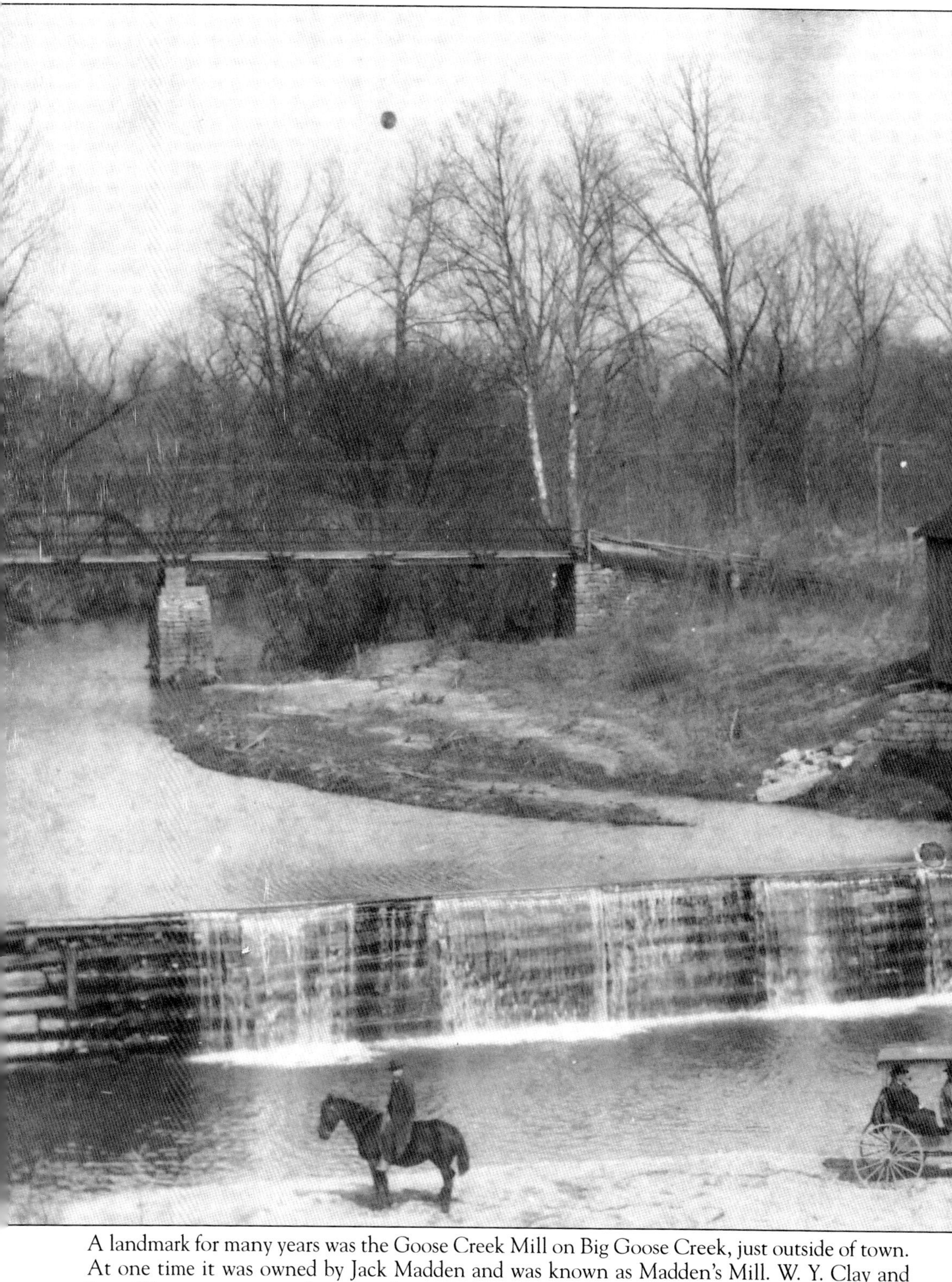

A landmark for many years was the Goose Creek Mill on Big Goose Creek, just outside of town. At one time it was owned by Jack Madden and was known as Madden's Mill. W. Y. Clay and Jesse West were owners when this photograph was made and they may be the men in the buggy.

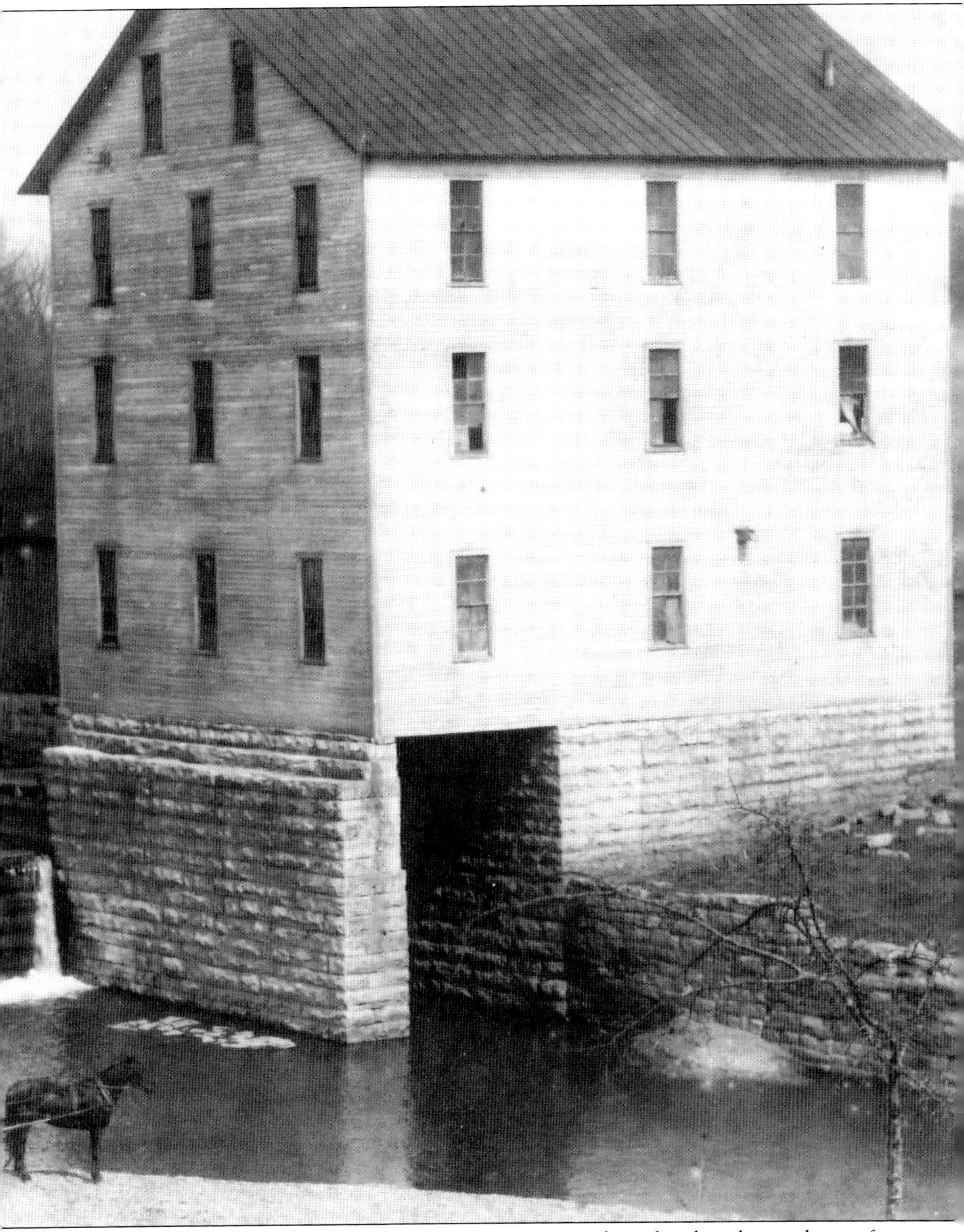

The mill was torn down before 1920. The cut stones were salvaged and used around town for construction. The rock foundation of the old Broadway Implement Company uses stones from the mill.

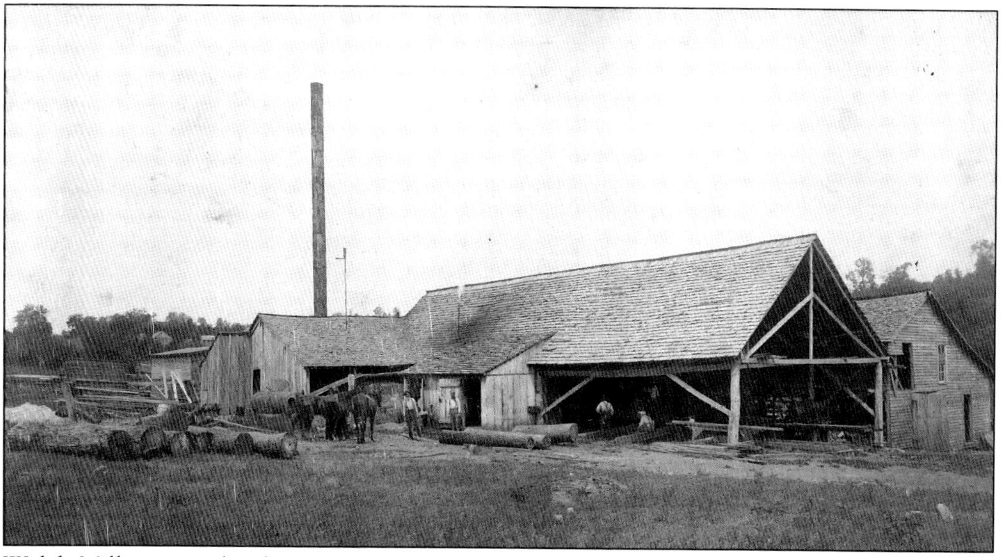

Welch Mill was another business outside of town. The mill produced lumber and millwork for home construction around the turn of the century. Mr. Welch's own home, still standing on Old Gallatin Pike, used lumber from this mill as well as the Hale home, later owned by Mr. and Mrs. William Massey, in East Hartsville. Mr. Welch was injured in an accident in the mill and carried to his home nearby. There he lay bedridden for over a year before dying of his injuries. The mill closed after his death and was eventually dismantled.

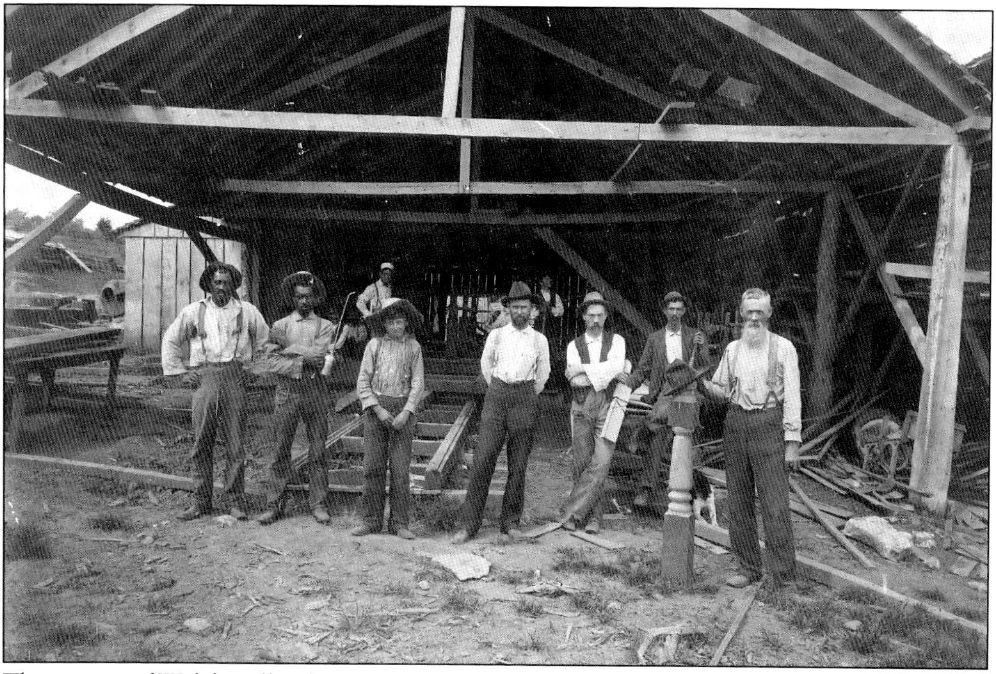

The interior of Welch Mill is shown here. Lumber, tools, and a newly turned newel post surround the workers of the mill in this photograph. On the far left is Nelse Martin, who later became the janitor of the old high school where he was affectionately called "Uncle Nelse." In the center is the mill owner, Robert Welch. One of the next two men is Mr. Hoel, who designed all of the gingerbread trim the mill produced. The last man on the right is Dick High.

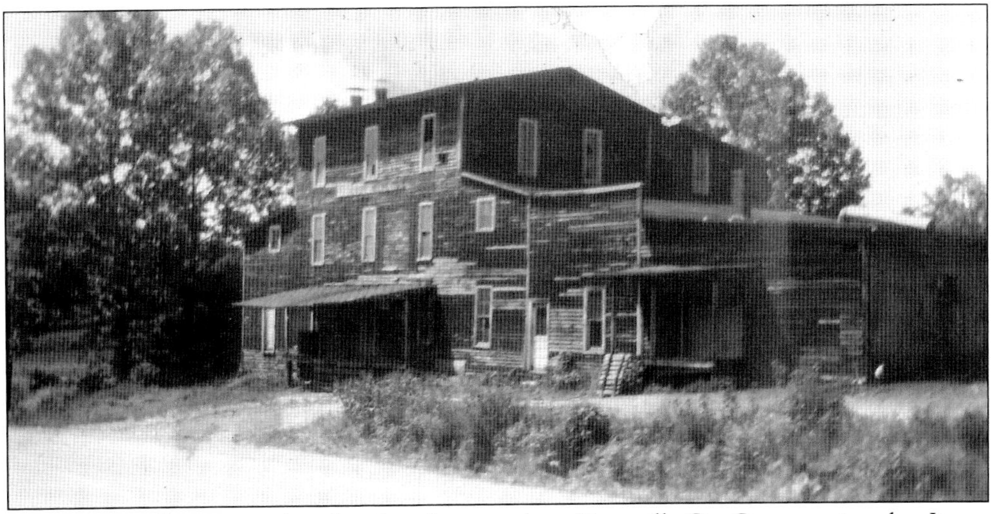

The rolling mill once stood at the edge of town, where Hartsville Gas Company is today. It was built in 1896 by Marcus D. Rickman and had a capacity of 100 barrels of flour daily. Marcus and his son Roy Rickman ran the mill producing Purity brand flour and White Pearl meal. The mill burned down in the 1960s.

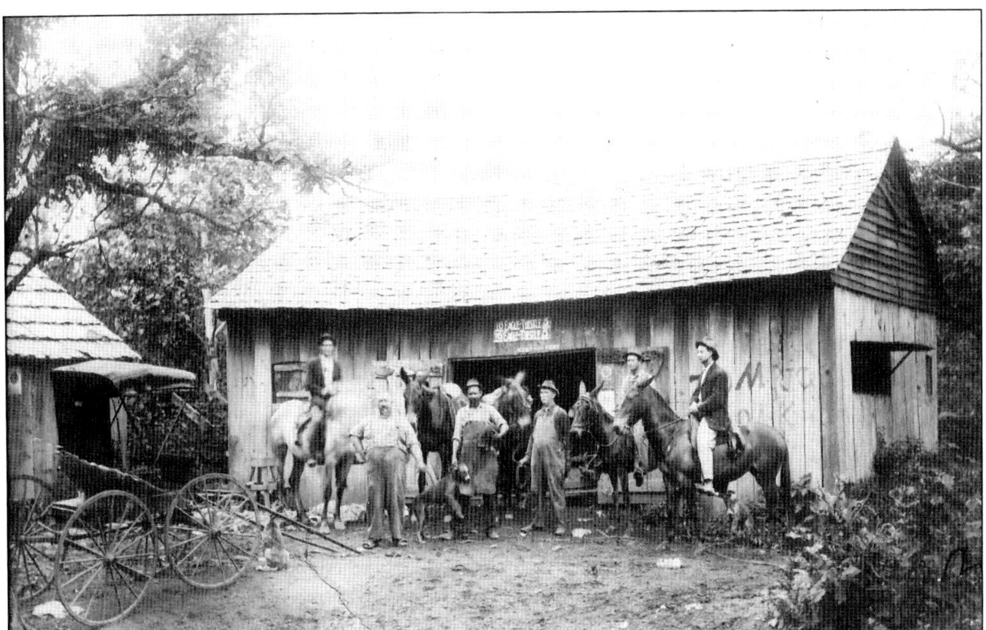

Ped Duncan's blacksmith shop stood in the Willard community, on a small island in Little Goose Creek, in the vicinity of the Willard Tobacco Factory. Mr. Duncan had no trouble swinging his large hammer, as he once tipped the scales at 300 pounds himself. Mr. Duncan is standing on the far left. The man holding the dog and cat is Jim Bivens.

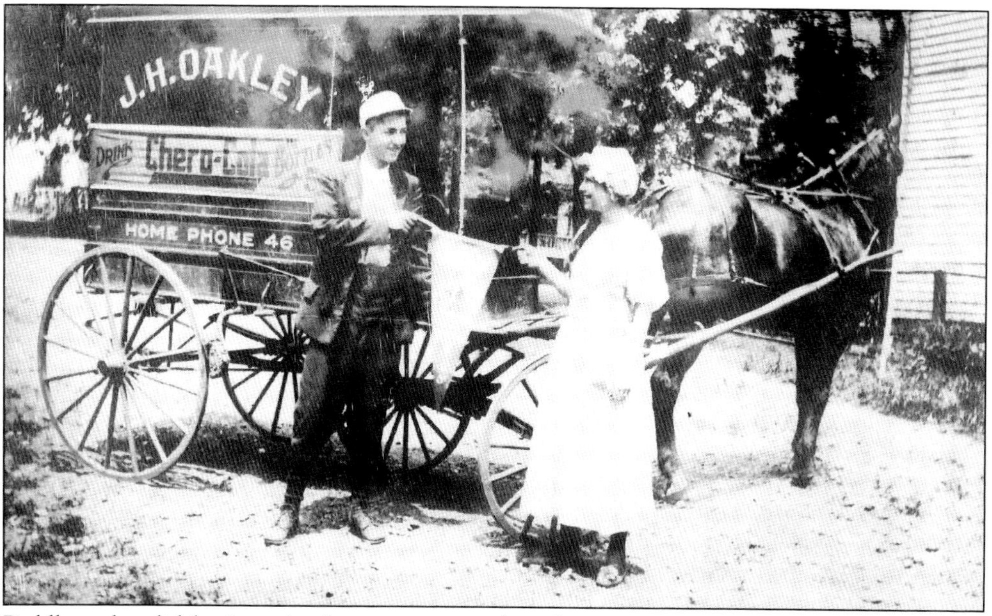

Peddlers also did business in the county, traveling from one community to another. Judson Oakley was one such entrepreneur. The banner on his wagon advertises, "CheroCola, In Bottles, 5¢." The banner he holds advertises the same. The young woman is Judson's wife, Edna Throp Oakley.

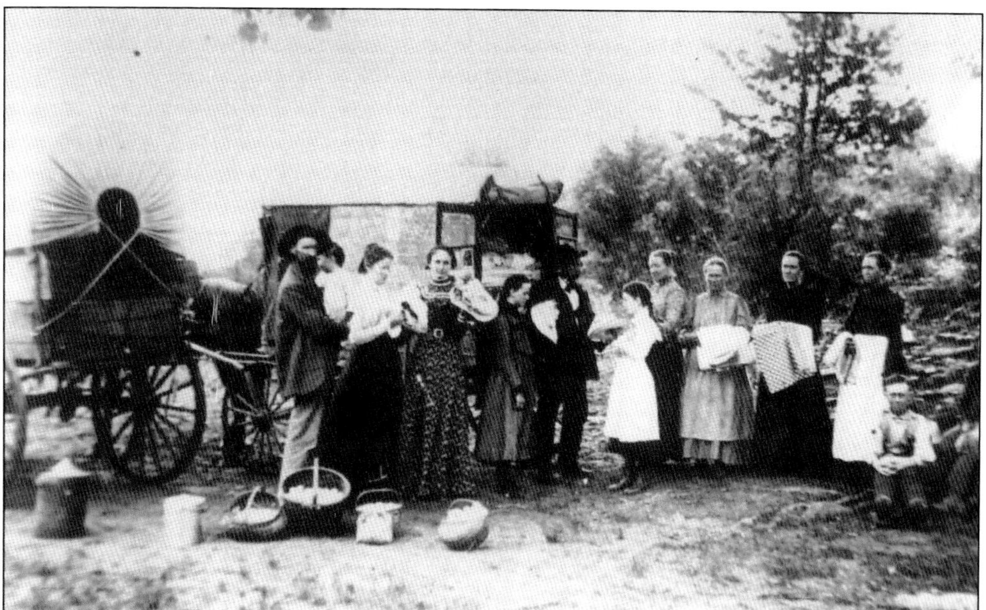

Peddlers often had to barter their goods, as this 1898 photograph shows. The peddler was Mr. Ellis and he is shown in the Old Bluff Springs area. In front are the eggs and butter the customers are using to barter. Left to right are: Joe Sanford (holding his granddaughter Vema Easton), Miss Willie Dies, Ollie Burton, Kate Sanford Burton, Mr. Ellis, Vesta Dies Massey, Sis Dies Cutrell, Mrs. Susan Burton, Nannie Dies, Jo Sanford, Lillard Sanford, John Fine Ash, and Donald Sanford.

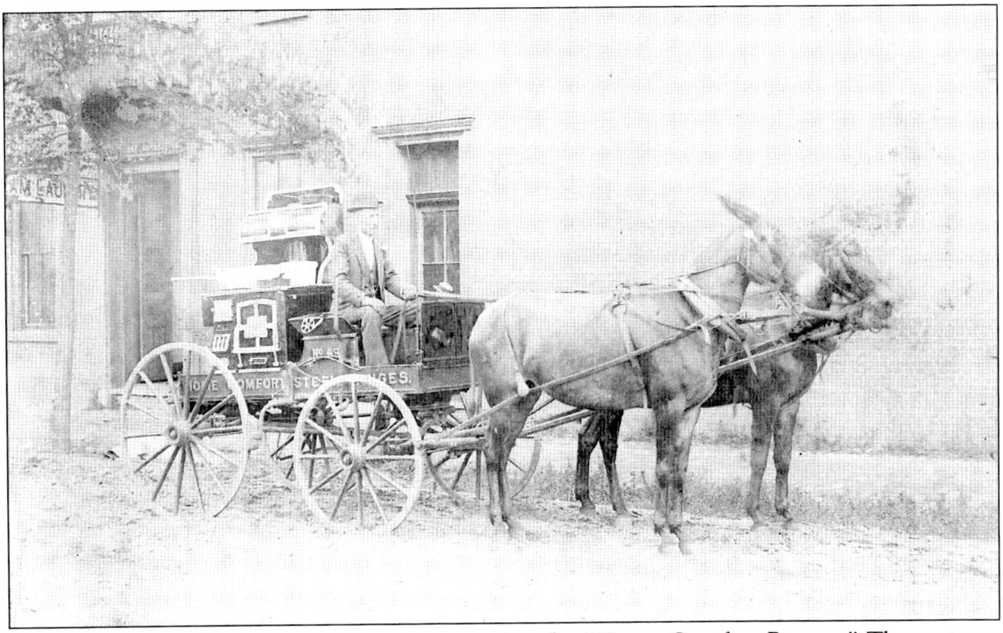

Uncle C. L. "Kit" Bennett was an area supervisor for "Home Comfort Ranges." These stoves were the latest in technology in their day and time. He is shown here delivering a new range. The two mules were his favorites. Their names were "Kate" and "Bird."

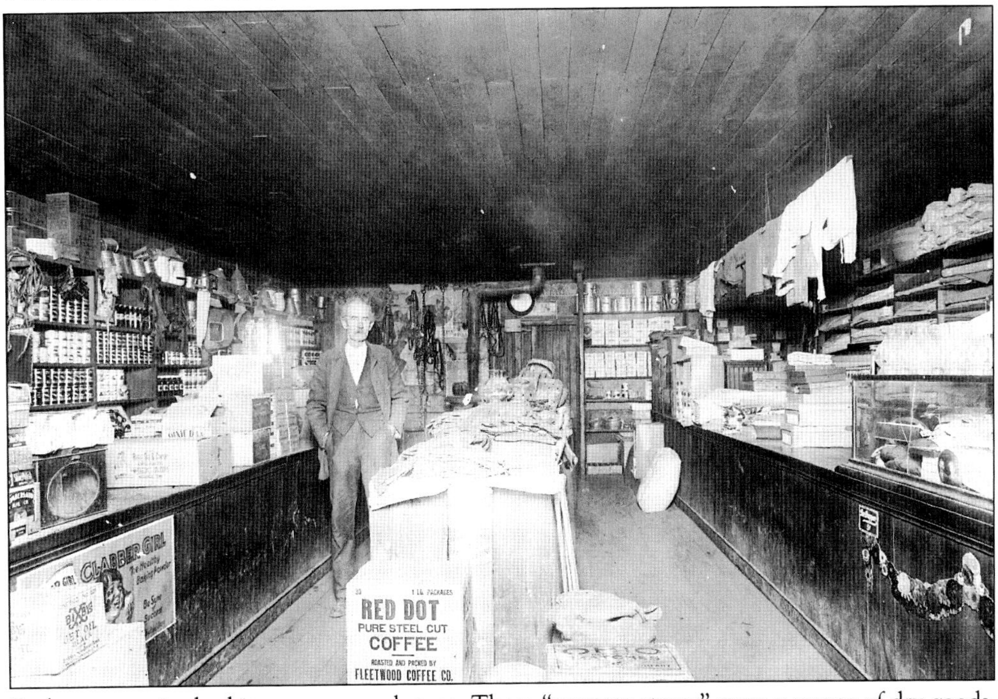

Each community had its own general store. These "country stores" were a source of dry goods, food items, hardware, and conversation. This 1925 photograph is of Willie Biggers in his store in the Beech Grove community. To the left was a room for grinding corn into meal. Another room in the back had a vinegar barrel, coal oil, and plow points. These small stores were the original "one-stop shop."

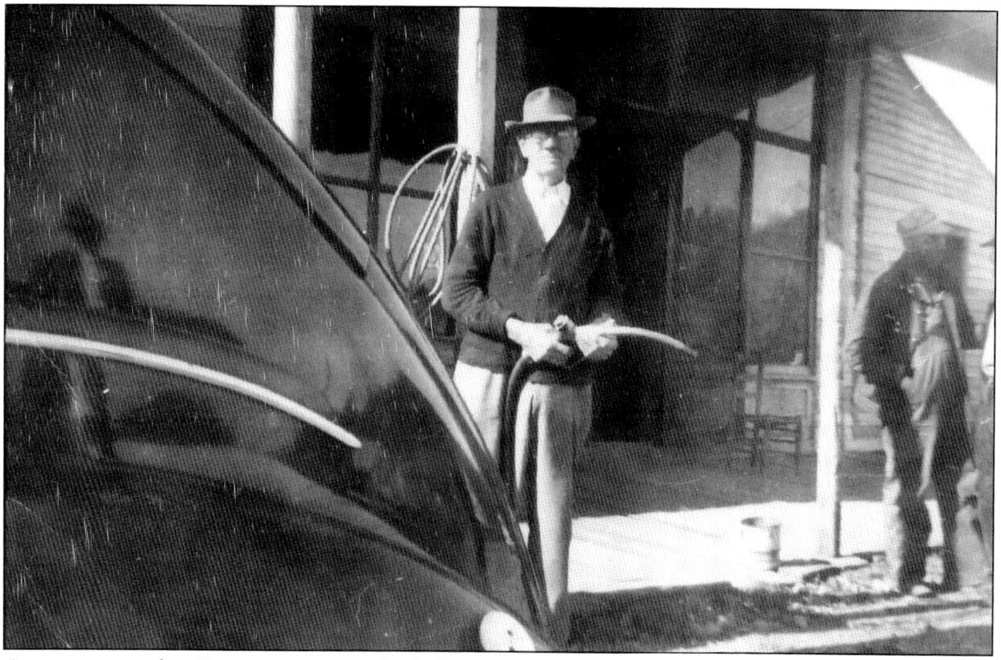

At one time, the Cato community had three general stores. Shown here in 1952 is Howard Beal in front of his store, which like many others, offered gasoline as well as staples. Mr. Beal purchased the store in 1915 and with his wife ran the store for over fifty years. The building burned in the 1970s.

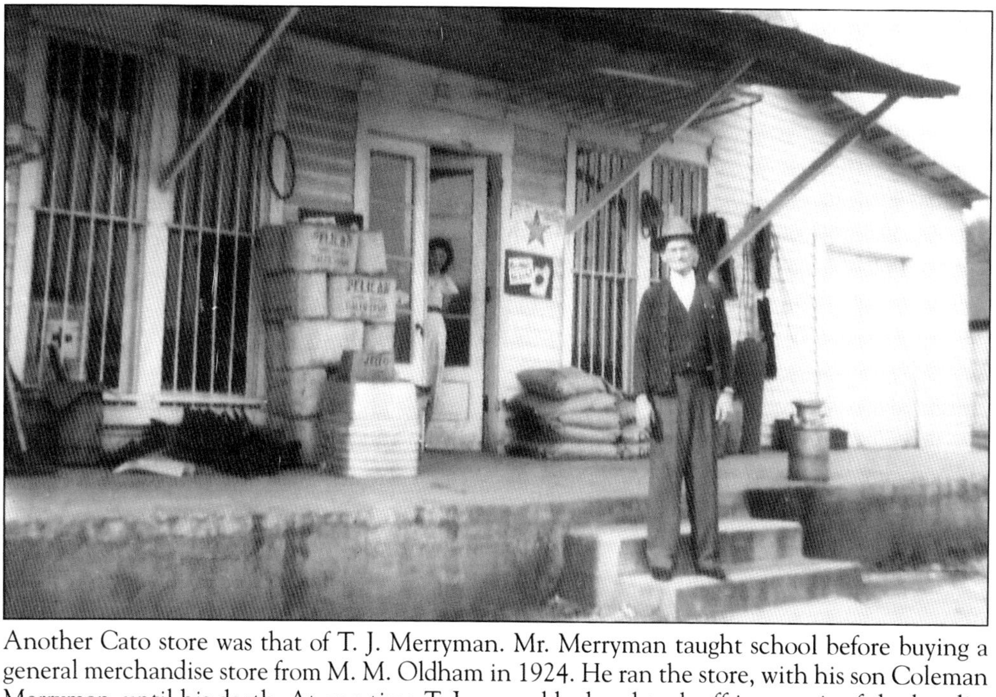

Another Cato store was that of T. J. Merryman. Mr. Merryman taught school before buying a general merchandise store from M. M. Oldham in 1924. He ran the store, with his son Coleman Merryman, until his death. At one time T. J. was robbed and took off in pursuit of the bandits when they fled. He didn't catch them although he hit speeds of 70 and 75 mph trying. He did, however, recognize one of the boys and they were caught and the money returned.

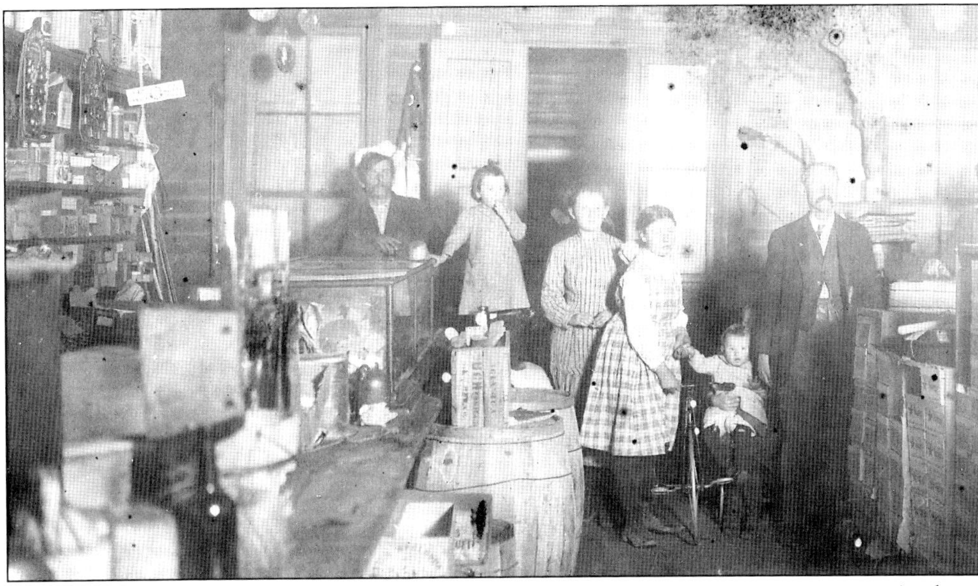

Jim Anthony's store stood on Old Gallatin Pike in the Walnut Grove community. Mr. Anthony is the man on the right. Barrels and boxes hold merchandise as every available inch of space is put to use. After Mr. Anthony's death, Beck Jackson ran the store. The store is no longer standing.

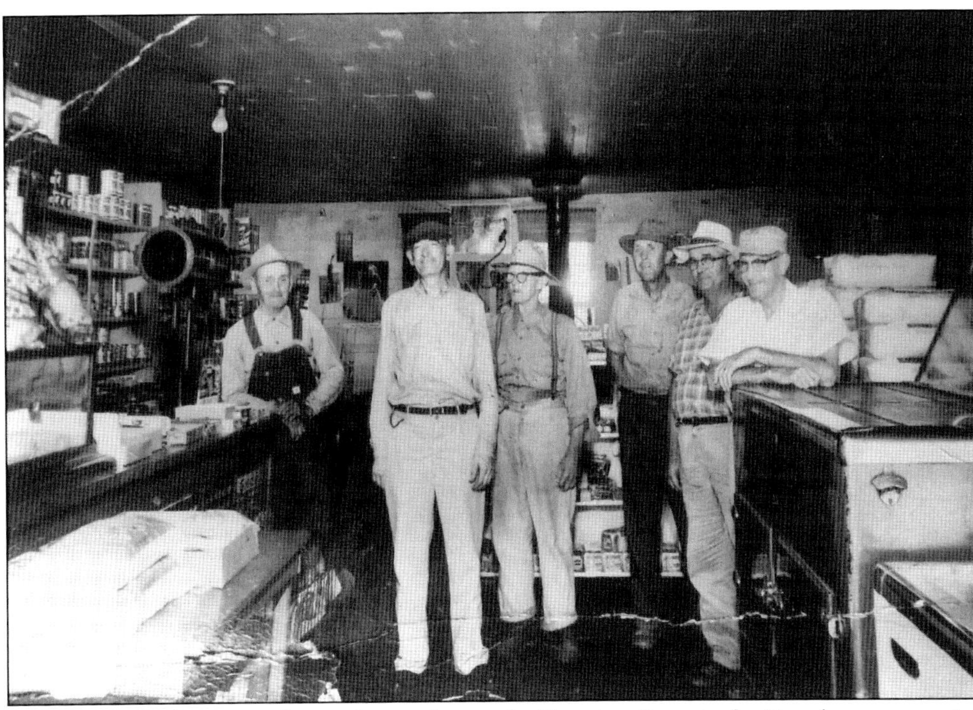

Tommy Stanford was one of several men who ran the Templow Store in the Templow community. The store was built in 1935 by Ollie Harper who was the first merchant. Mr. Stanford is shown here with several "locals." Left to right they are: Claude Carr, Leonard Fuller, Don Carr, Buck Harper, Frank Allen Fuller, and Mr. Stanford.

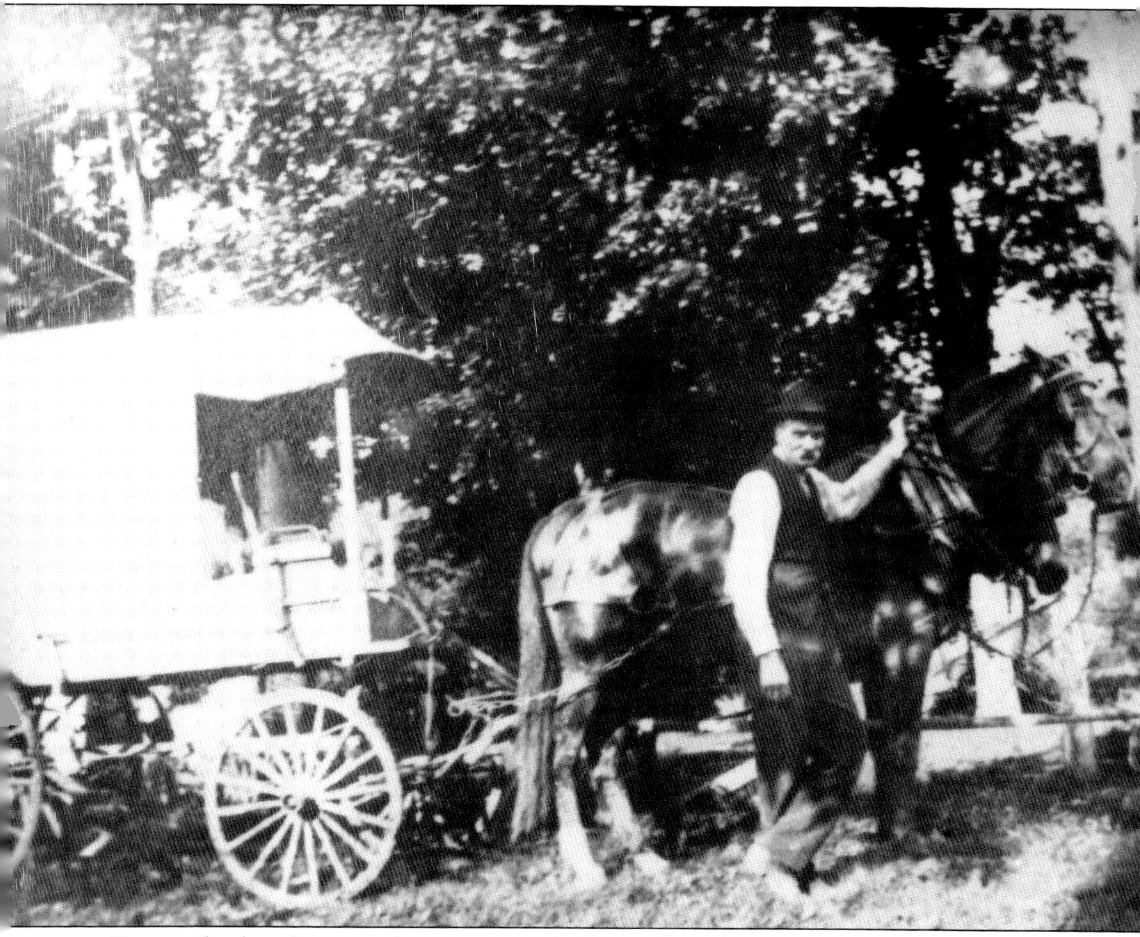

Despite the fact that a good country store had everything from apples to zippers, many people in rural areas didn't have transportation to get to a store or to carry their goods back home. Peddlers such as Mr. Etheridge, shown here, catered to residents who enjoyed the priviledge of "shopping at home," long before the Home Shopping Network was created. Etheridge traveled the back roads of the county around the turn of the century and into the 1920s.

Three

TRAVEL

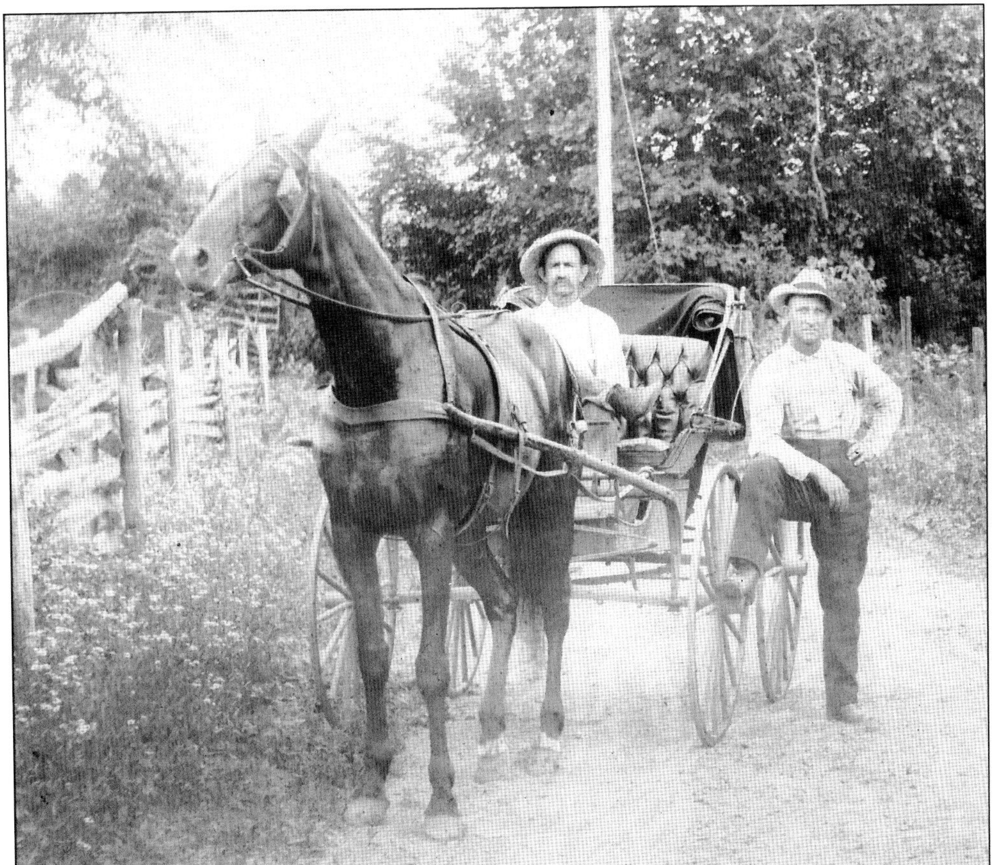

Buggies were the accepted mode of travel when this photograph was made around the turn of the century. This quiet country lane with its rail fence was typical of most roads in the county. The gentleman with his foot on the wheel of the buggy is M. M. Kirby, father of Mary Agnes Kirby Chitwood. The man in the buggy is unidentified. In just a few short years the buggy would become a relic of the past.

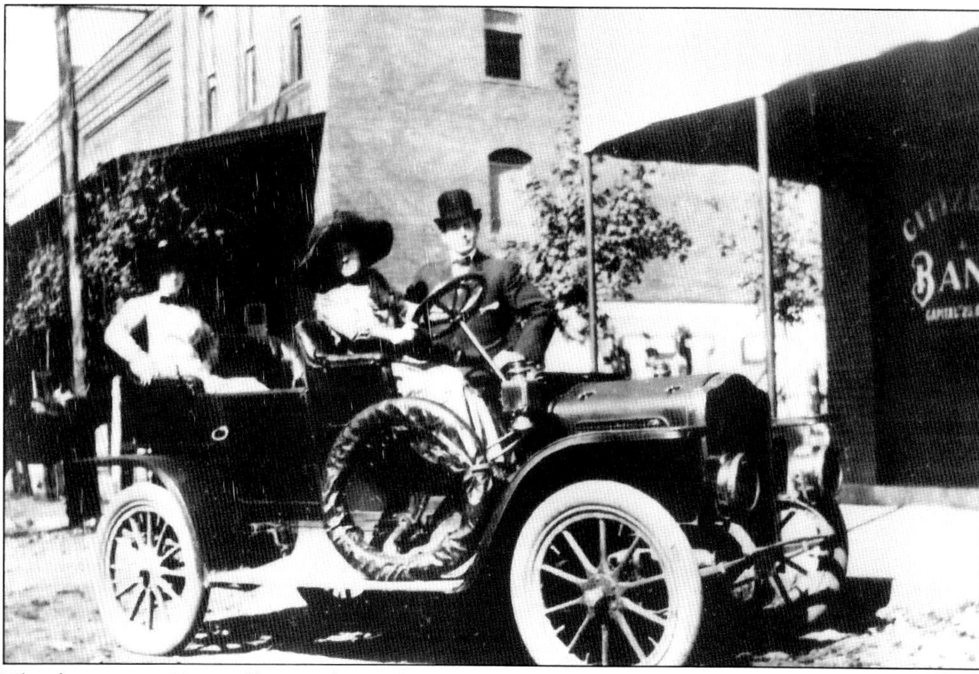

The first car in Hartsville was this White Steamer. In this photograph, thought to have been made in 1905, the steam-powered car is parked in front of the old Citizen's Bank on Main Street. The car was owned by Mr. A.C. Welch who purchased it in Washington, D.C., and drove it to Hartsville. The driver in the photograph is Miss Will Earl Hale. Mary Langford sits in the rear. The man is unidentified.

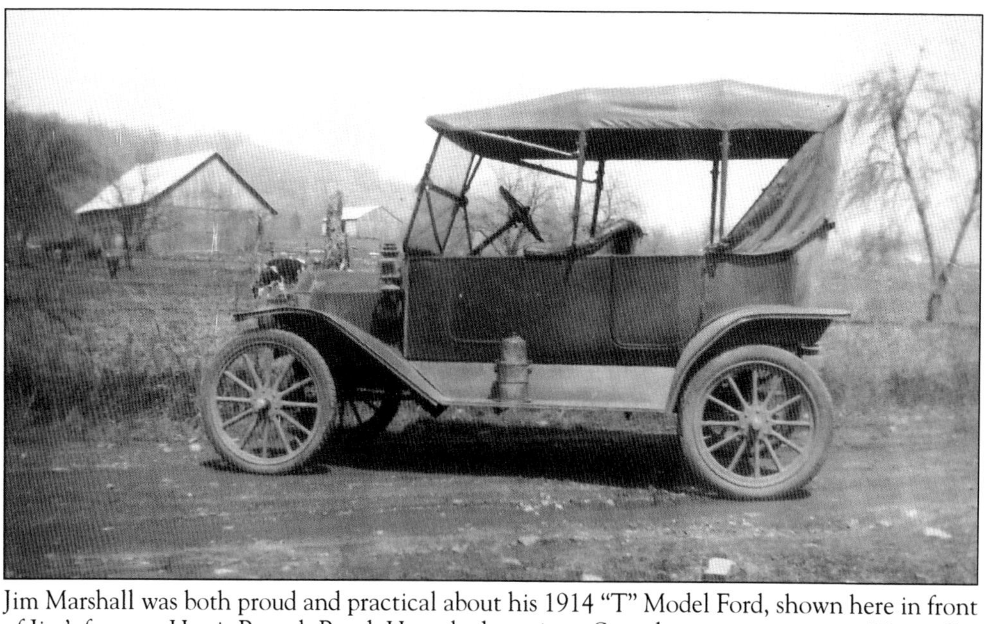

Jim Marshall was both proud and practical about his 1914 "T" Model Ford, shown here in front of Jim's farm on Harris Branch Road. He only drove it on Saturdays to go to town in Hartsville, and Sundays to go to church in Green Grove. The rest of the week he kept it in his shed. There, he used a jack to place a bench under each axle so that the car sat off the ground all week, protecting it from wear and tear.

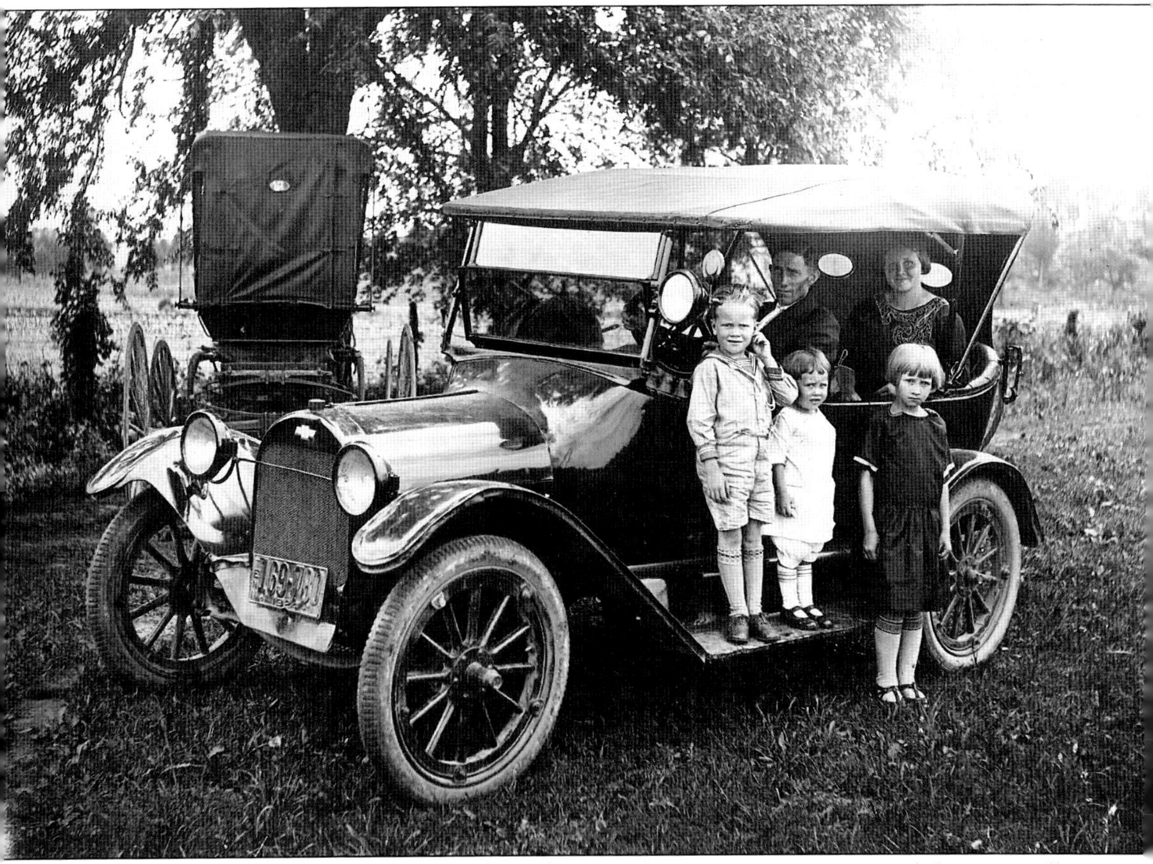

In 1924, when this photograph was made in the Providence community, automobiles were still the new boy on the block and many people continued to use horses and buggies. As the picture shows, the buggy and horses tied up behind the car were yet to be replaced by any Tin Lizzie. Justifiably proud of their new vehicle are Robert McKee and his wife Georgie Pruett McKee. Their children, posed on and by the running board, are Buddy, Maggie, and Robbie.

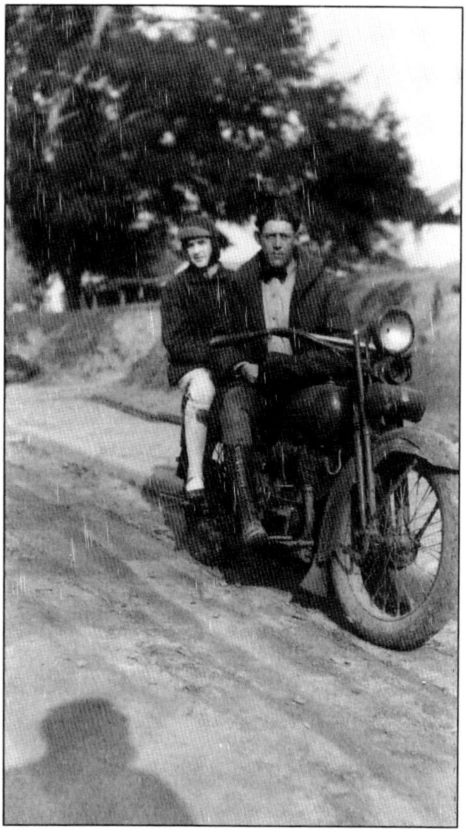

A young George Terry and an unidentified friend perch on this early model motorcycle in the late 1920s. Many a local chicken, dog, or cow was spooked when George rode this around home in the Providence community. Remembering that most county roads were unpaved until after World War II, one cannot envy his ride much.

Styling in cars had changed considerably when this photograph was made in 1938. The car's large grill and headlights stand out, plus its wire rims. The door opened backwards by today's standards. The young ladies seem more interested in the photographer. They are Katherine McMurtry (left) and Iris West Reese (right). The gentleman is Seldon West, Iris' grandfather.

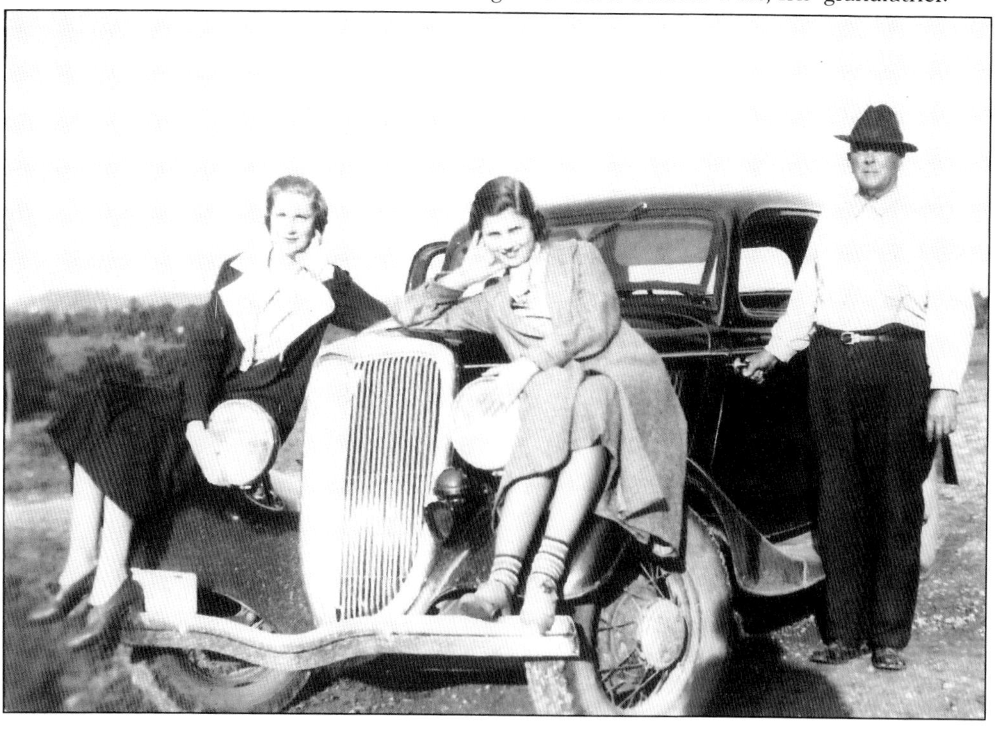

Trucks have been no less an important part of the community's past. In 1944 this truck was being used by the Holder Brothers at their stockyards in Hartsville. The stockyards are still in the Holder family today. Note the license plate in the shape of Tennessee. At one time a person could request the same number tag from year to year. This tag number was used by the Holders for many years.

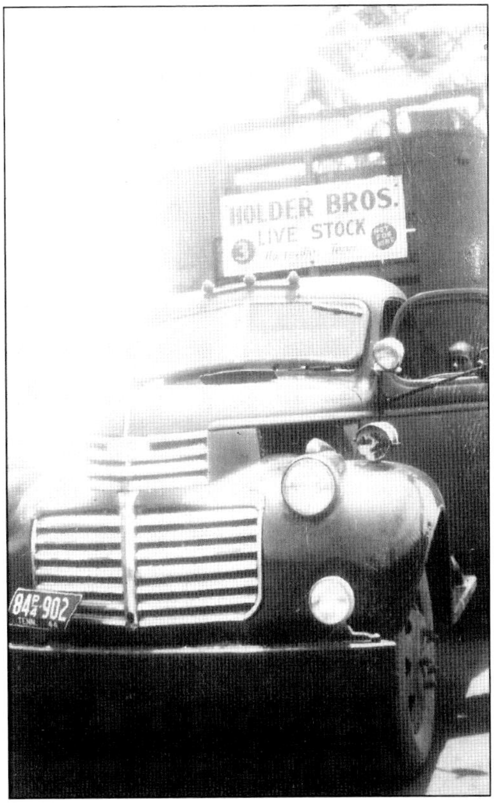

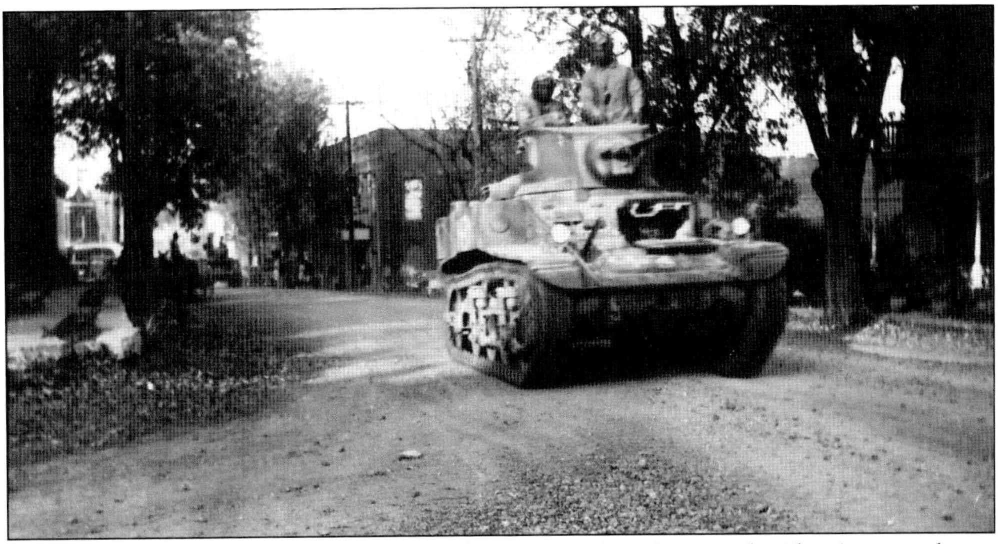

A different type of vehicle rolls up Church Street in this photograph. The Army tank was one of many that traveled the dirt roads of the town and county during World War II when maneuvers where being held in middle Tennessee. Because the hills and climate in this area closely resembled that of Germany, military maneuvers were conducted over a large part of rural middle Tennessee. The soldiers, many from up north, were made to feel welcome by the local folks and many husbands and wives met during maneuvers. In the background is the Eveska Theatre.

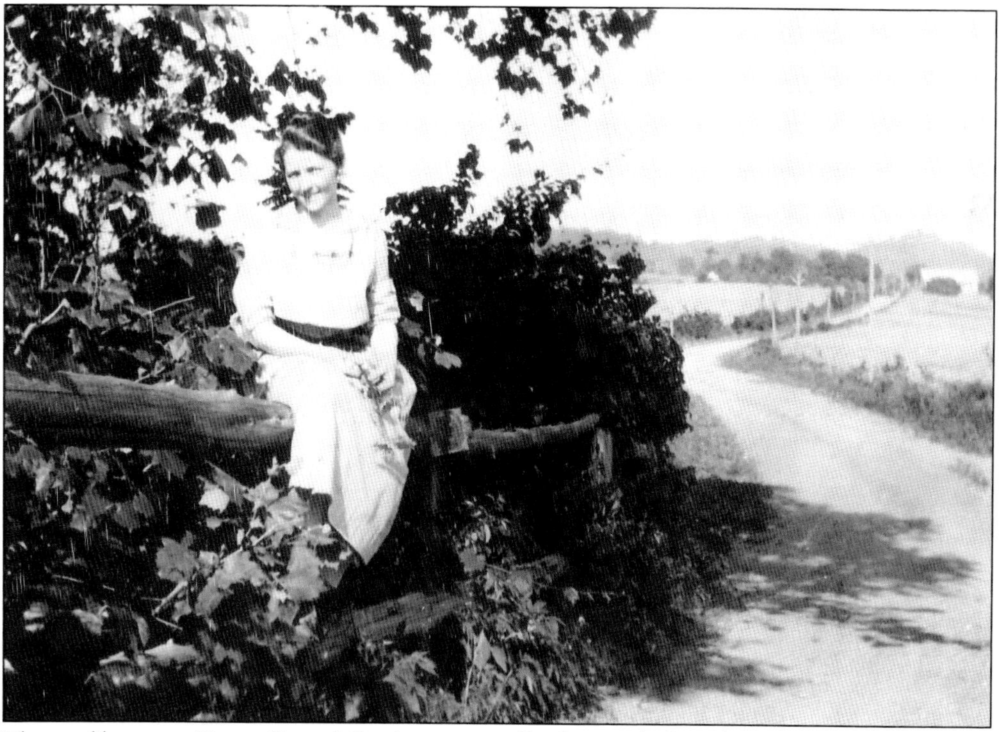

The road between Hartsville and Carthage was still a dirt road when this photograph was made. Nan Haynie poses on the fence surrounding the farm she and her husband Henry owned on Old Carthage Highway, now Highway 25. Their farm, now owned by H. B. Cunningham, was on the edge of town, just this side of Big Goose Creek. The photograph dates from the 1920s.

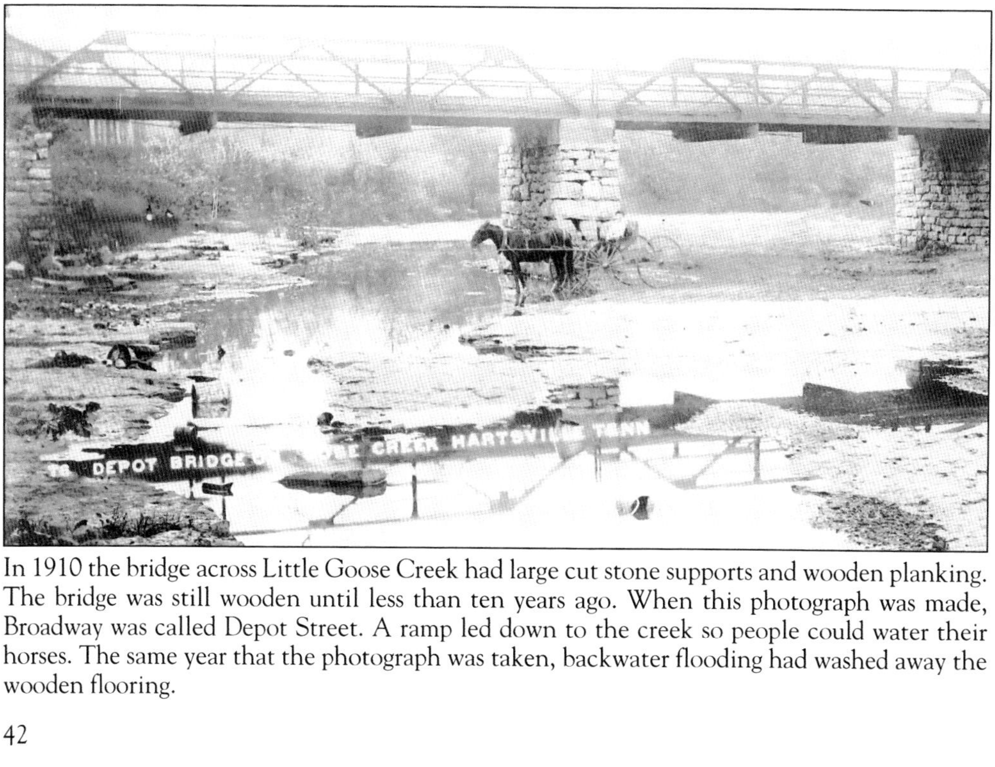

In 1910 the bridge across Little Goose Creek had large cut stone supports and wooden planking. The bridge was still wooden until less than ten years ago. When this photograph was made, Broadway was called Depot Street. A ramp led down to the creek so people could water their horses. The same year that the photograph was taken, backwater flooding had washed away the wooden flooring.

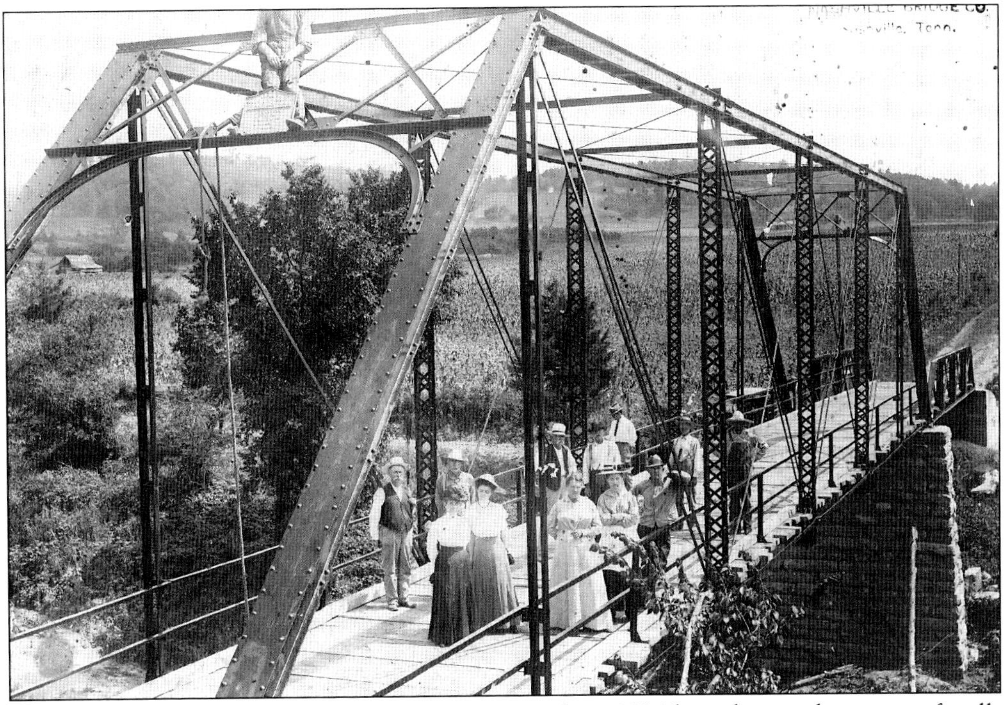

The completion of this bridge over Big Goose Creek in 1896 brought out this group of well-dressed citizens. The bridge was built by the Nashville Bridge Company. The stone for the foundation is impressive; each stone was hand-cut to fit. The iron framework was "modern" at the turn of the century. Notice the thickness of the wooden planks used for flooring. The gentleman on the far left in the vest and straw hat was Mr. Richard Love, chairman of the County Court bridge committee.

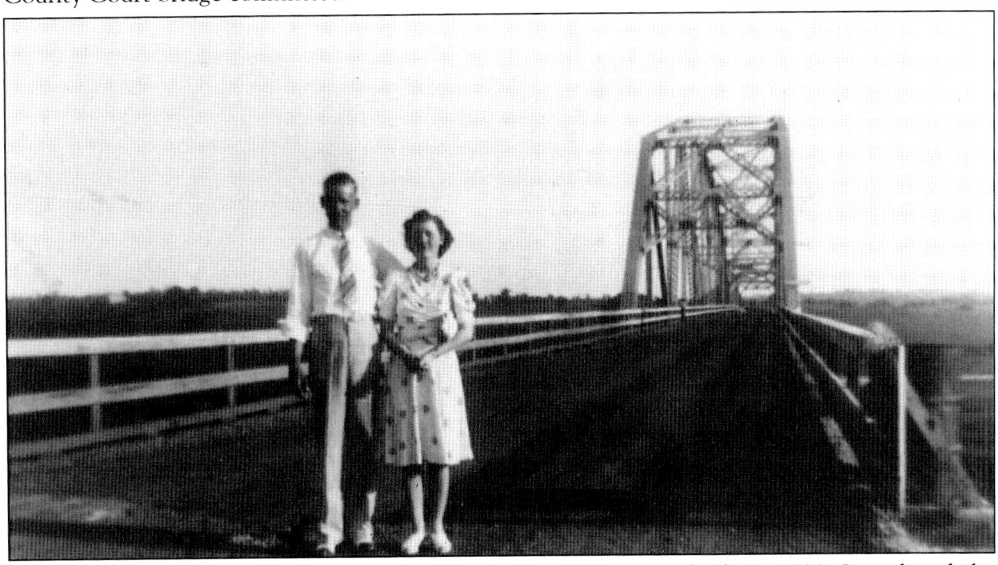

The Coleman Winston Bridge over the Cumberland River was built in 1929. It replaced the ferry at Lowe's Landing. Mr. Winston had become instrumental in getting the state to build the bridge, as had other prominent citizens. It was replaced in the 1980s with a new concrete span. This photograph shows the old bridge around 1940. Shown are Mr. and Mrs. James Taylor.

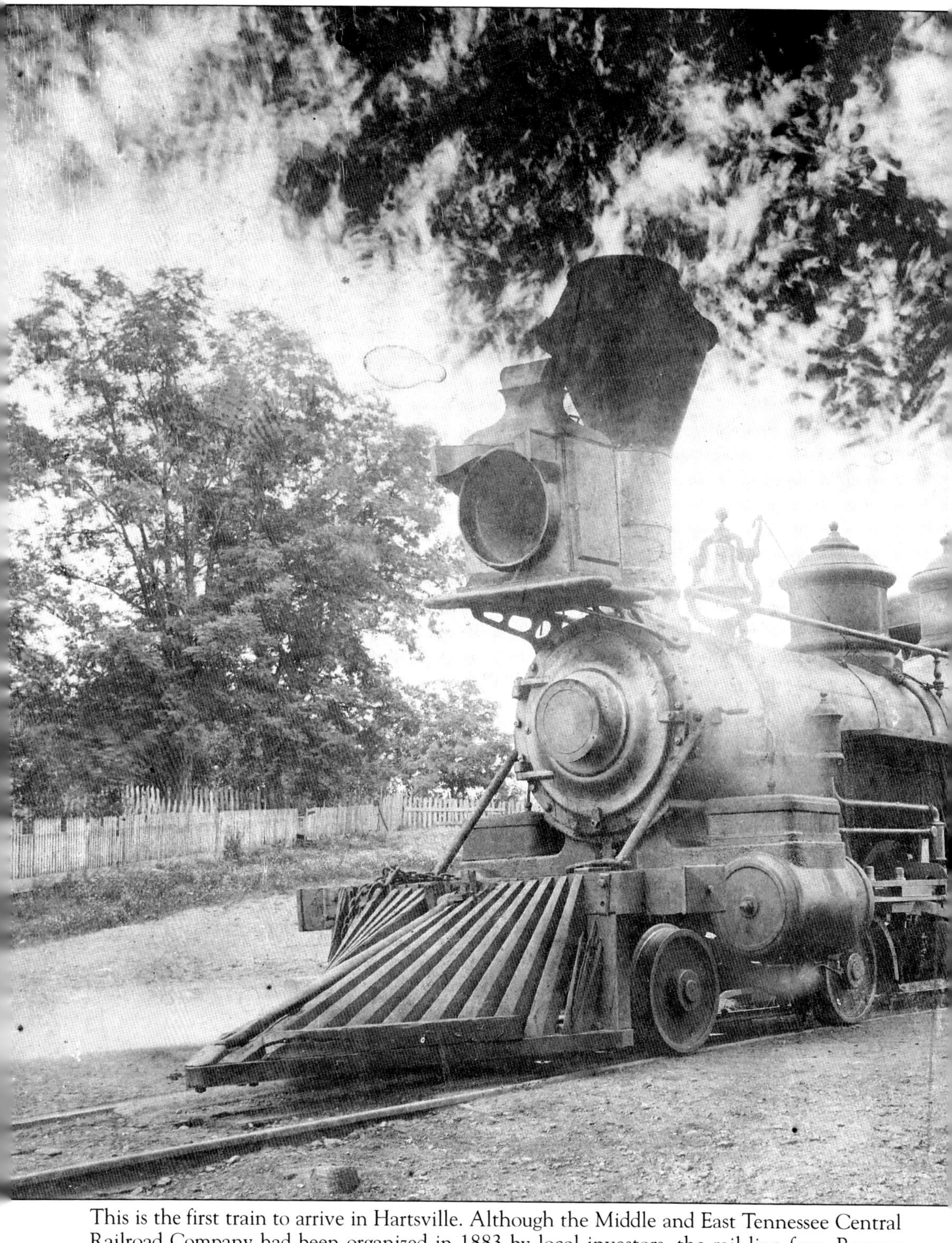

This is the first train to arrive in Hartsville. Although the Middle and East Tennessee Central Railroad Company had been organized in 1883 by local investors, the rail line from Rogana (in Sumner County) to Hartsville was not completed until January 1, 1892. Later that same

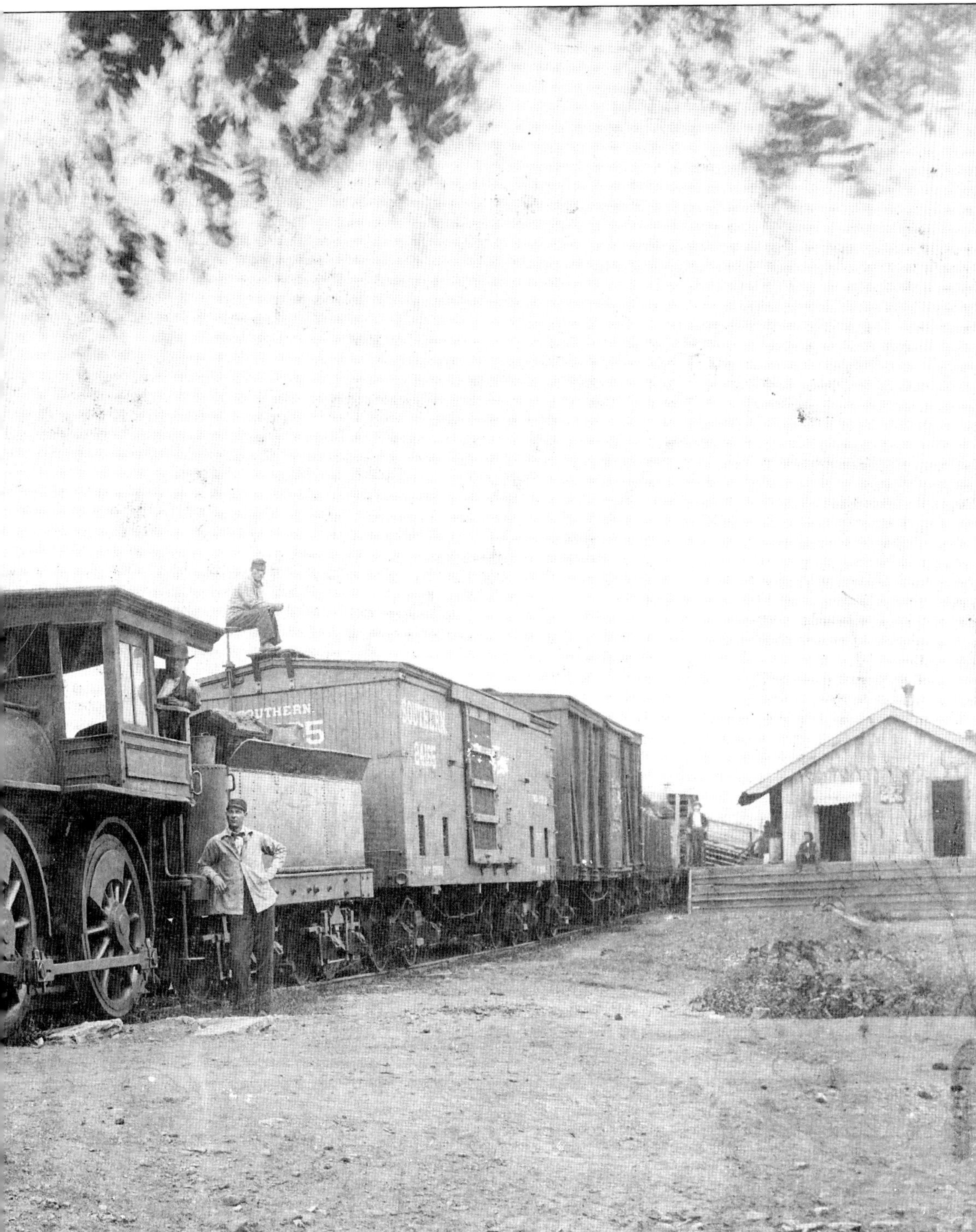

year, the first locomotive to travel the line pulled into Hartsville. The building shown is part of the present depot. Two of the men in the photograph are identified as Walter Fiddler and William Fisher.

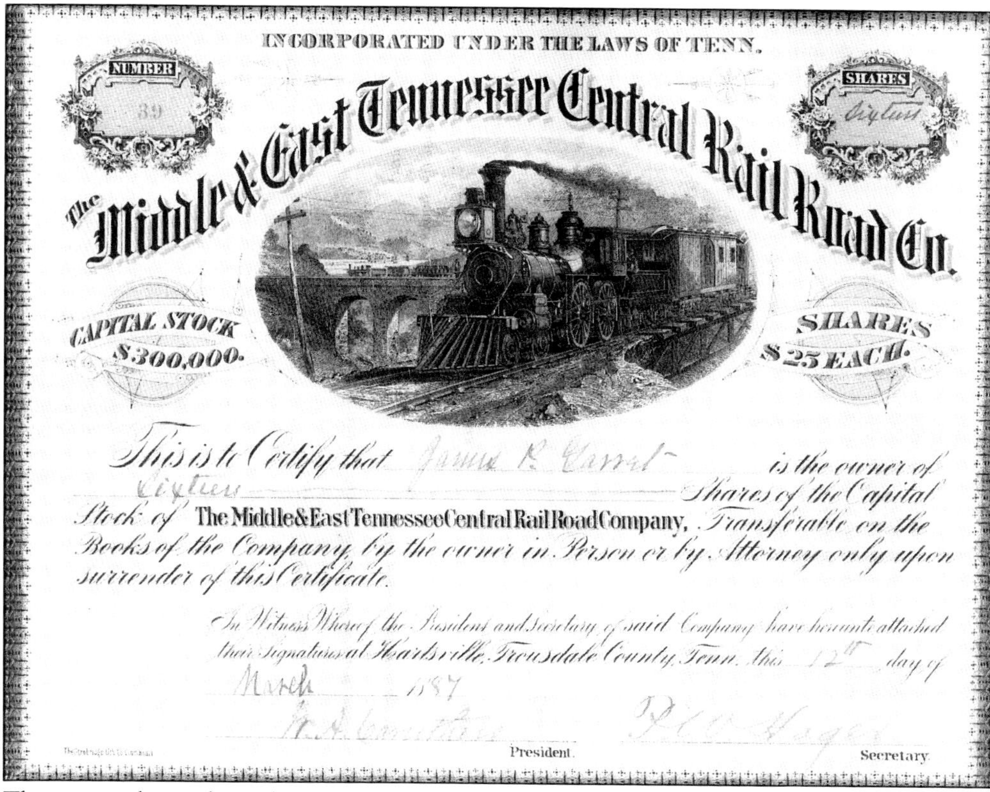

INCORPORATED UNDER THE LAWS OF TENN.

NUMBER 39

SHARES Sixteen

The Middle & East Tennessee Central Rail Road Co.

CAPITAL STOCK $300,000.

SHARES $25 EACH.

This is to Certify that ______ is the owner of Sixteen Shares of the Capital Stock of The Middle & East Tennessee Central Rail Road Company, Transferable on the Books of the Company by the owner in Person or by Attorney only upon surrender of this Certificate.

In Witness Whereof the President and Secretary of said Company have hereunto attached their Signatures at Hartsville, Trousdale County, Tenn. this 12th day of March 1887

President

Secretary

This is a stock certificate from the Middle and East Tennessee Central Railroad Company. The Railroad was organized on February 19, 1883 by several Trousdale County investors at $25 a share with a capital stock of $300,000. The line was to extend from Gallatin to Knoxville but got only as far as Hartsville. It was sold under foreclosure in 1897 and eventually became part of the Louisville and Nashville (L & N) Line.

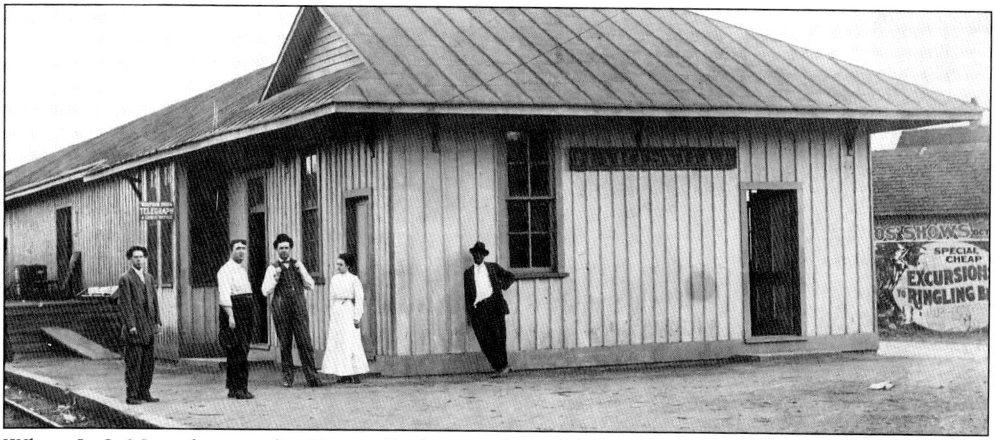

When L & N took over the Hartsville line it also added onto and improved the depot. This photograph was made after 1906 when L & N took over. The depot building is still standing despite the fact that the last train ran in 1978 and the tracks were taken up soon after. The building has been restored and today houses a museum. The woman in the photograph is Ida Hammond, clerk, and one of the men is Jim Bob Hall, the agent. Note the sign advertising "cheap excursions to the Ringling Brothers Circus."

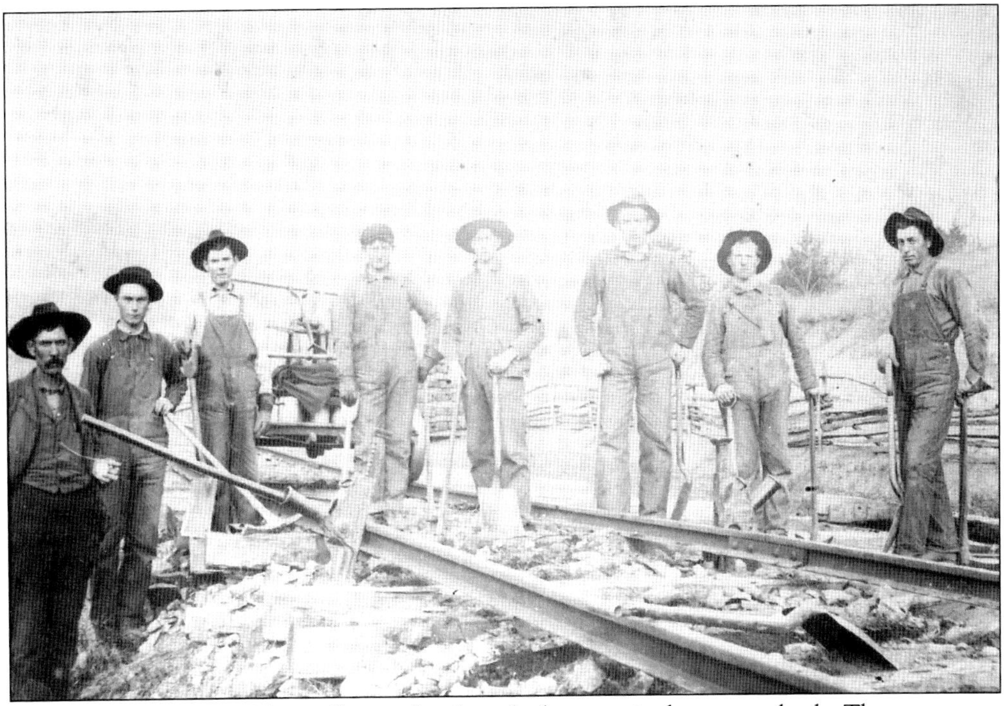

Building the line into Hartsville was hard work that required a strong back. These men are shown laying track for the Middle and East Tennessee Central Railroad, around 1890 or 1891. The line extended from Rogana to Hartsville, a total of 11.38 miles. The financially strapped line ended their efforts at Hartsville, despite plans to go even eventually to Knoxville.

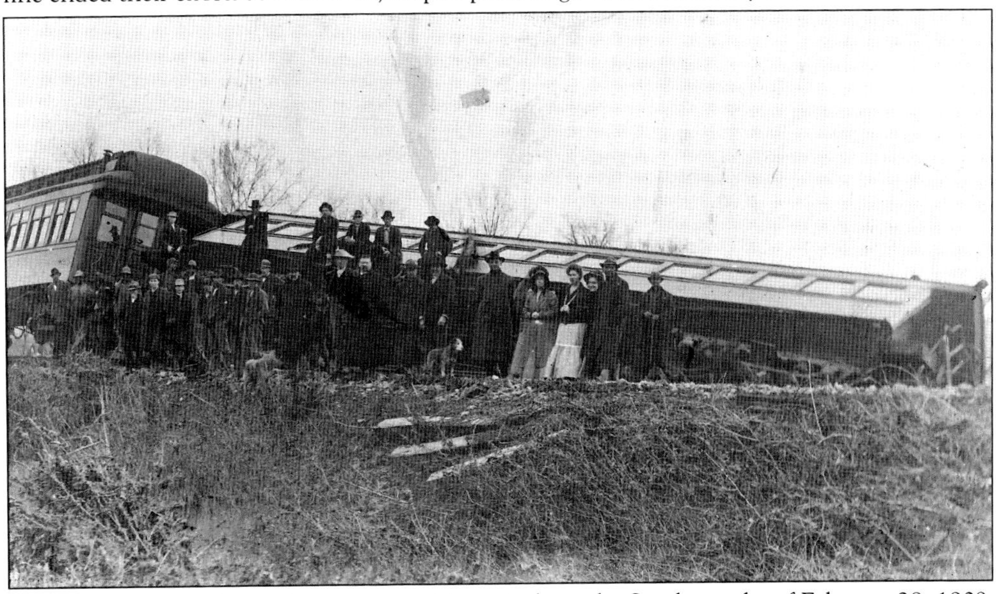

The train ride into Hartsville was not without its hazards. On the night of February 28, 1909, backwater caused by heavy rains washed away part of the railbed, causing this wreck. The next morning local citizens flocked to see the damage and have this picture taken. It is believed that there were no serious injuries. The wreck occurred at "Dalton's Station," a stop on the line just before Hartsville.

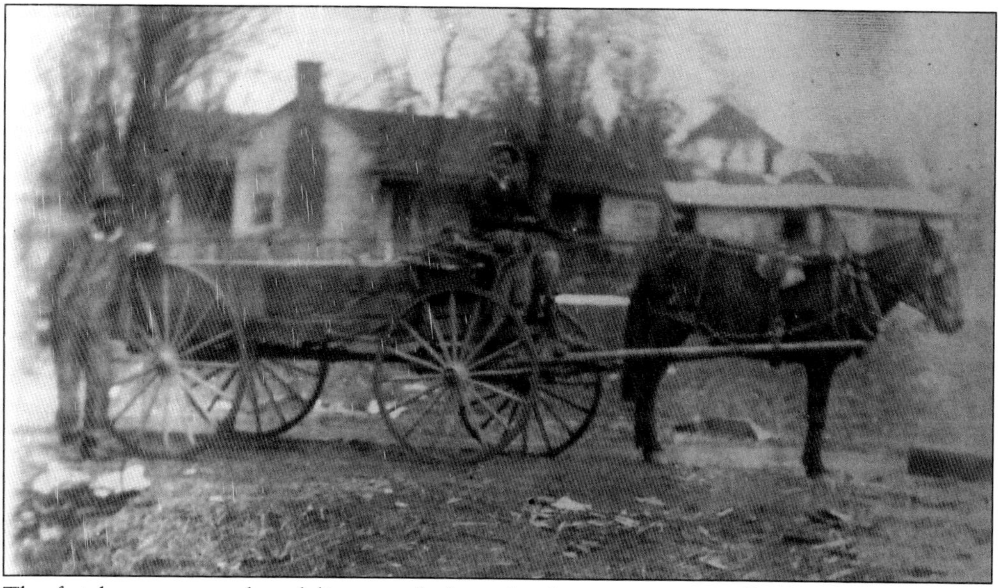

The freight wagon used to deliver goods from the depot to town. Millard "Pa" Carter is the driver. Mr. Carter drove the freight wagon for many years and was a regular around town. The other gentleman is Edgar Dean McCadden.

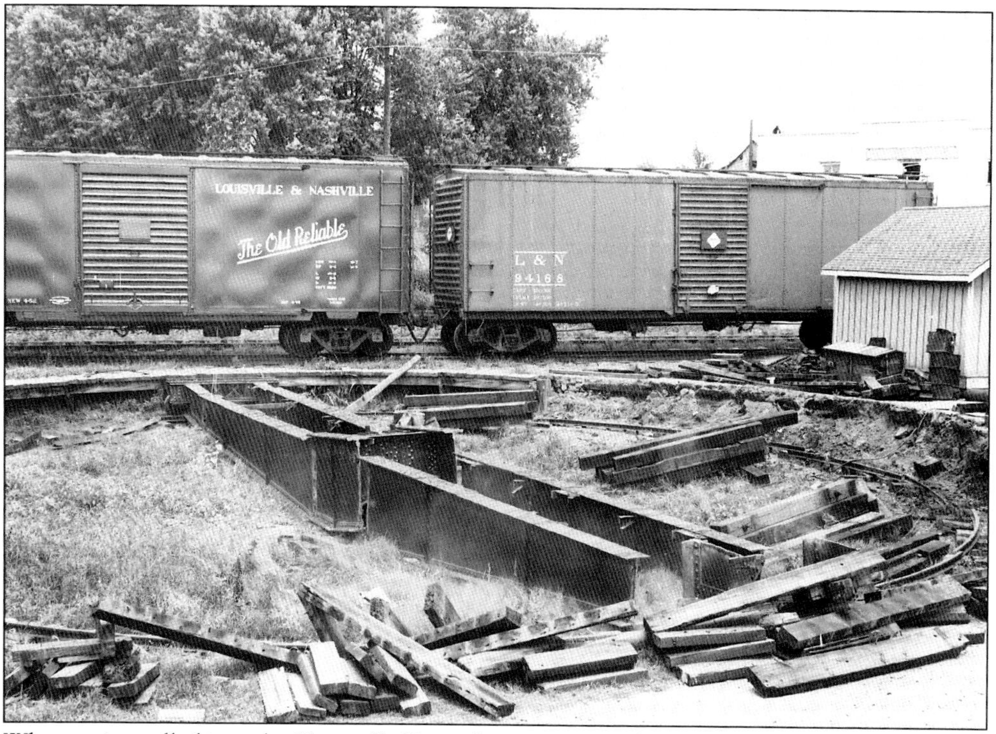

When trains pulled into the Hartsville Depot because it was the end of the line, a turntable was needed to turn the engine around. The Hartsville turntable was so well balanced that according to old timers, an engine weighing fifty tons could be turned by only two men. The turntable was dismantled after regular passengers service stopped in 1953. The photograph shows the turntable being taken apart.

Four

THE RIVER

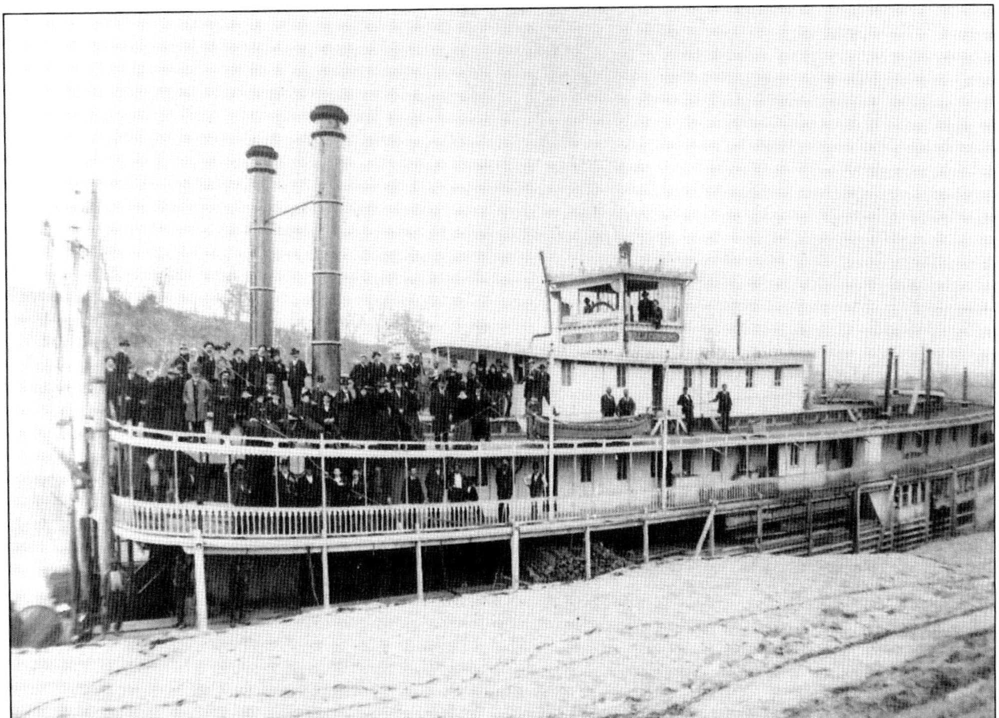

Hartsville was no stranger to river travel when this photograph was made in 1897. Since 1798, when the Hart family opened Hart's Ferry, the Cumberland River has been a major travel route. The boat pictured here, the *Will J. Cummings*, piloted by Capt. W. S. Bowman, was a packet. When it came to Hartsville on March 2, 1897, for a daytime excursion trip, it was a famous boat. A year earlier it lost the only side-by-side steamboat race on the Cumberland when it raced the *R. Dunbar* piloted by Capt. Tom Ryman Jr.

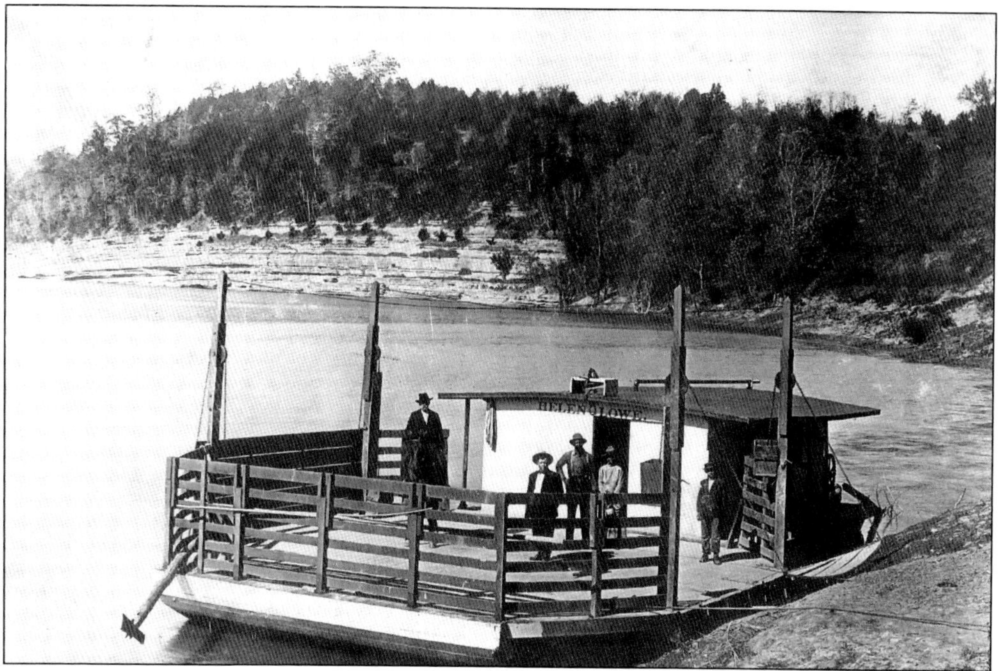

This is the ferry at Lowe's Landing on the river. Today, the location is often referred to as Taylor's Landing, for the Taylor family that farms the land around it. Lowe's Ferry connected Hartsville to the Providence community and Wilson County. After a tragic accident when a car drove off one end of the ferry and its driver was drowned, the public pressed the state to consider a bridge. In 1929 the Coleman Winston Bridge was completed and the ferry ceased to operate.

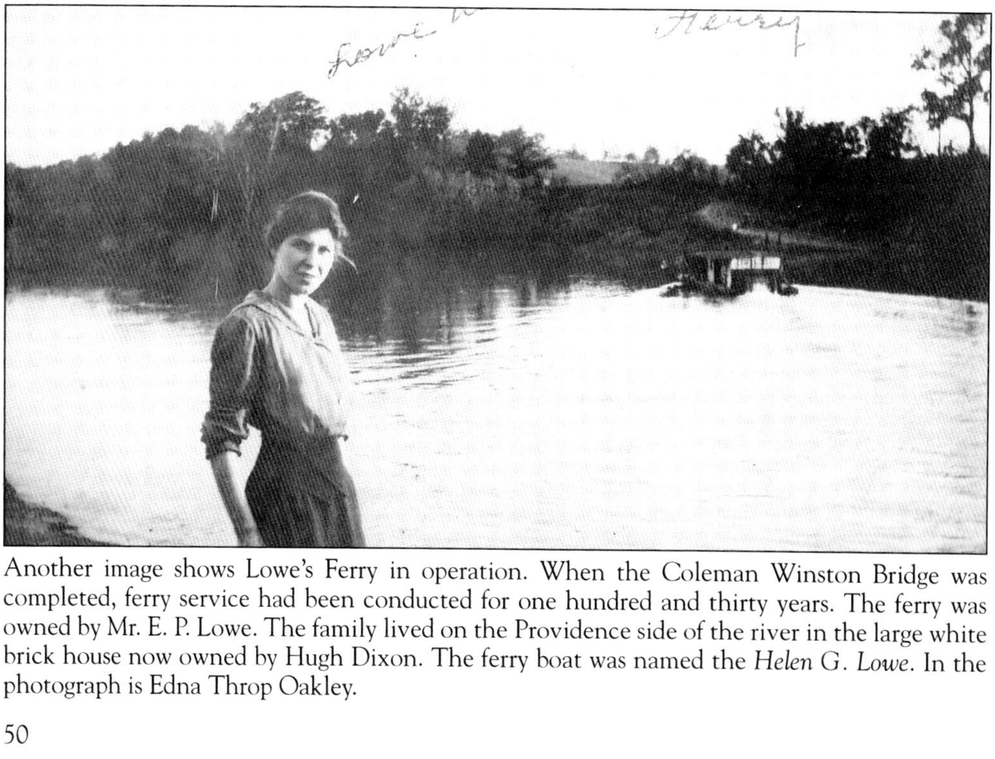

Another image shows Lowe's Ferry in operation. When the Coleman Winston Bridge was completed, ferry service had been conducted for one hundred and thirty years. The ferry was owned by Mr. E. P. Lowe. The family lived on the Providence side of the river in the large white brick house now owned by Hugh Dixon. The ferry boat was named the *Helen G. Lowe*. In the photograph is Edna Throp Oakley.

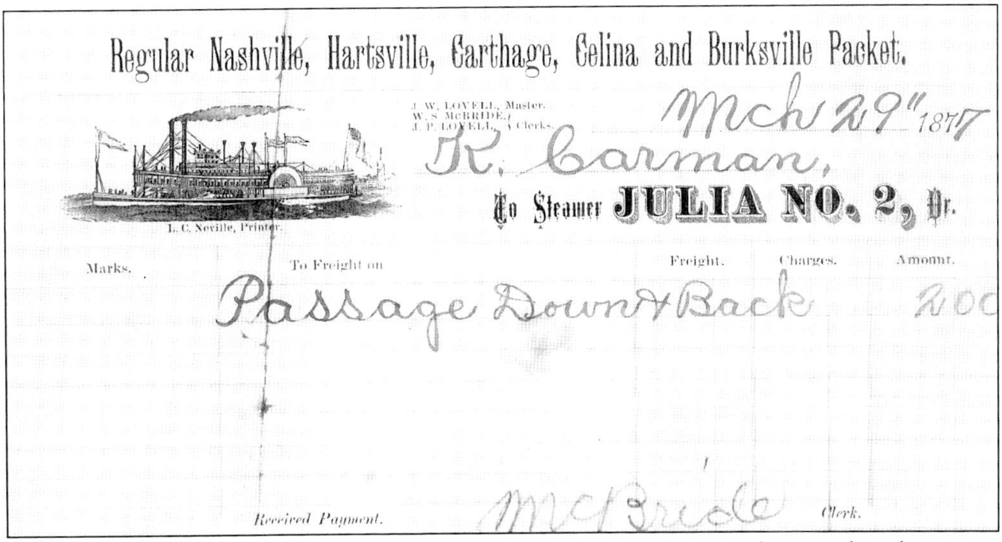
Regular Nashville, Hartsville, Carthage, Celina and Burksville Packet.

J. W. LOVELL, Master.
W. S. McBRIDE, J. P. LOVELL, Clerks.

Mch 29" 1877

R. Carman,

To Steamer JULIA NO. 2, Dr.

L. C. Neville, Printer.

Marks.	To Freight on	Freight.	Charges.	Amount.
	Passage Down & Back			2 00

Received Payment. McBride Clerk.

This ticket dated March 29, 1877, shows Hartsville as a regular stop for a packet ship going upriver. Besides Hartsville, the towns of Carthage, Celina, and Barksville, KY, are listed. The cost for the journey? Two dollars to Nashville and back. Later in the summer, when the water level dropped, boats could not make the trip up river. Eventually the Corps of Engineers would build a system of locks to ensure year-round travel.

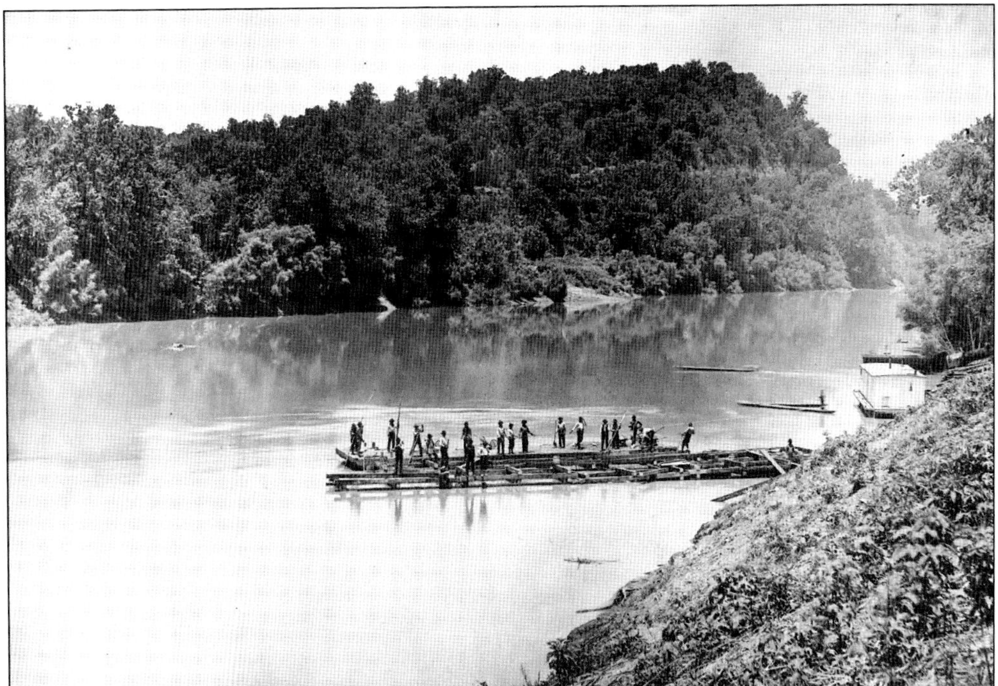

In 1894 construction was begun on Lock #5. This lock, with one side touching Trousdale County and the other side adjoining Wilson County, began with the building of a coffer dam to hold back the river from the site. In this photograph, dated June 2nd of that same year, men and equipment are just arriving. The bank on the far side is Trousdale County.

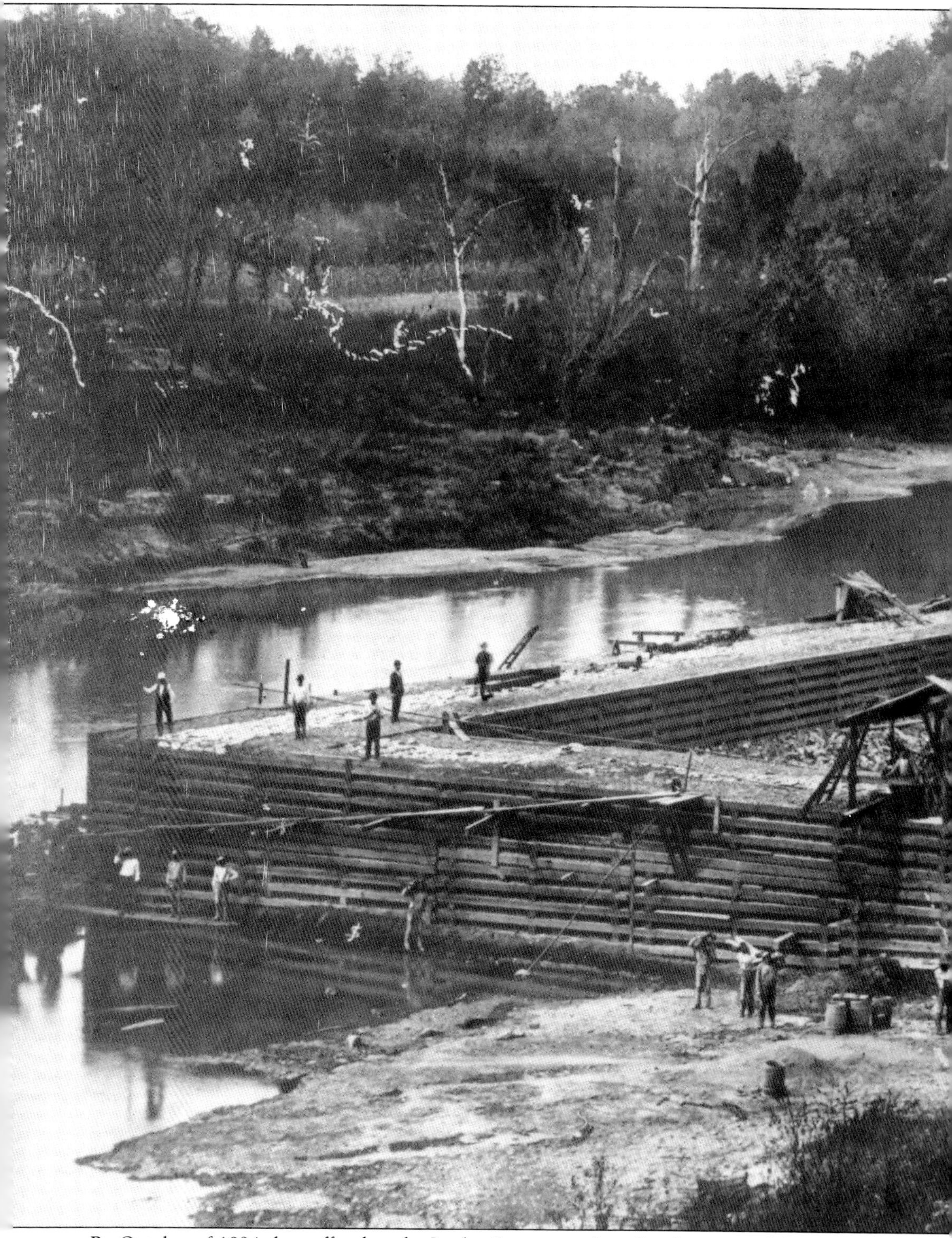

By October of 1894 the coffer dam for Lock #5 was complete. By this time of the year, based on low rainfall, the river bed is noticeably shallow. The lock system would prevent that in the

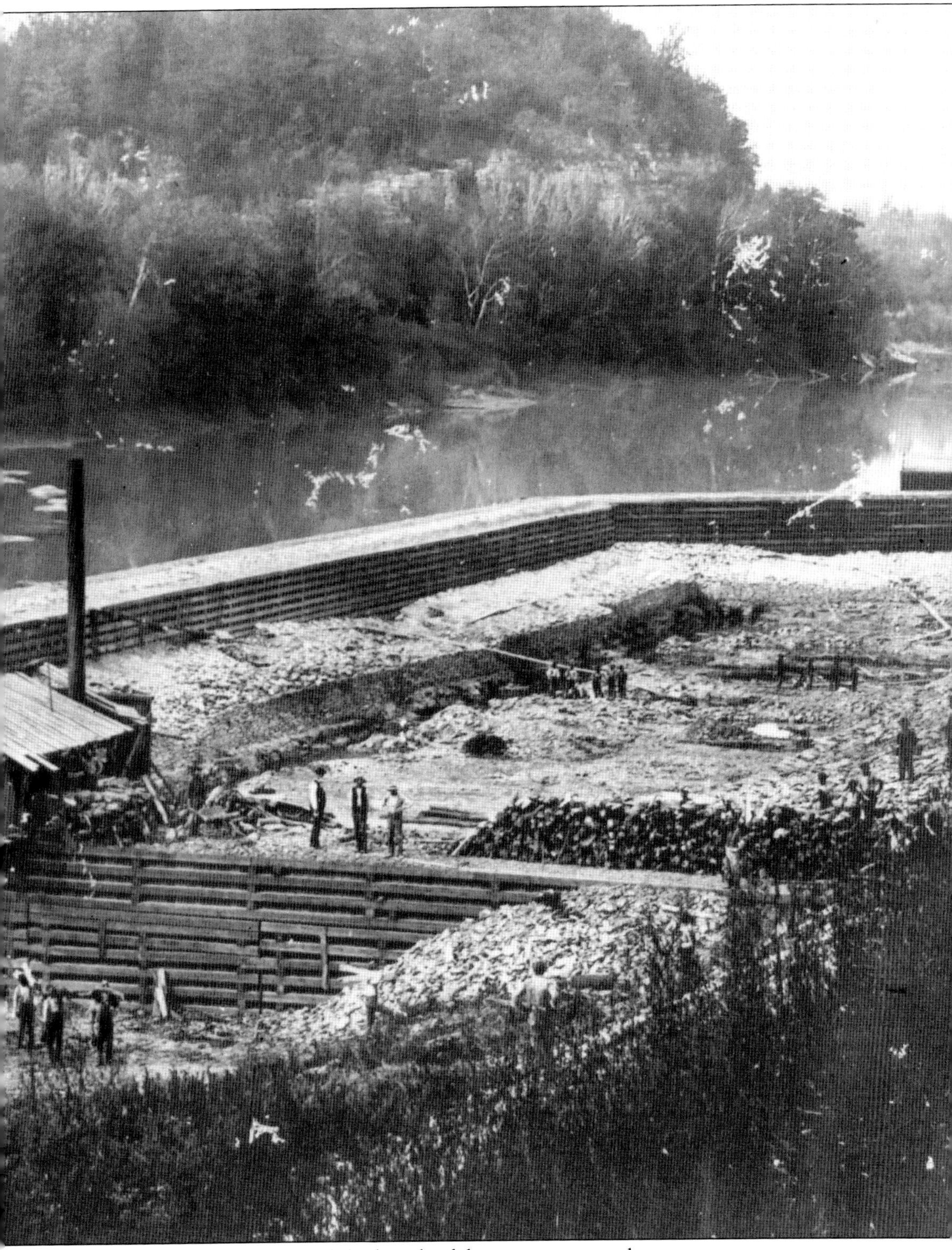

future and allow boats to travel the length of the river year-round.

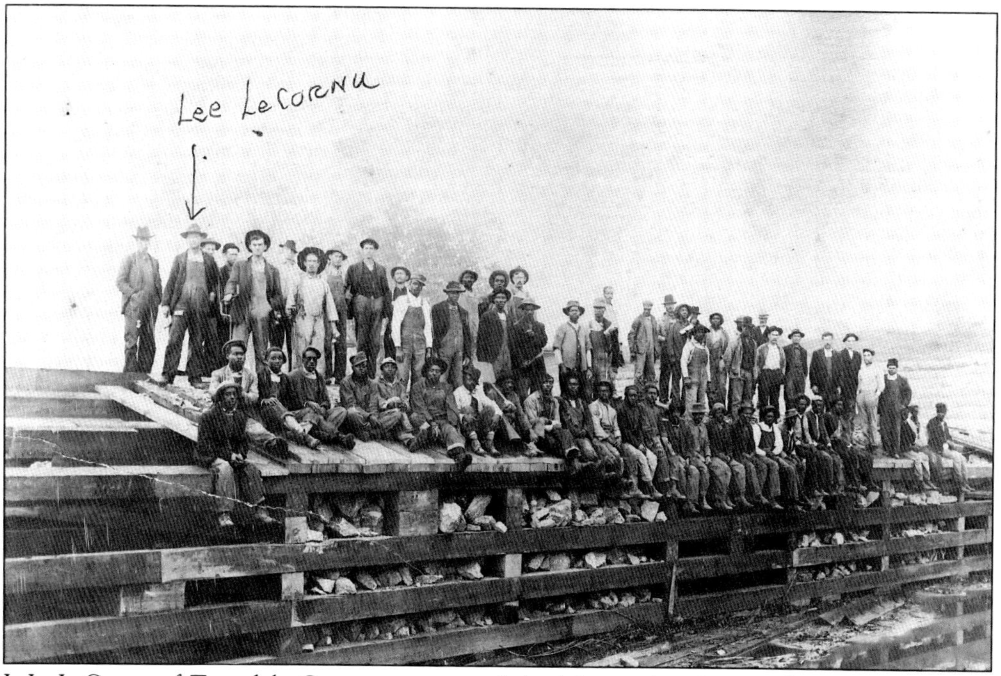

J. L. LeCornu of Trousdale County was one of the laborers hired to work on Lock # 5. He would walk to work everyday from his home upriver. The walk, several miles, was through woods and fields—not on a road or a path. J. L. or " Lee" is the second man from the left end of the top row.

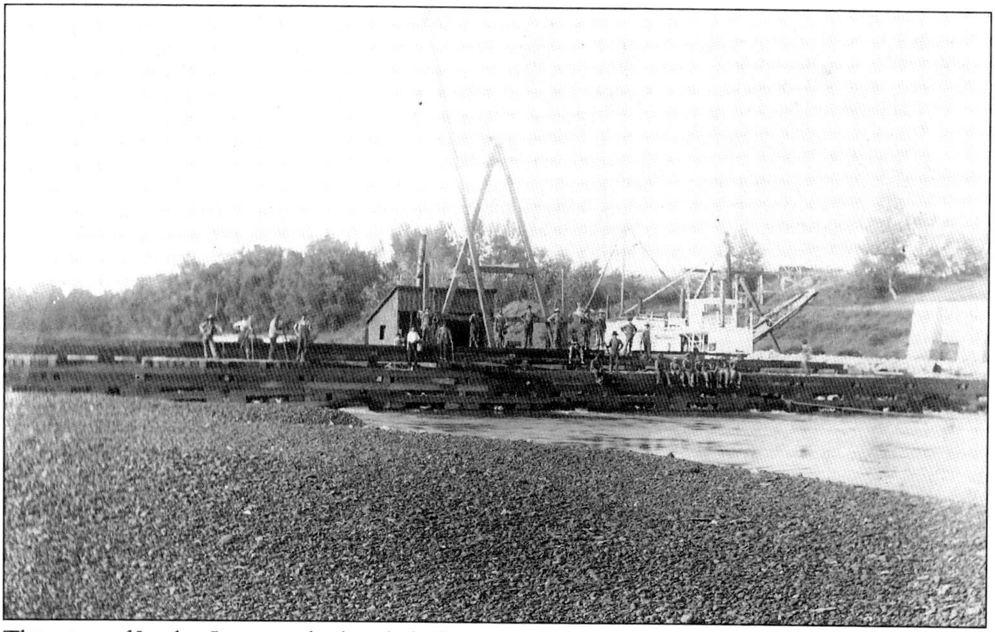

This view of Lock #5 was made shortly before completion. The photograph was made standing on the Trousdale County side of the river. It would be another twenty years before construction would start on Lock #6 further up river, but still in Trousdale County.

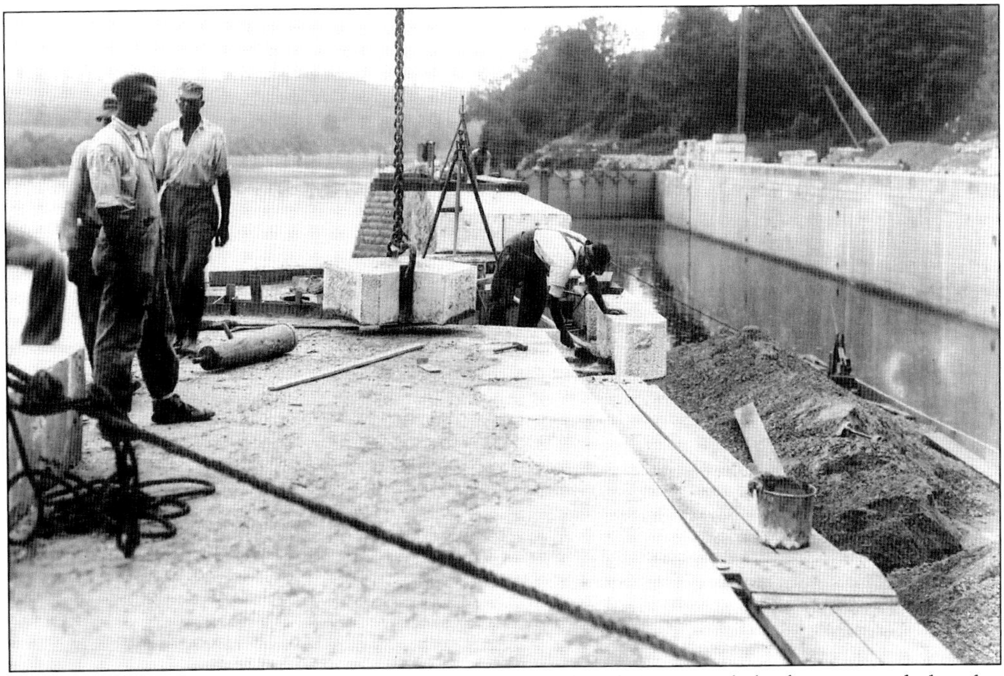

Construction of Lock #6 began in late 1913. By July of 1914 work had progressed this far. Stone cutters from Italy were brought in to cut the stone facing on the lock. Here workmen are putting mortar between the stones.

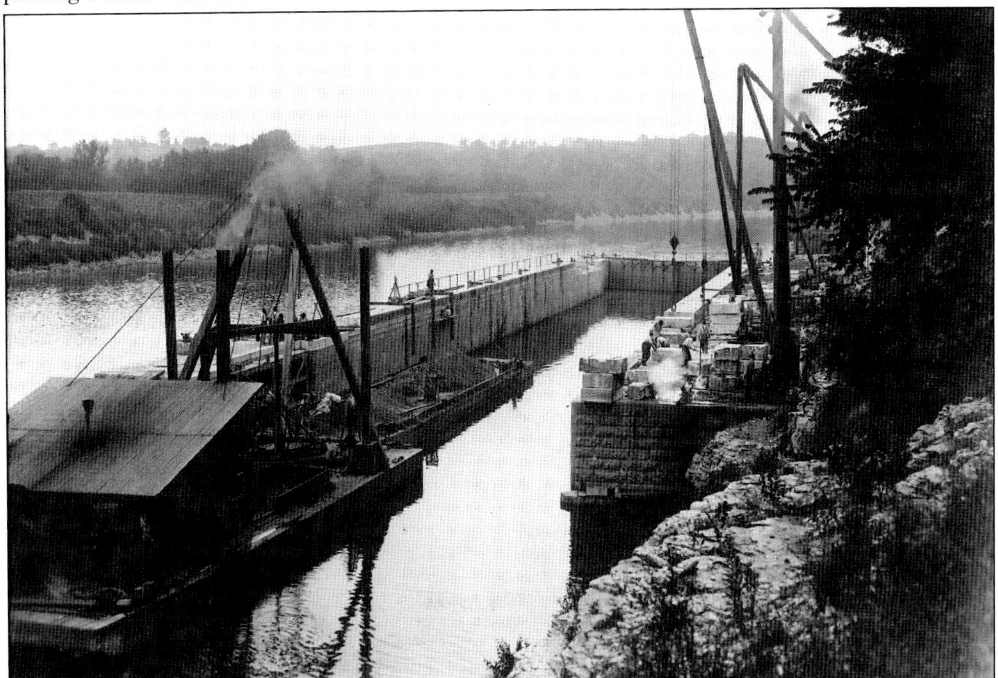

This is another view of construction on Lock #6. Further upriver, past Rome, another lock would be built. The locks were used until the construction of Old Hickory Dam in the 1950s. Then, they were partially blown up. Some of the rock walls can still be seen at the water's edge.

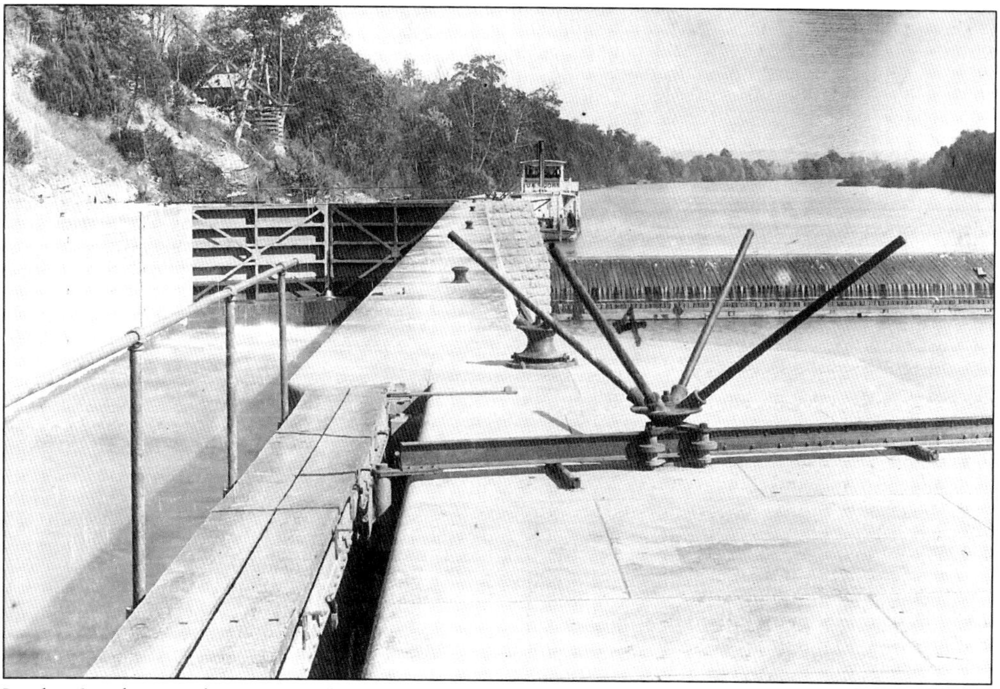

Lock #6 is shown after its completion, looking up river. The lock gates can be seen to the right. Immediately in front are the levers that were turned by the Lock Keeper to open and close the lower gates. The boat in the background is the USS *John*, a Corps of Engineers boat.

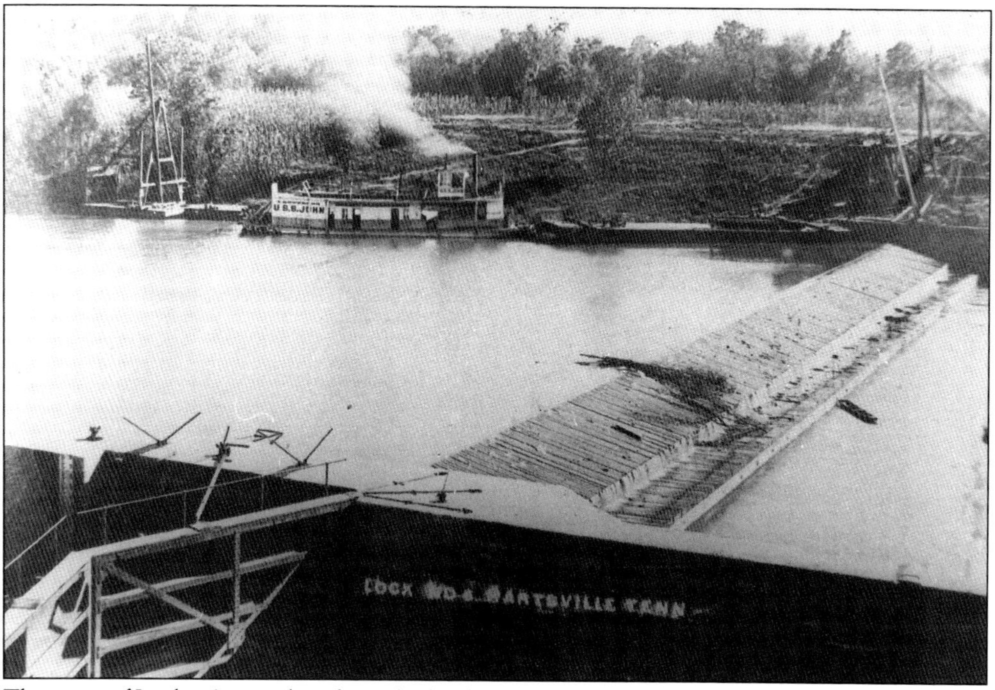

This view of Lock #6 was taken from the bank. Here it is easy to see the difference in the levels of the river that the dam was able to create. Local residents were fond of fishing below the dam and around the lock wall.

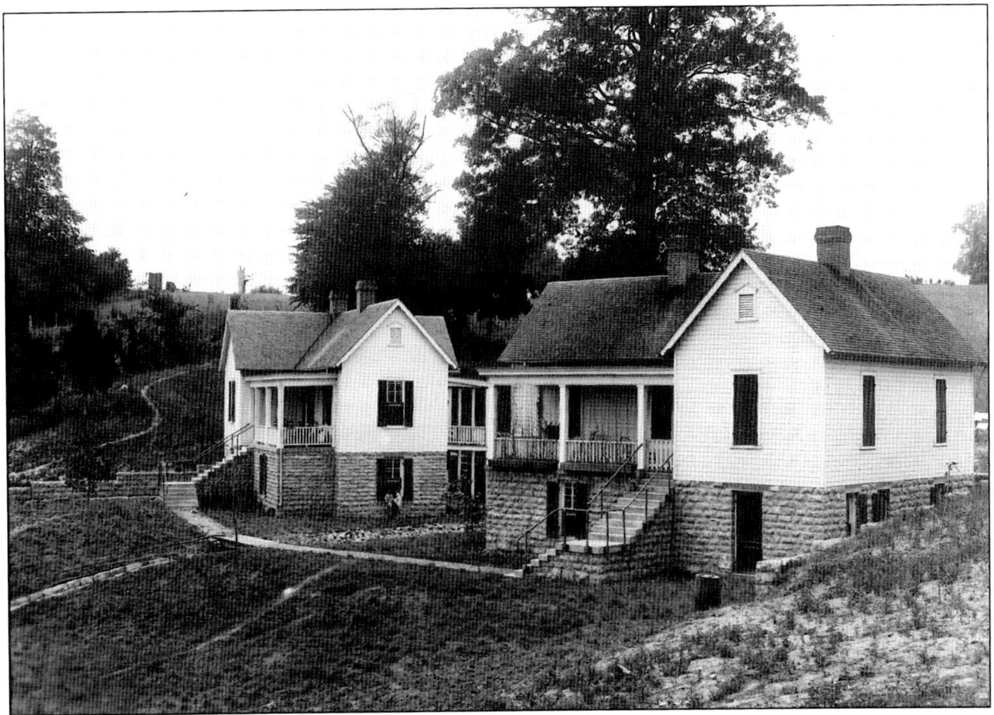

The lock keepers' homes at Lock #6 were of sturdy rock construction and sat on the hill overlooking the lock. The grounds around the lock and the houses were kept up and always neat in appearance. As a result the lock became a popular place for picnics and outings. The homes were demolished when Lock #6 was.

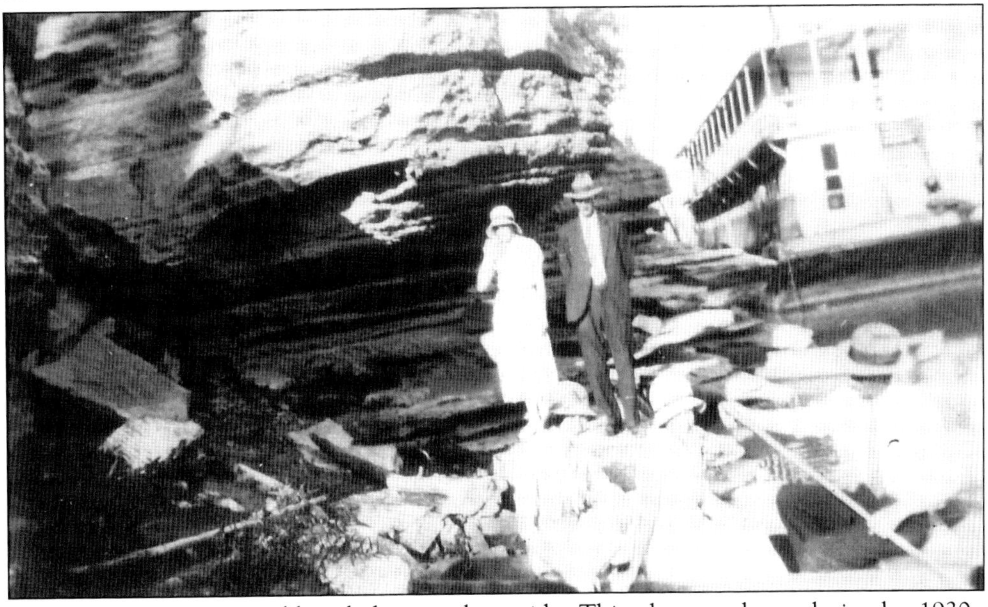

A picnic at Lock #6 could include a rowboat ride. This photograph, made in the 1930s, shows members of the Castalian Springs Methodist Church on such a picnic down by the water's edge. One member of the group shown is Katherine McMurtry. Note the large boat in the background.

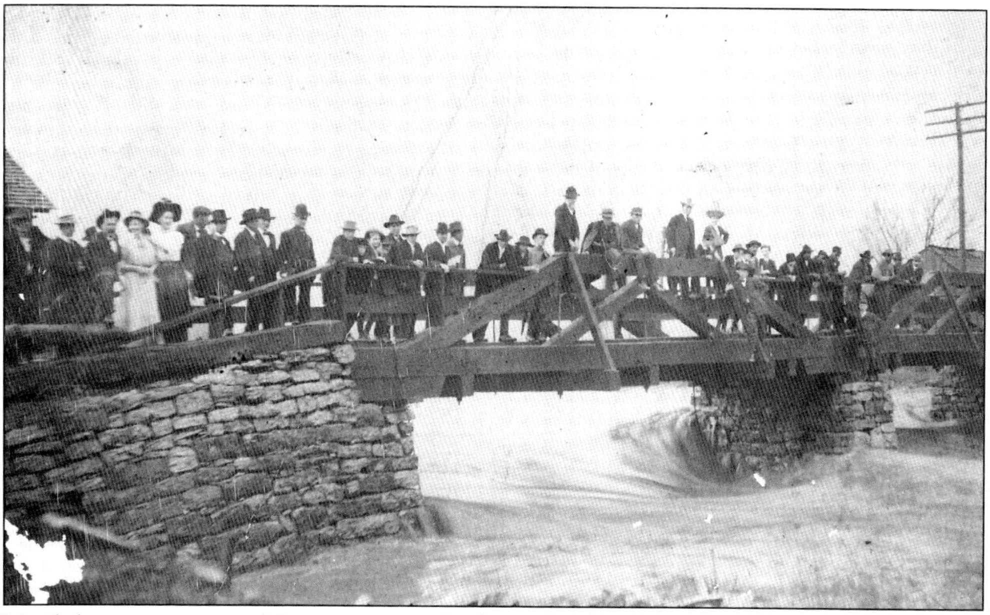

Until the construction of dams upriver and other controls, Trousdale County had been subject to flooding. The worst flood in memory was the flood of 1926/27. Heavy rains began the 14th of December and continued through the first week of January. They produced the longest period of flooding the county had seen. This view of the bridge over Little Goose Creek on Broadway, shows the fury of the flood.

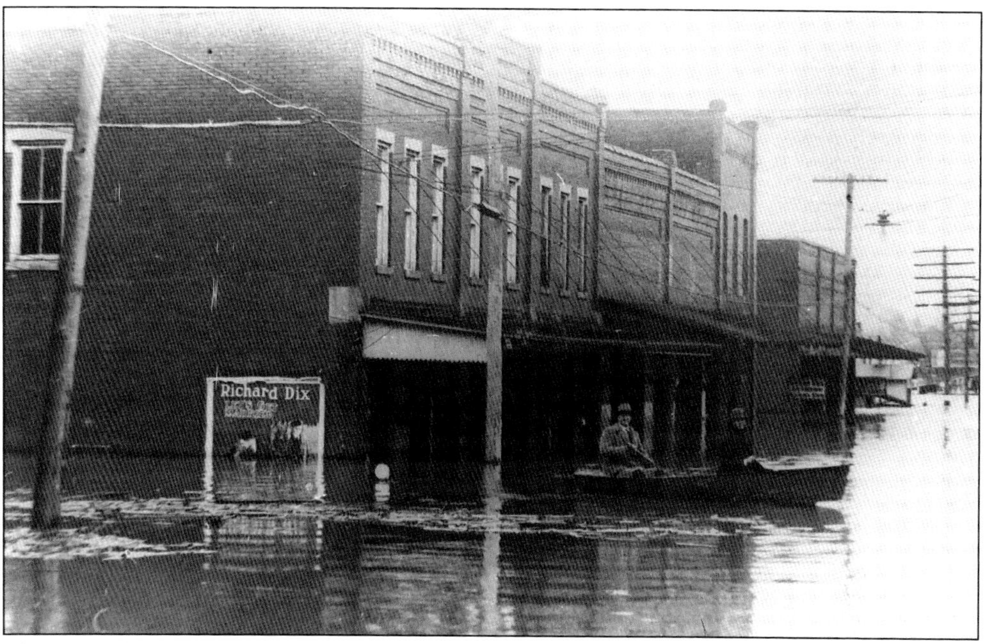

The entire downtown area of Hartsville was flooded. The high-water mark was more than 4 feet deep in businesses on the south side of Main Street and deeper still on the north side, as seen here. The round glass ball that appears to be floating in the center of the photograph was the top of a stoplight system used in 1926. The light stood in the center of the road. Richard Dix, the name on the poster, was staring in a movie at the Hartsville Theatre—also under water.

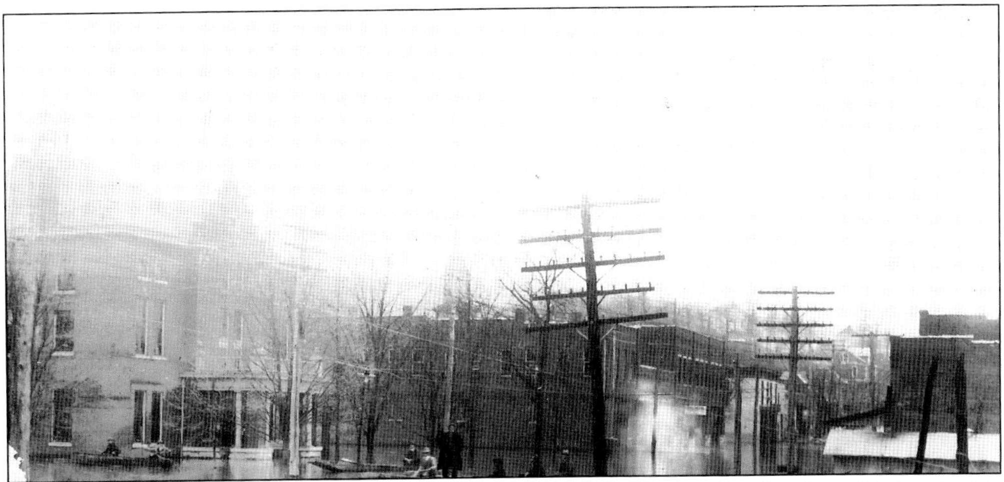

People were able to canoe through the county courthouse during the flooding. To locals this is referred to as "backwater" because it actually is the Cumberland River backed all the way up Little Goose Creek. Since the mouth of the creek is about 3 miles from town, the extent of flooding can be imagined.

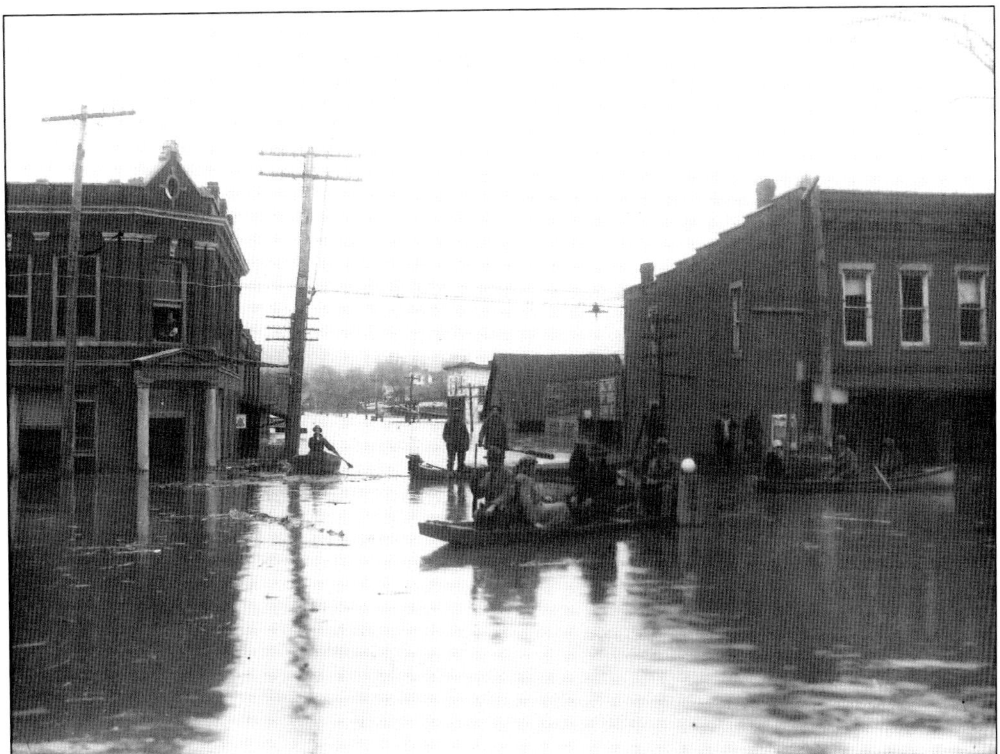

To the left is the old Bank of Hartsville building. The upstairs housed the telephone office. The traffic light for the south side of the street can be seen in this photograph. Merchants in town suffered considerable damage. Although many of them anticipated flooding, they did not place their stock high enough off the floor, and the waters rose far higher than they expected.

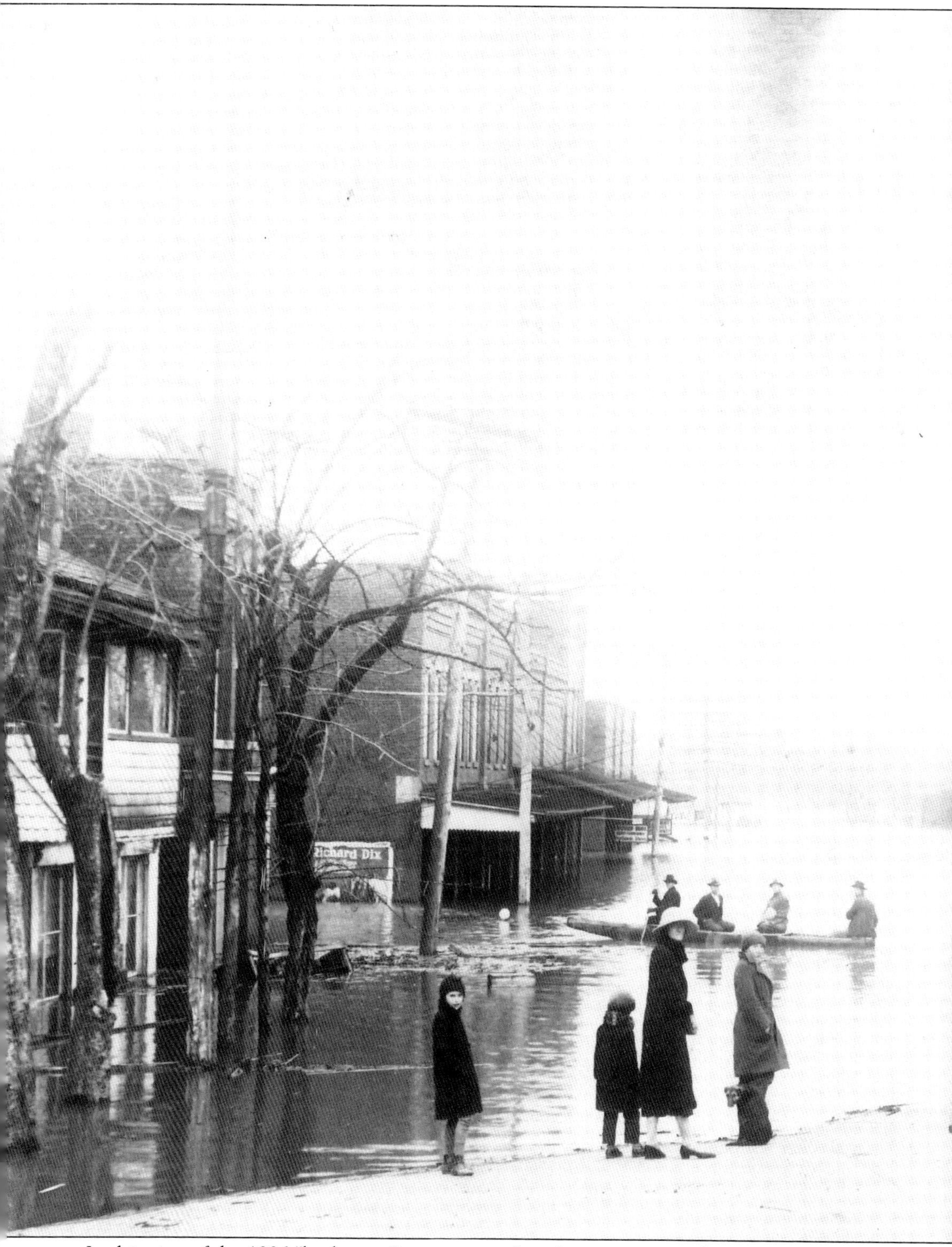

In this view of the 1926 "backwater" one can see that the main street of Hartsville has changed little. With the exception of the two frame structures, one on each side of the street closest to

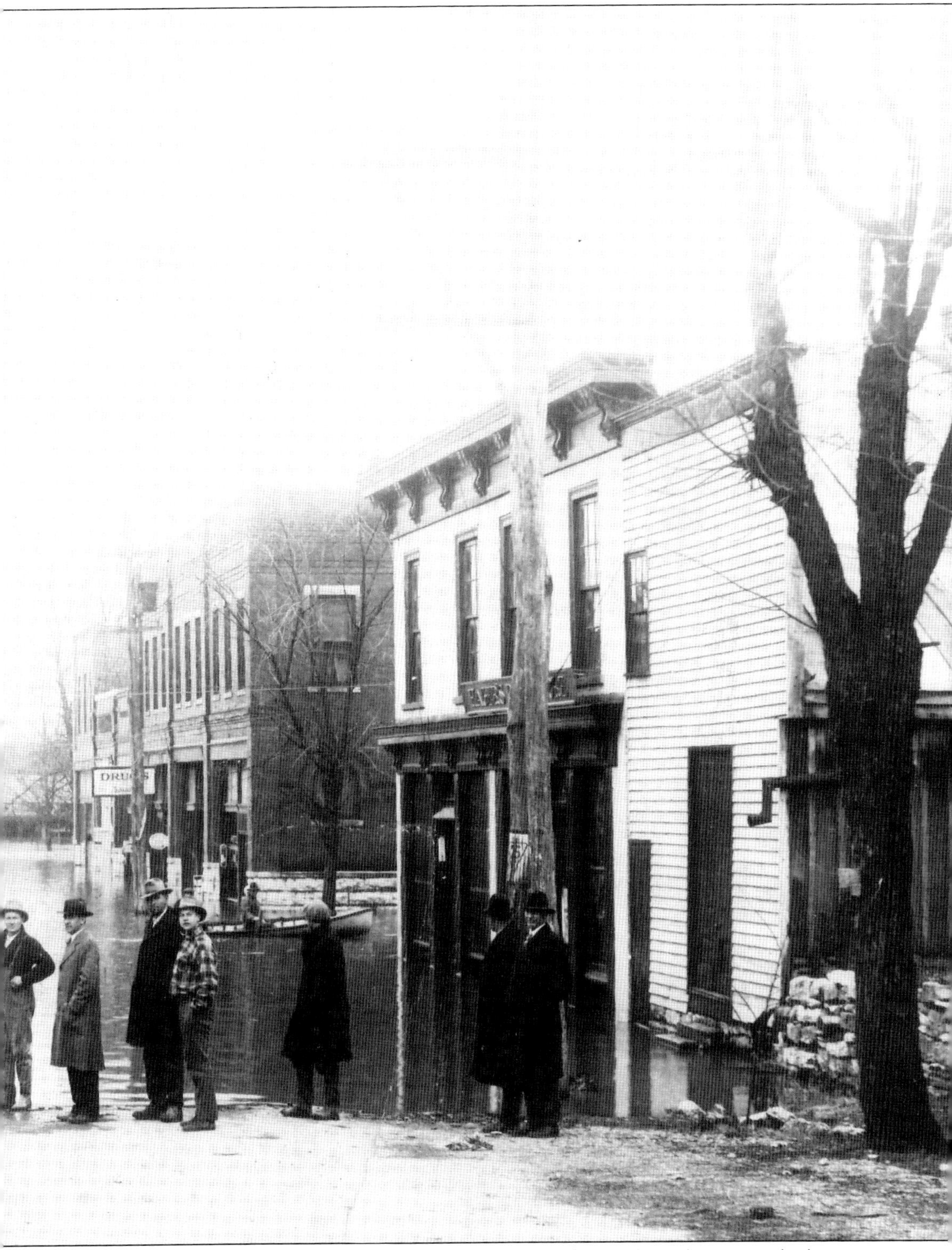

the camera, the buildings in the photograph are still standing today. The view is looking east from Jail Hill, or Post Office Hill today.

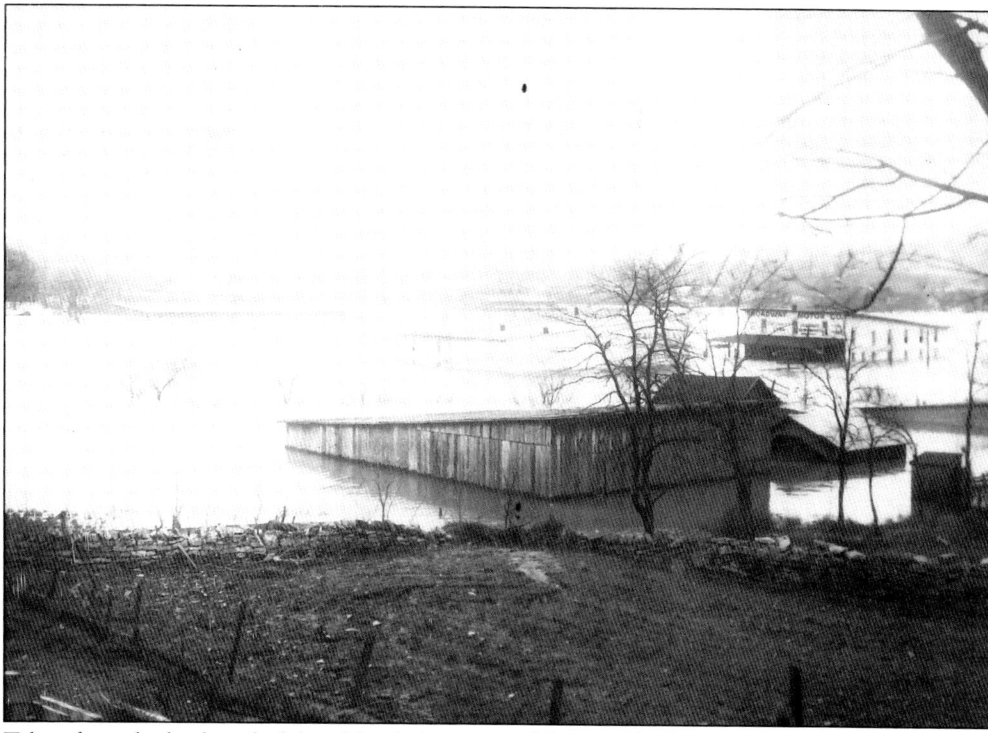

Taken from the backyard of the old jail, this view of the 1926 backwater shows North Hartsville and Broadway. The wooden buildings in the immediate foreground are no longer standing. In the rear are several of the county's tobacco warehouses, most still in use today.

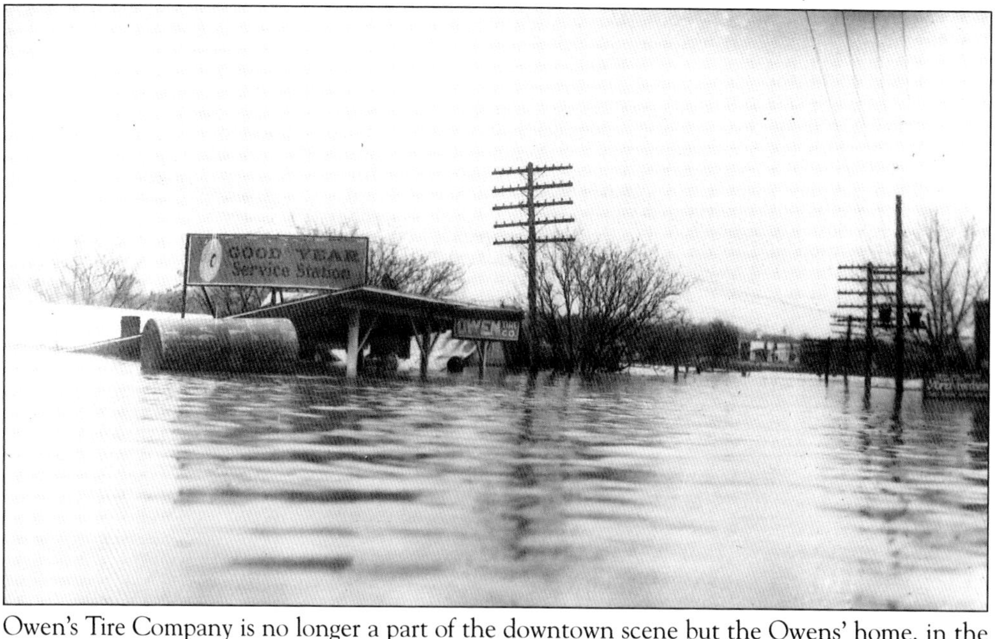

Owen's Tire Company is no longer a part of the downtown scene but the Owens' home, in the background, is recognizable to most residents. The Owens' home is still standing today. For many years it was the home of "Miss Pearl" Thompson. Today, Mr. and Mrs. Andy Vaught live there. The Co-op building and White's Exxon station sit where the tire company was in 1926.

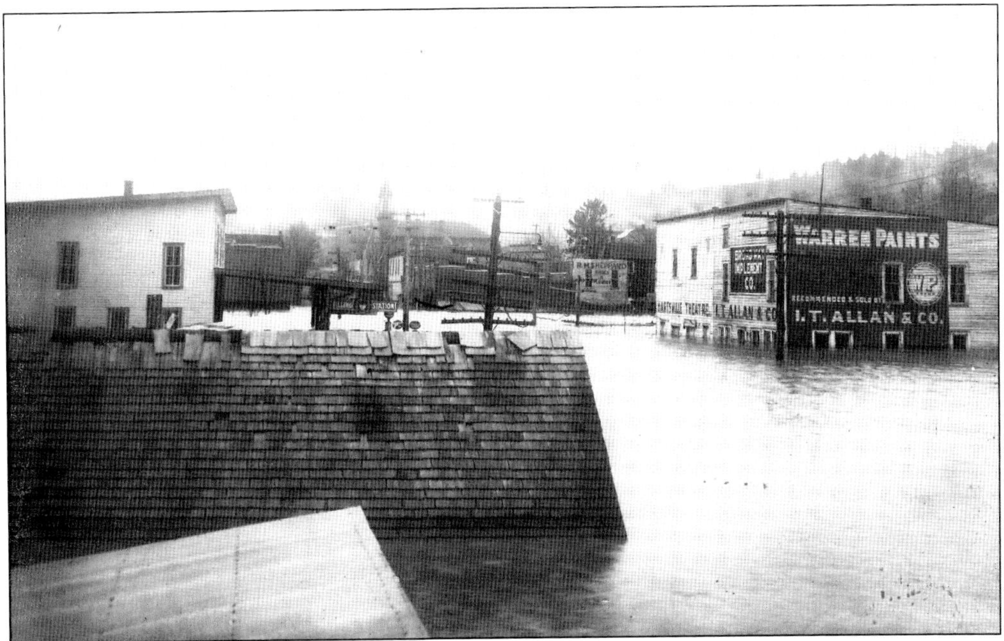

Broadway Implement Company, I. T. Allan and Company, the Hartsville Theatre, and R. M. Sheppard—Tinner and Plumber, are no longer familiar Hartsville names. In 1926 they were all doing business. This photograph was taken looking south on Broadway. None of the wooden buildings in the foreground are still standing today.

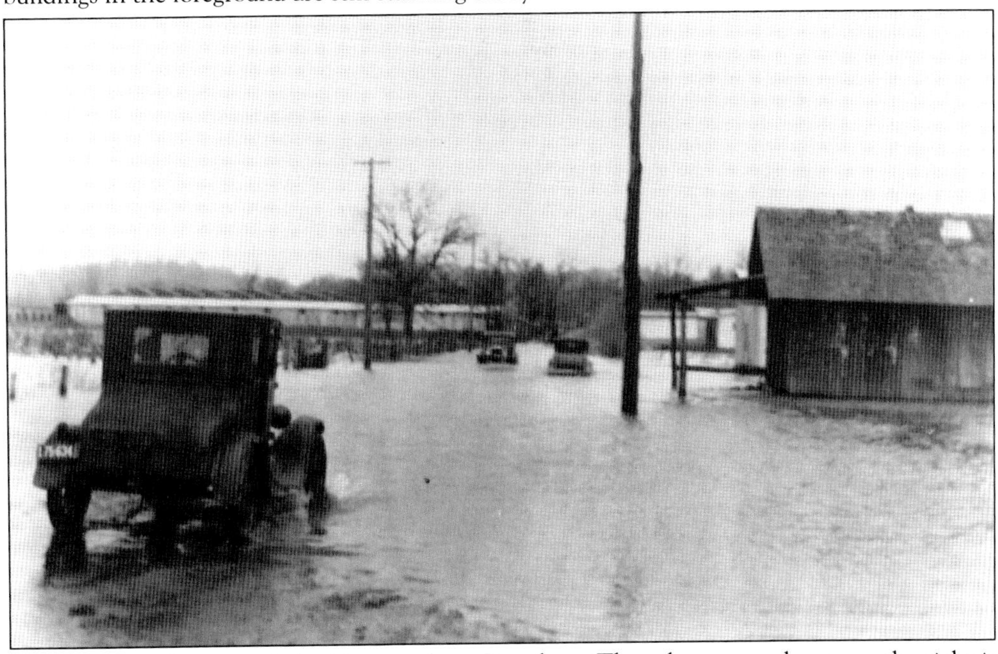

This photograph was made looking north on Broadway. The tobacco warehouse on the right is Farmer's Warehouse, still in use today. The building at the right was Claydie Jones' blacksmith shop. These vintage cars, with their high axles, were not intimidated by the water on the roadway. Although this flood in 1926 was the one for the record books, another flood in 1946 was almost as high.

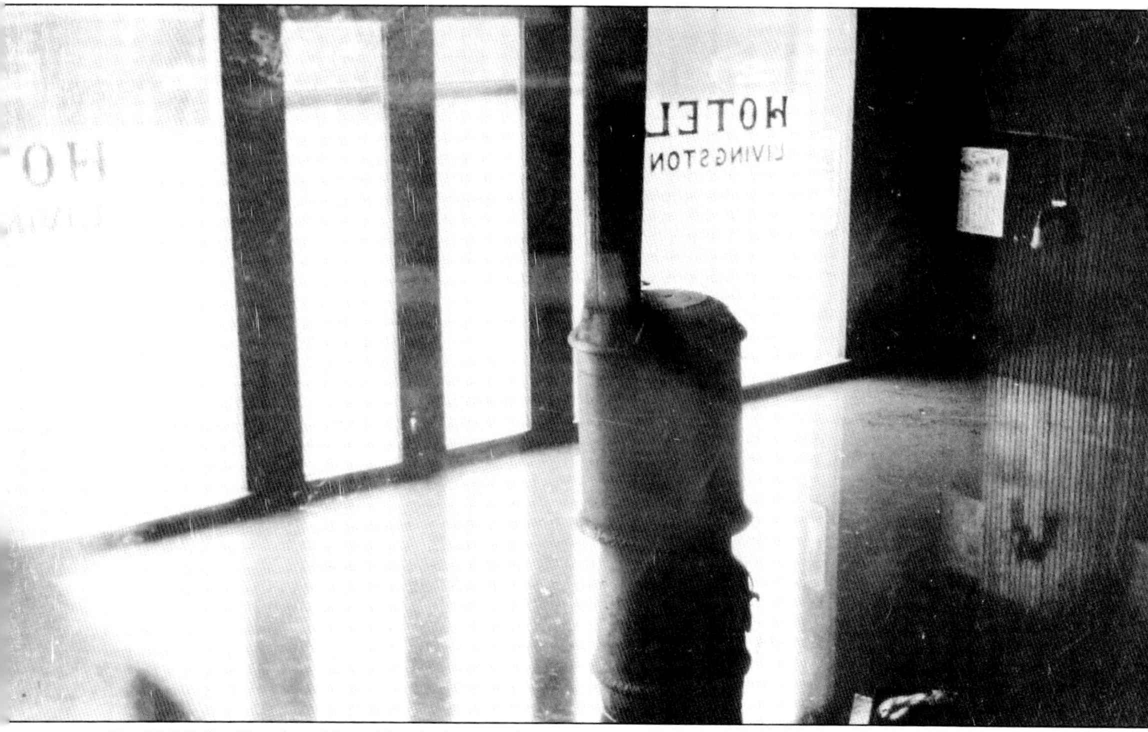

By 1926 the Rankin Hotel had changed its name to the Hotel Livingston. This photograph was made during the great flood from the staircase in the lobby of the hotel. The large pot-bellied stove in the center of the photograph was used to heat the lobby in the days before central heat. Late one night during the flood the phone in the lobby began to ring and would not stop. Manager J. H. McCormach was awakened and left his upstairs room. Wearing his hip boots he descended the stairs and waded across the lobby. He answered the phone to hear a woman say, "I am calling from Lafayette and I heard that water was knee deep in the hotel in Hartsville—is that true?" We cannot print Mr. McCormach's reply.

Five

Churches and Schools

Beech Grove Methodist Church began in 1834 in the Beech Grove community of the county. The original church was log and was replaced by this structure around the turn of the century. The building was brand new when this photograph was made. The church is still active today and this building still in use. Because of the county's early settlement, most of its churches have long and active histories.

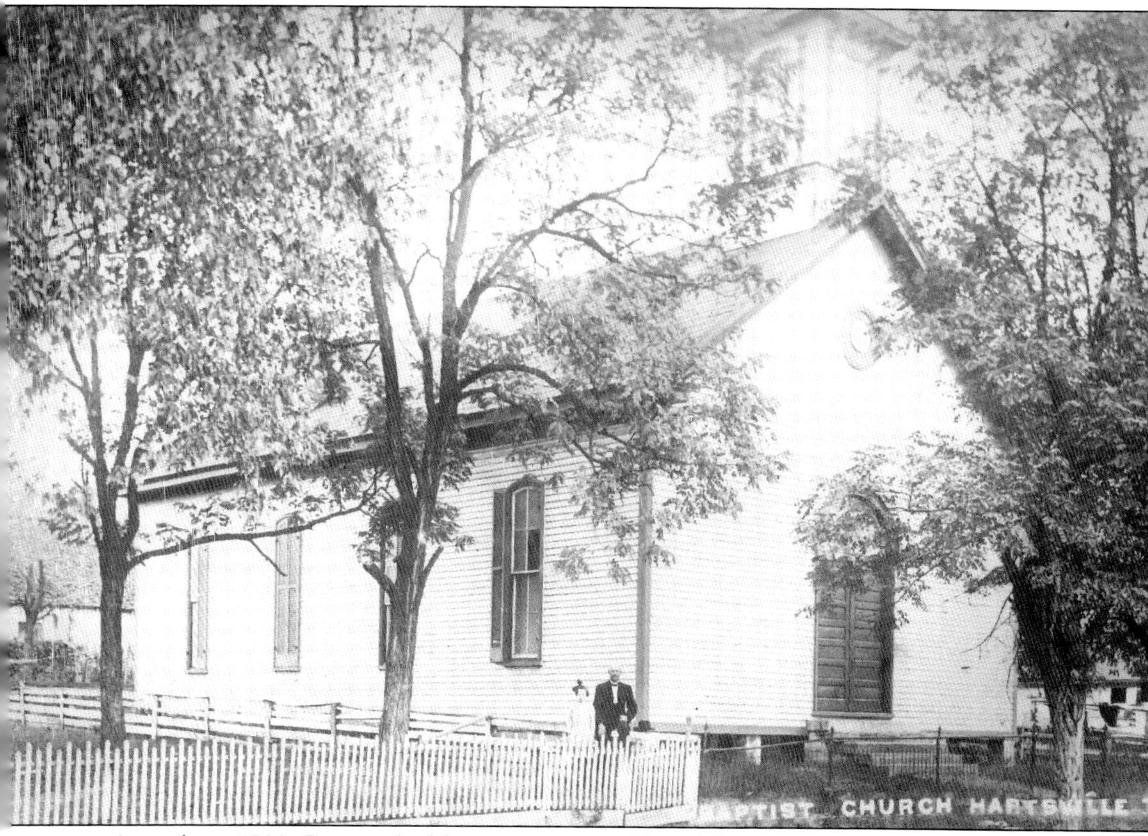

As early as 1800, Baptists had been meeting in Trousdale County. The Dixon Creek group organized March 8th of that year. In Hartsville several denominations shared a building until the mid-1800s. The church pictured was built around 1871 for use by the Baptist congregation. The building still stands today on Church Street. It has been bricked since this photograph. The man in the picture is Rev. John T. Oakley with his granddaughter.

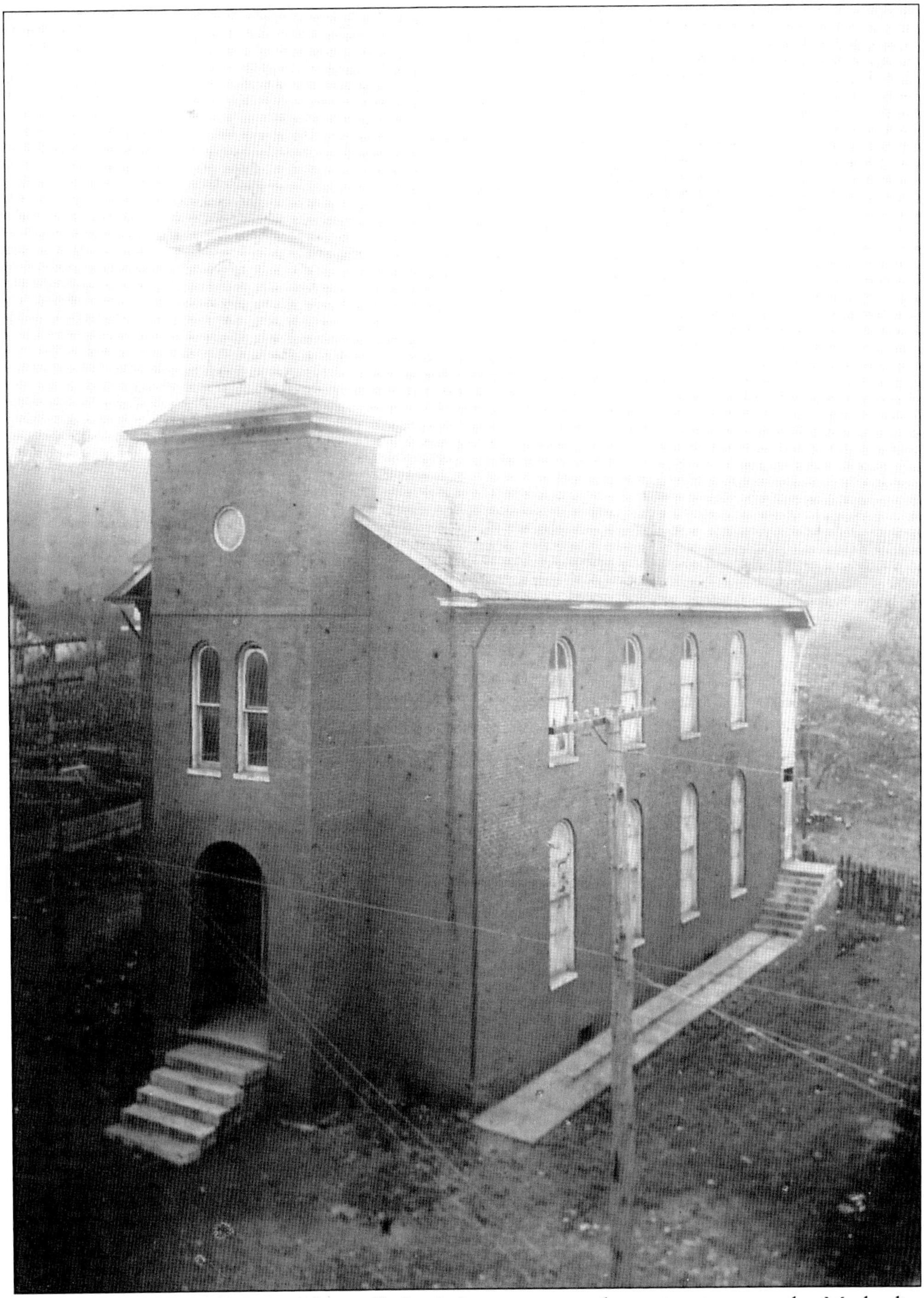

The first church building in Hartsville built by a separate denomination was the Methodist church, shown here. It was built around 1843. It was an impressive one-story brick building. In 1850, the newly organized Masonic Lodge added a second story to the church for use by that group exclusively. The church was used by Union Troops during the Civil War. Today this still imposing structure is the Russell Popcorn Factory.

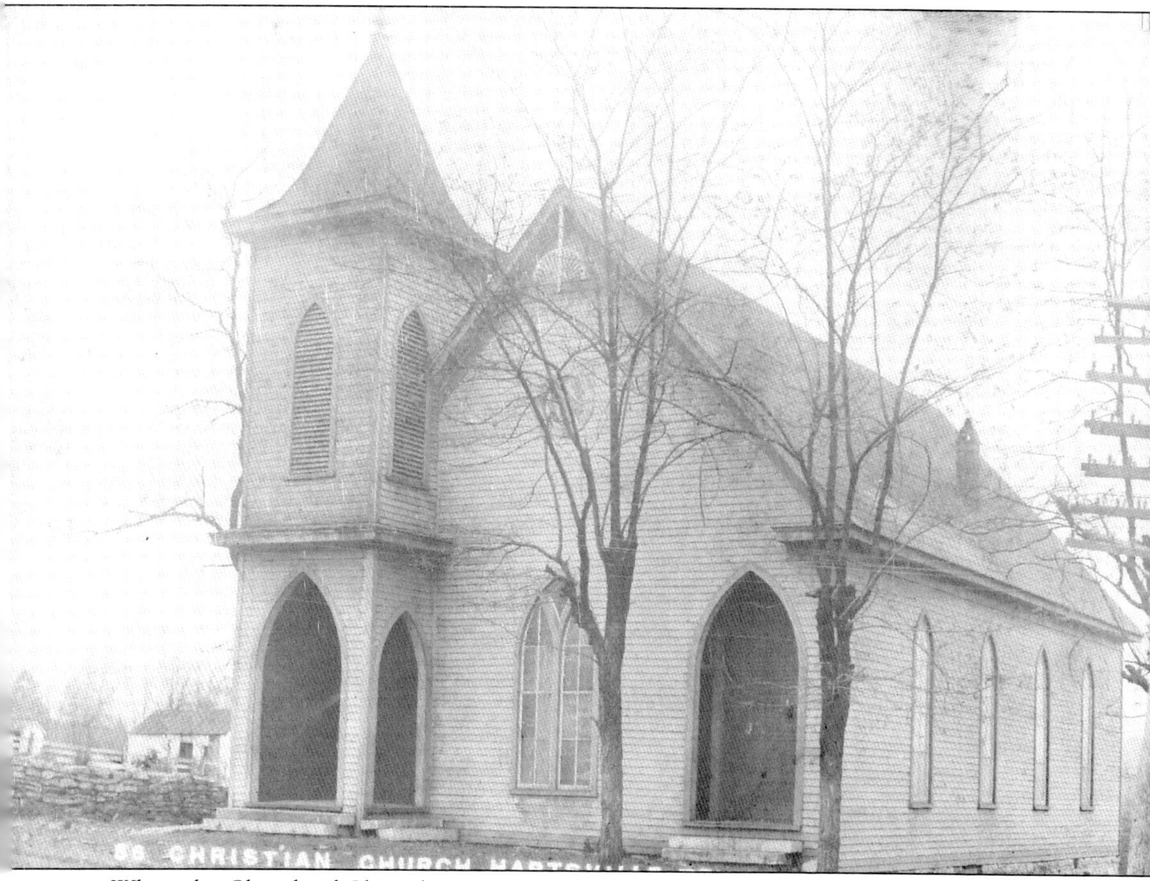

When the Church of Christ began in Hartsville it was 1842 and numbered twenty-six men, thirty-six women, and two servants. By 1871 the congregation had built this gothic arched building. It stood where the U.S. Post Office is today. At one time it was called the Christian Church. In 1961 the congregation moved to a new location on Halltown Road and this building was torn down.

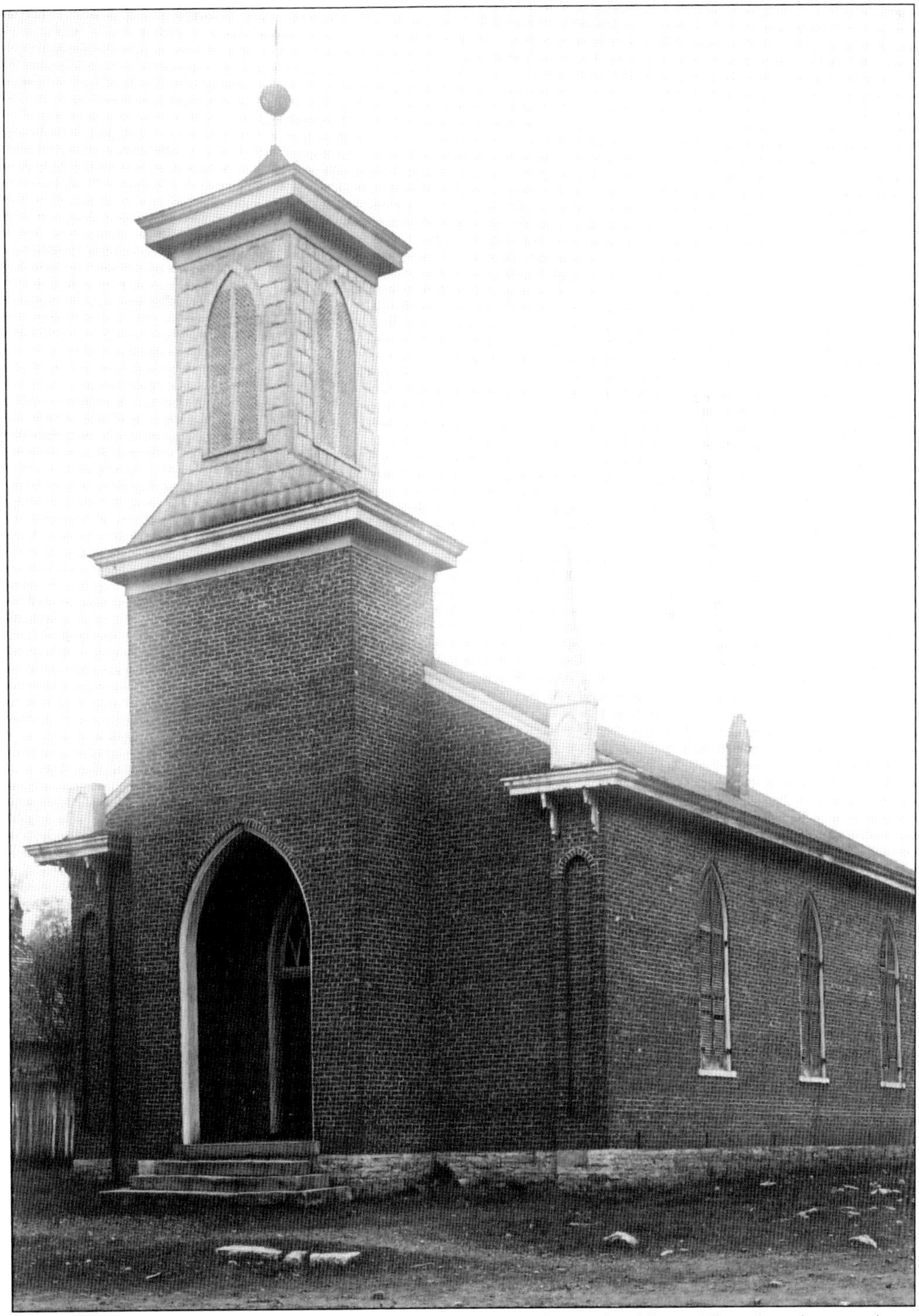

In 1852 the Presbyterian congregation built this handsome building. The church met there for almost one hundred years until declining membership led to its closing in the 1940s. At that time it was partially dismantled, and turned into a two-story business structure. Today the building houses Flowerland.

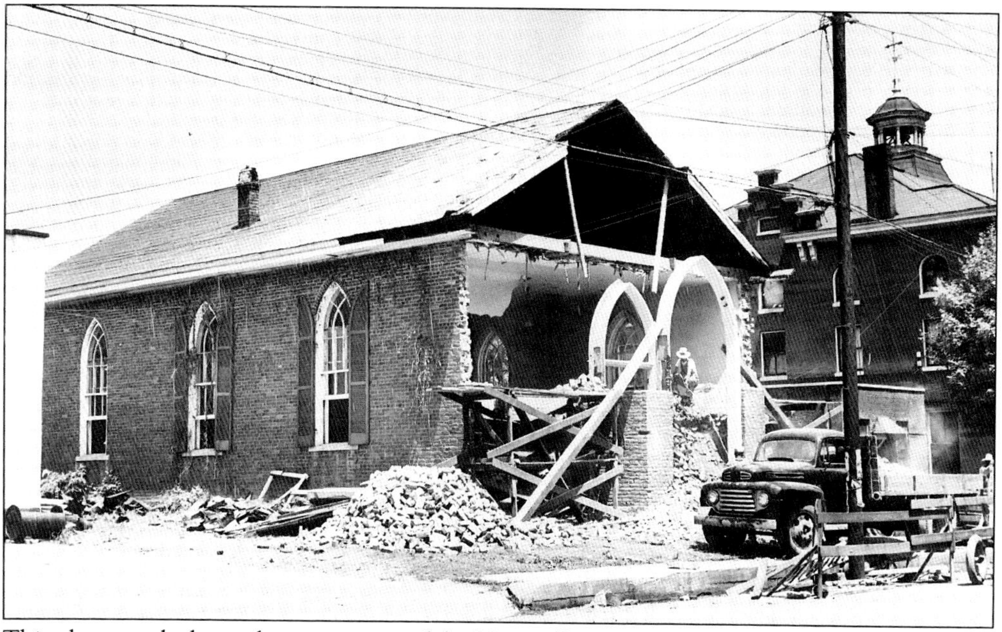

This photograph shows the renovation of the Hartsville Presbyterian Church in the 1940s. The windows were bricked in, the roof raised several feet and a second floor created in the space. The doors of the old church and several windows were taken and used in the remodeling of the Key United Methodist Church.

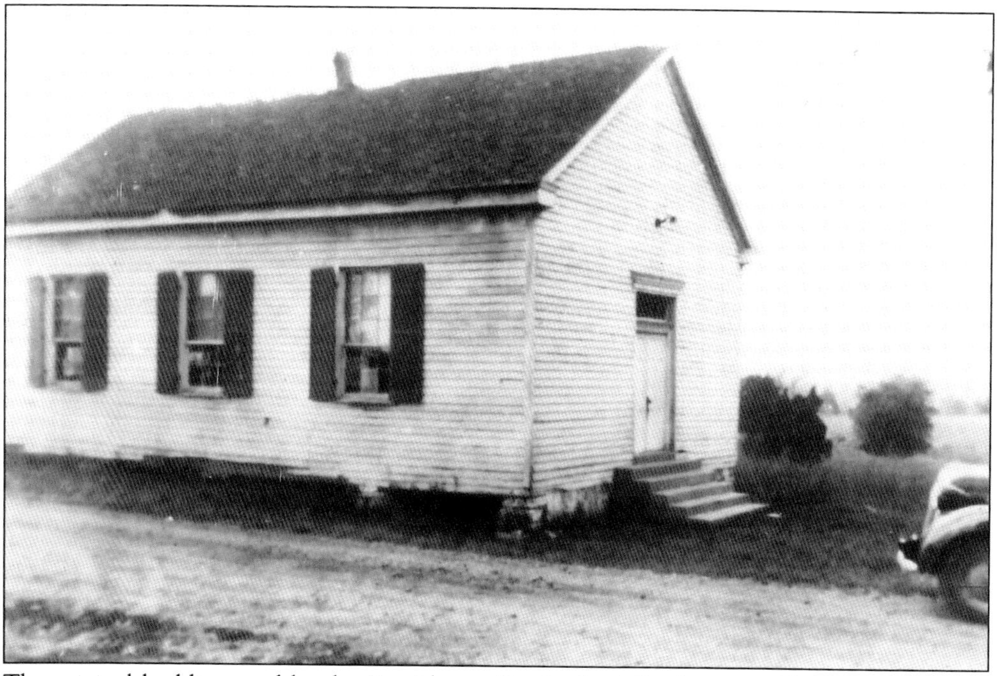

The original building used by the Providence Cumberland Presbyterian Church was built in 1822. Shown here, it was still in use In 1941. It was built of logs and weatherboarded. An early member spoke about the structure as being built under the "providential guidance of God" and choose to call it the "Providence Church"—soon the community took the same name.

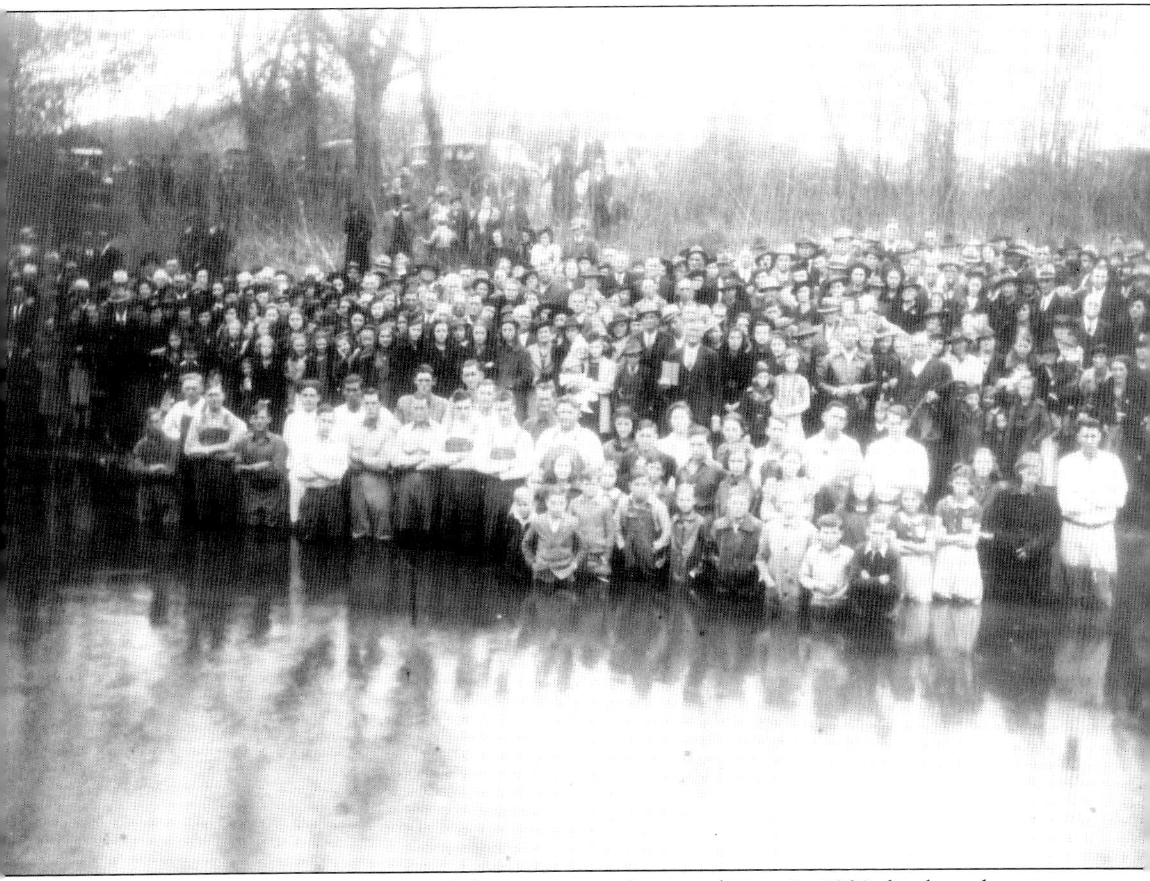

Baptism in the creeks and springs of the county is a long tradition. In 1939 this large baptism took place on Big Goose Creek. The people were members of Goodwill Missionary Baptist Church. Brother Calvin Gregory of Lafayette did the baptisms. Among those being baptized are: Britton Linville, John Martin, Edwin Martin, George Taylor, Alex Ray, Nora Scruggs, Risey Scruggs, Annie Parris McCormack, and Roxy Mae McCormack.

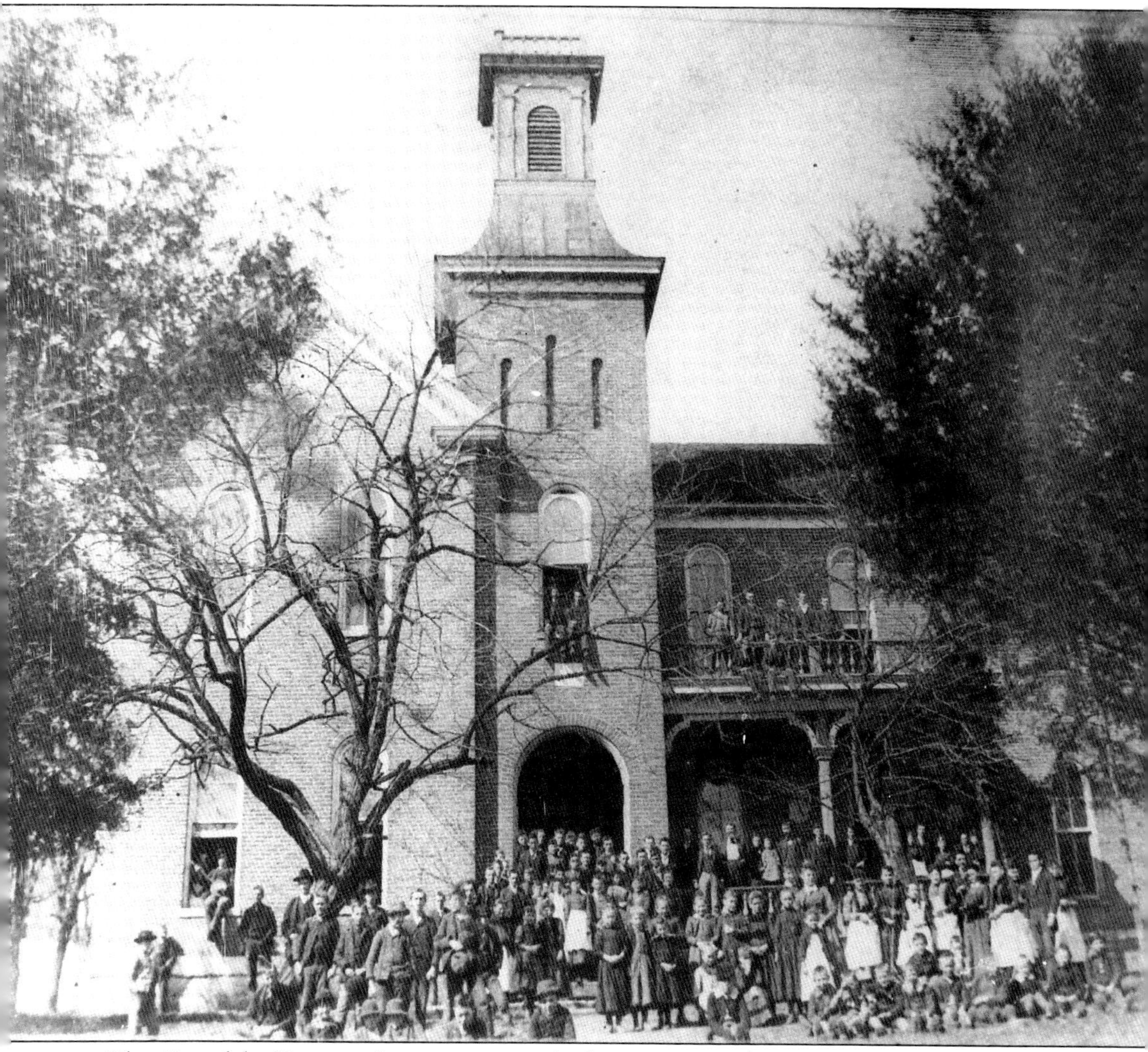

The Trousdale County education system had its roots in the Hartsville Masonic Institute. Operating from 1868 to 1910, it then became Hartsville Academy, which eventually became Trousdale County High School. The building, shown here in 1891, was built in 1870 after an earlier one burned. A new school was built in 1919. In the 1970s this building was demolished, and the Academy Apartments occupy the site today.

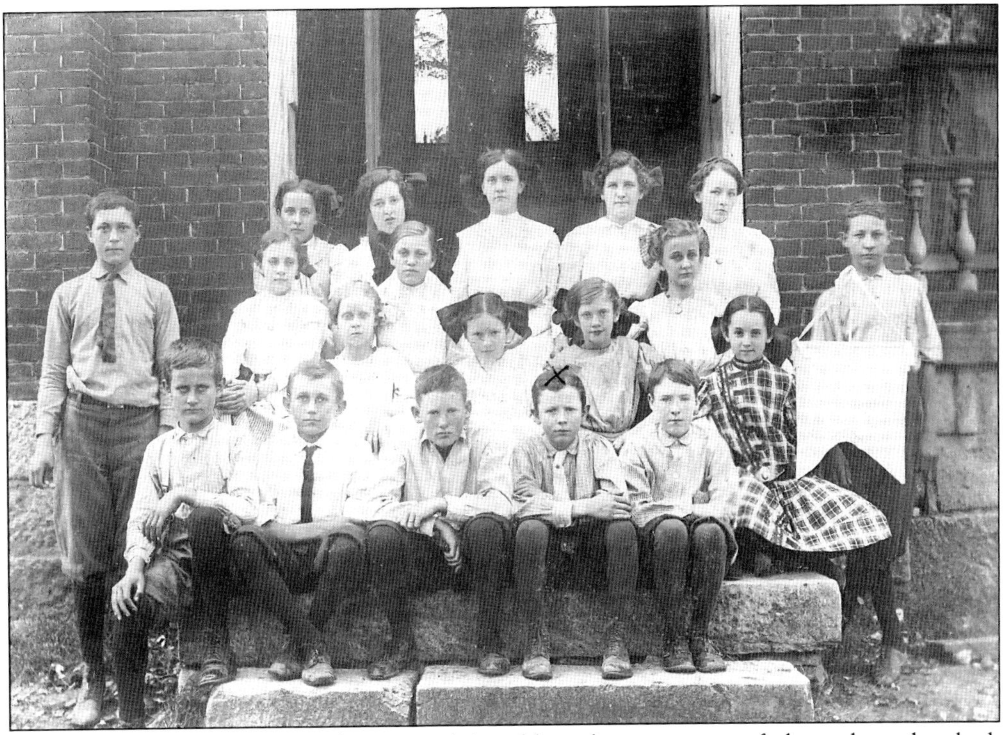

In this photograph, taken on the steps of the old academy, a group of eleventh graders look serious and proper. Note the large stones used in the school's foundation and steps. The boy on the first row with the "x" is Alfred Lauderdale. The photograph was made in 1908.

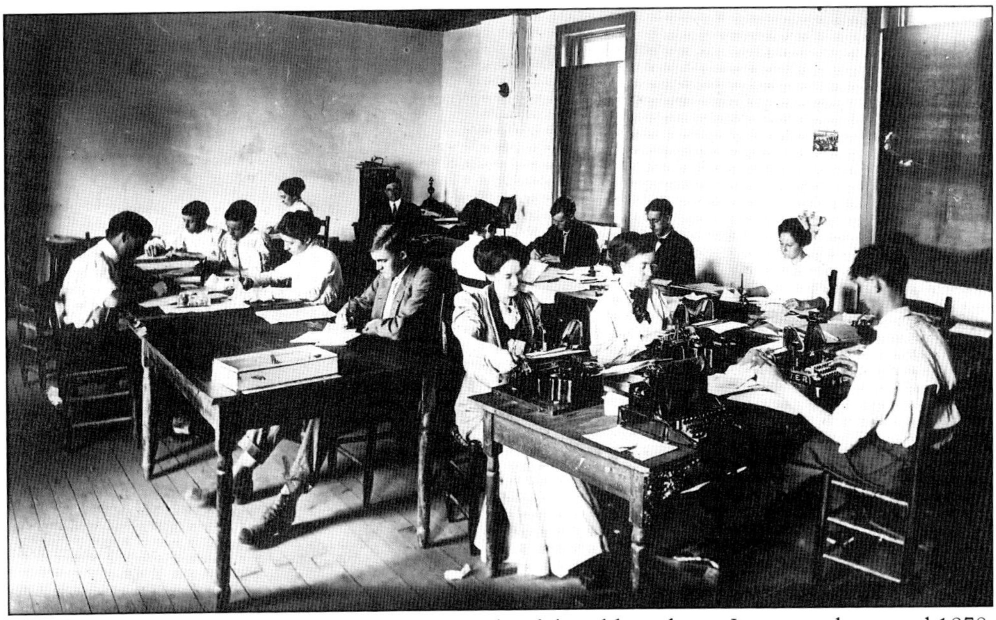

This is the only known photograph of the inside of the old academy. It was made around 1878, when it was still known as the Hartsville Masonic Institute. The students shown are in the "Commercial Room," learning to use some very early examples of typewriters.

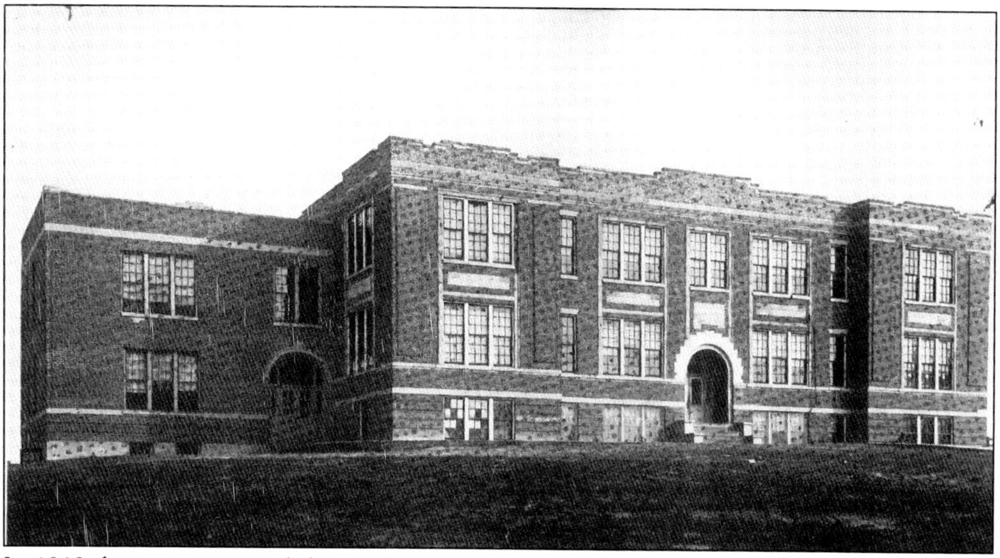

In 1919 the county erected this modern three-story brick school on a hill overlooking town. The earlier school had been on the south side of Little Goose Creek. When "backwater" was up, students from the north side couldn't get to school. This location was chosen so that more students would be able to attend when flooding became a problem. It was replaced in 1952.

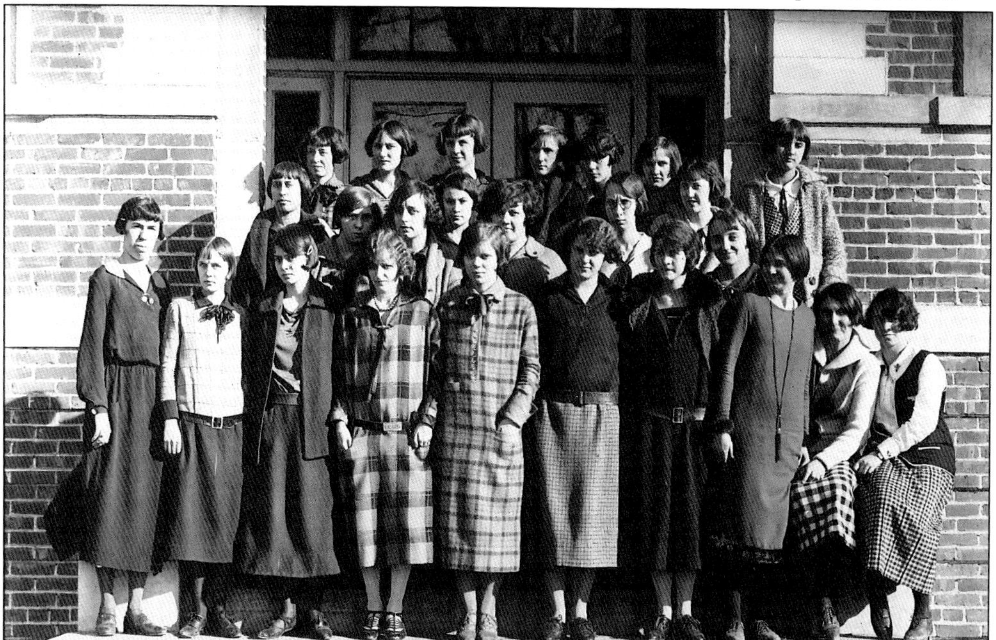

If you look closely at this 1925 photograph made in front of the old high school you will notice the similarity of the ladies' haircuts. It was the "style" of the time. Pictured, from left to right, are: (first row) Lucy Brock (teacher), Eloise Hall, Leonora Bratton, Elizabeth Crenshaw, Ruby Stubblefield, Mildred Hickman, Mary Perkins, Edna Bradley, Margaret Eason, Marie Ward, Elizabeth Langford; (second row) Eugene Burton, Ada Martin Cornwell, Lois Dalton, Lorene Bell, Eliza Duncan, Mary Lou Bell, Katherine Dalton, Eddie Brown; (third row) Beatrice Duncan, Thankful (?) Duncan, Anise Frye, Louise Oldham, Mayme Cothron.

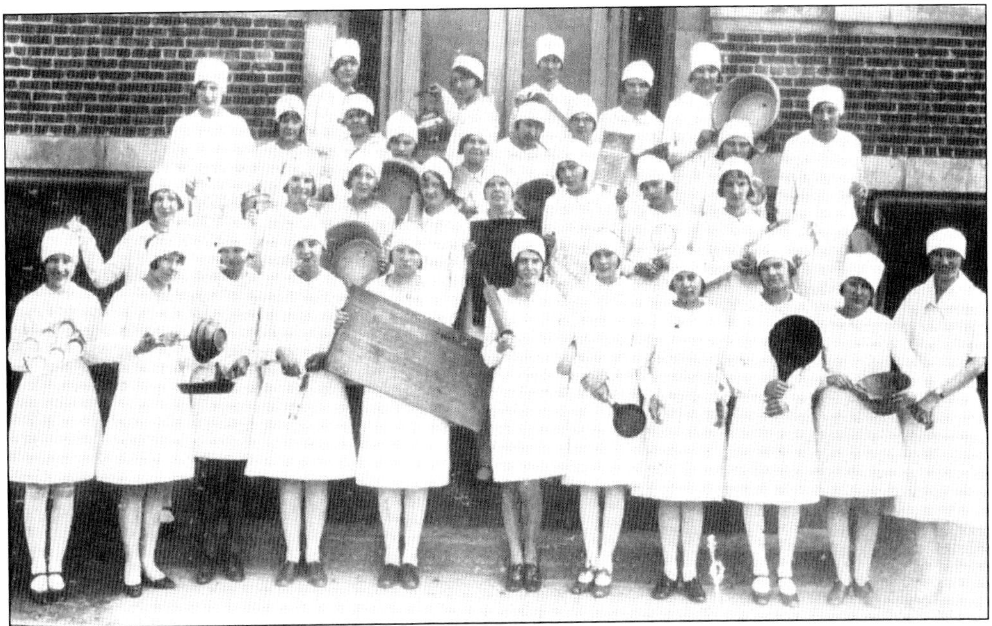

The Future Homemakers of America Club at the high school look prepared to whip up more than just biscuits in this photograph taken in 1928. The girls composed a poem that began with these lines: "The Home EC. Class of '28, Bet your life they're up to date."

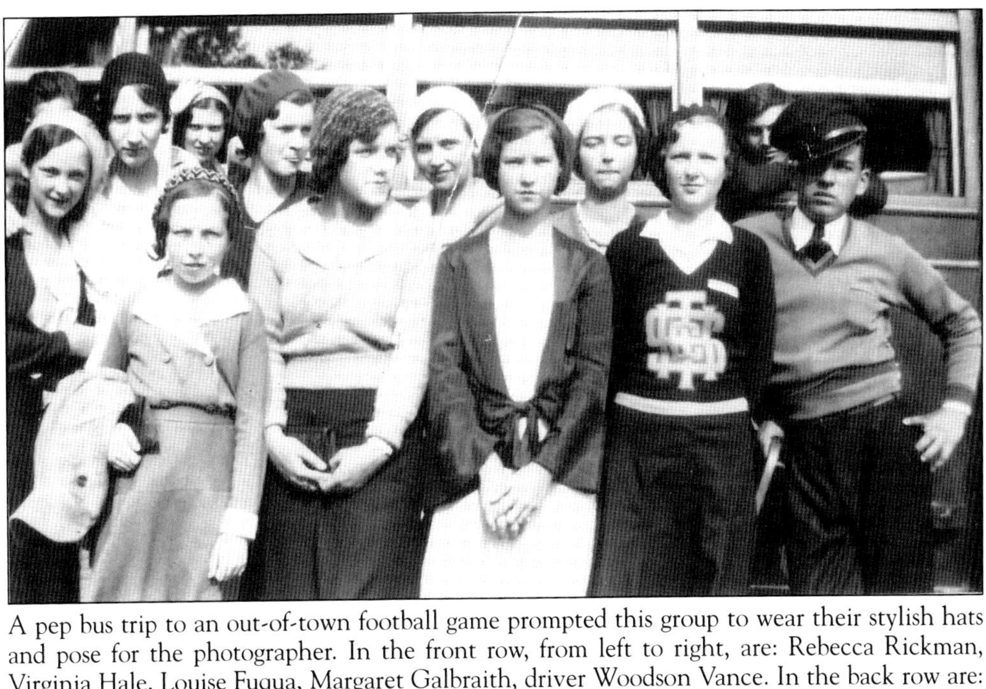

A pep bus trip to an out-of-town football game prompted this group to wear their stylish hats and pose for the photographer. In the front row, from left to right, are: Rebecca Rickman, Virginia Hale, Louise Fuqua, Margaret Galbraith, driver Woodson Vance. In the back row are: Lillian Allen Merryman, Virginia Winston, Margaret Rickman, Mary Agnes Kirby, Evelyn Wiles. Helen Bratton and J.C. McMurtry are in the bus windows.

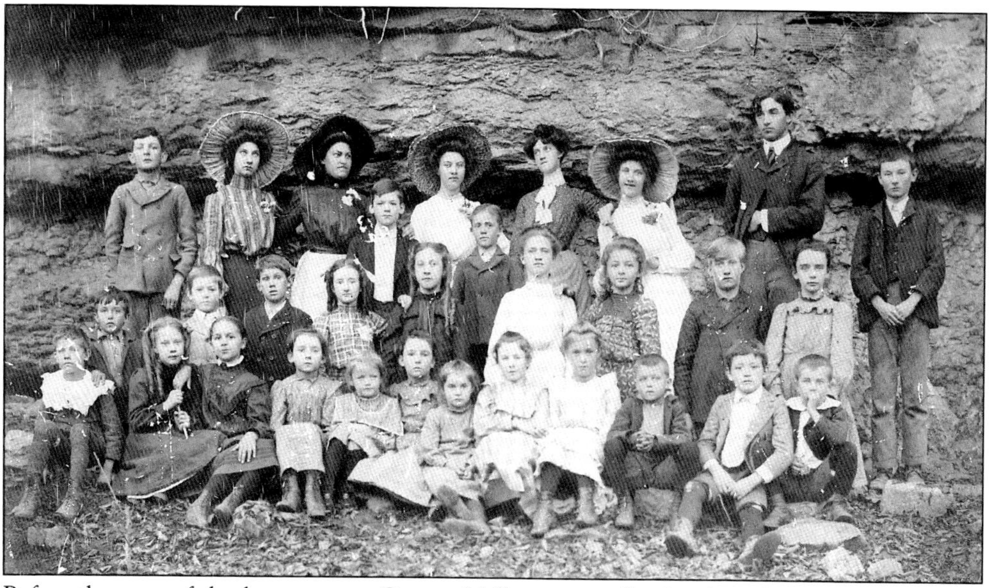

Before the turn of the last century, Grange Hall was a small school in the third district. The photograph was taken by a rock bluff close to the one-room school. The school was torn down years ago. The teacher is Pat Kerr. The school was filled with children from the Stubblefield, Marshall, Gross, and Rankin families, all residents of the area.

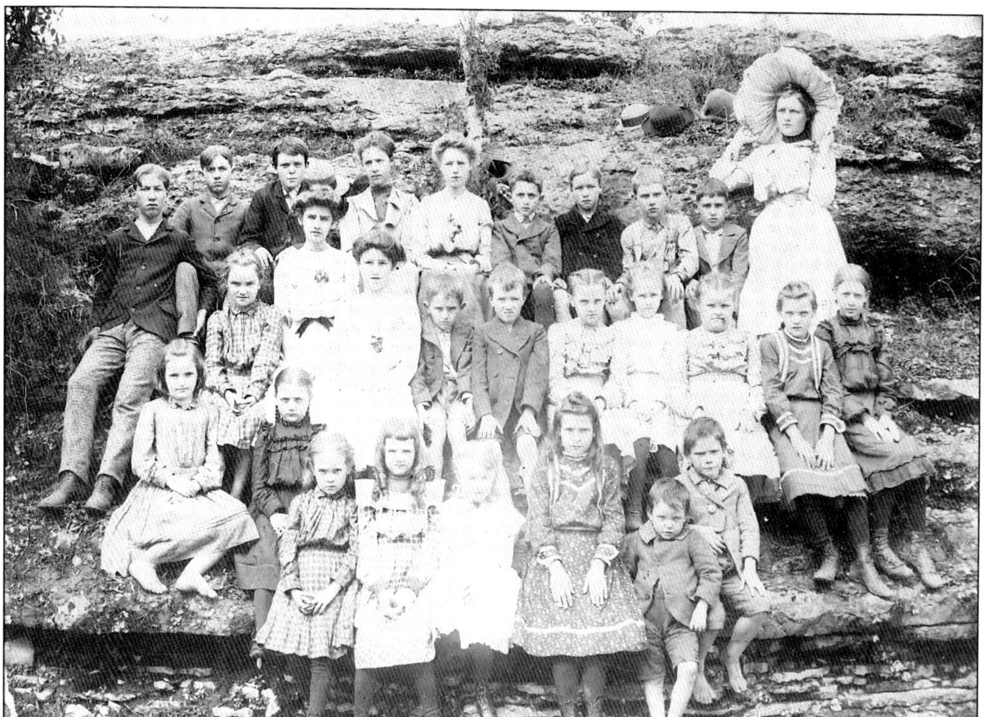

Sulphur College was actually a small school in the community started by a Mr. LeSuer, a veteran of the Civil War. This photograph was taken around 1900 on a rock outcropping directly behind the school. The school closed in 1918. Several years ago, the abandoned building burned.

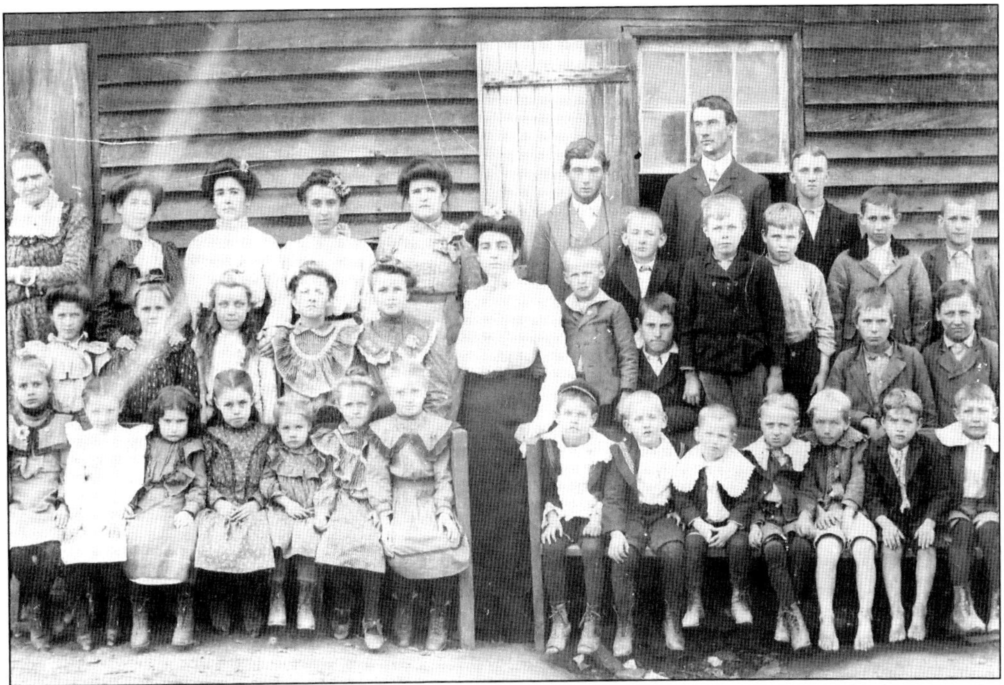

The Pumpkin Branch School began in 1804, as a subscription school, open only five months of the year. In 1902, when teacher Violet Leigh posed with her students, it was part of the public school system. At least one of the students was "heads taller" than the teacher. The older woman on the left was Mrs. Bill During, a visitor. Note the barefooted boys in the front row.

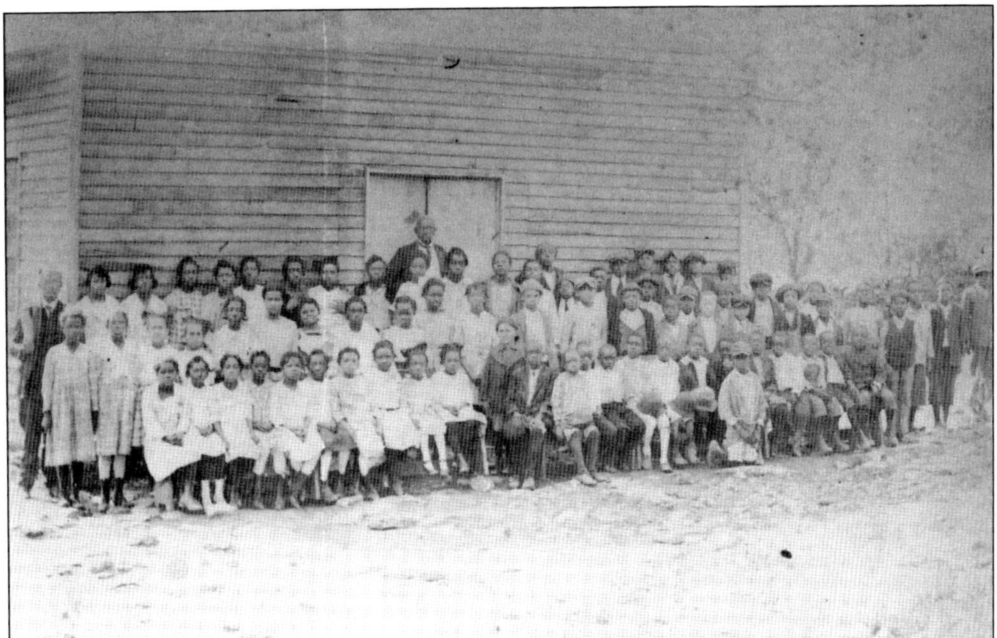

The School in the Woods was the only school available for children in the black community for many years. The building was built as a church in 1886 and soon after began to do double duty as a school. It was used until 1923 when Ward School was built.

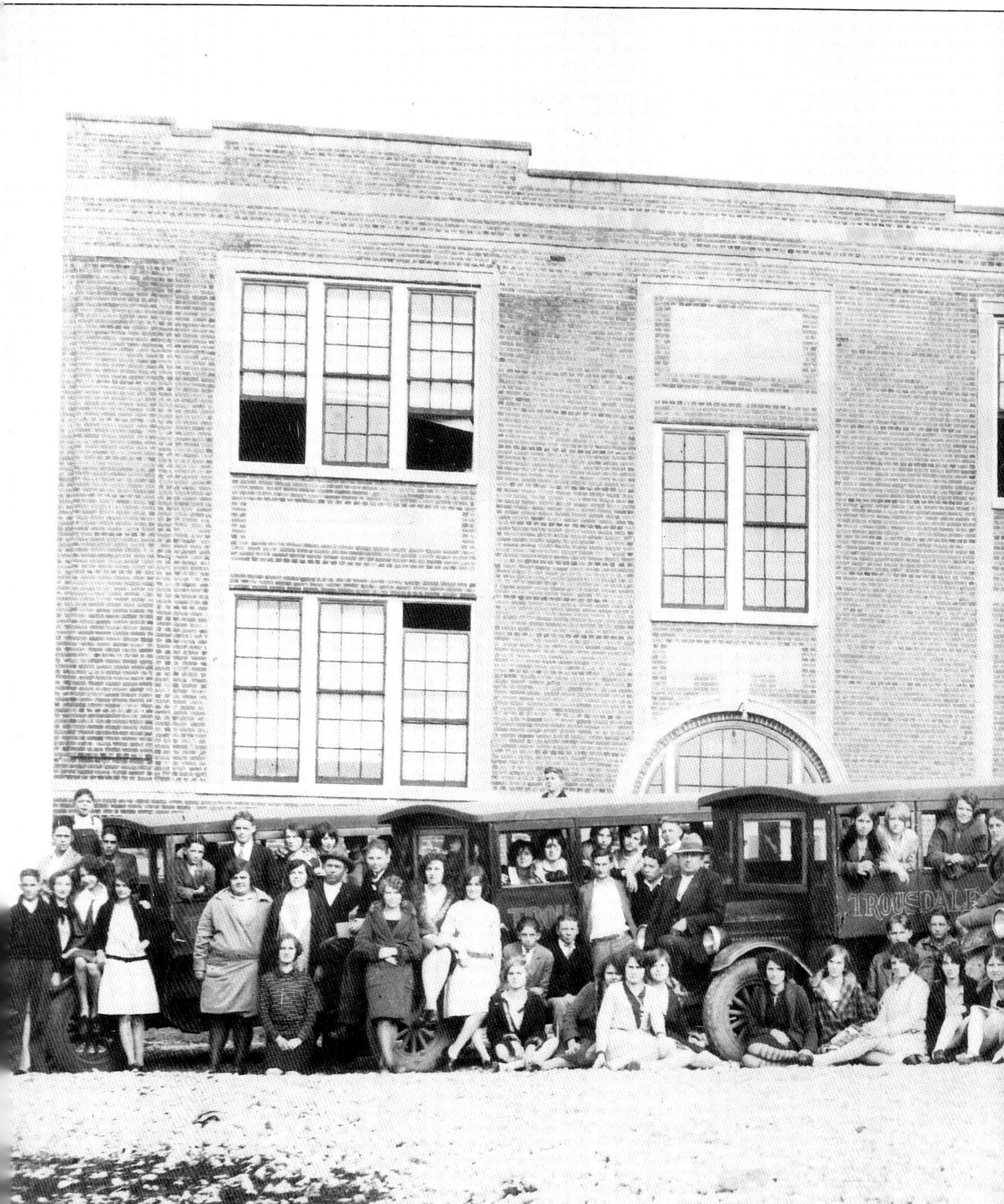

The first school buses used in Trousdale County lined up for this photograph in 1927. The buses had wooden bodies. Only high school students were allowed to use the buses, as most communities still had their local schools for the lower grades. If a football player rode the bus,

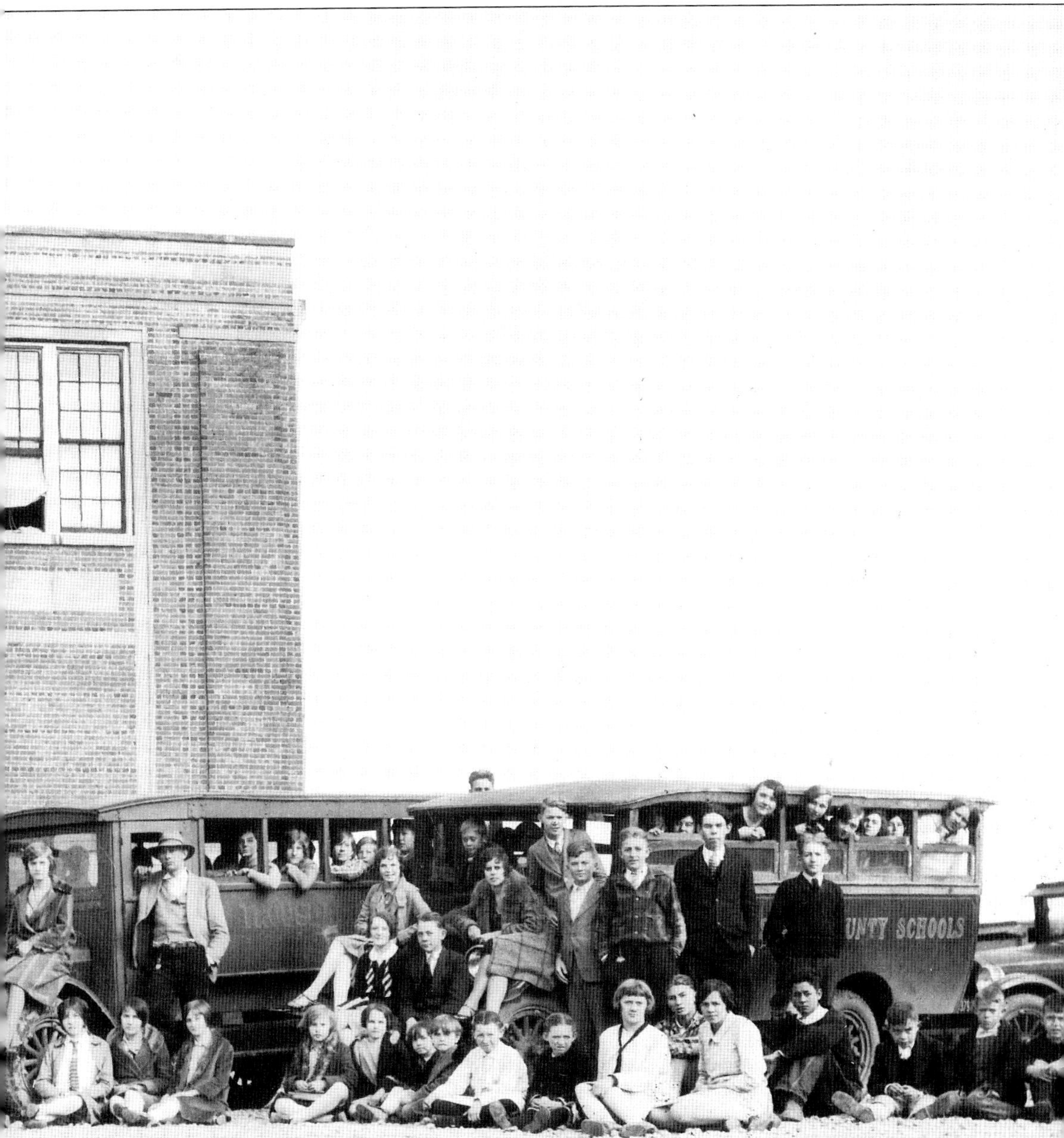

the other students had to sit on the bus and wait until football practice was over before the bus would leave. The drivers were: Thurlow Gregory (Cato route), Berlin Jones (Bartheia), Howard McClard (Beech Grove), H. H. Lipscomb (Walnut Grove), and Ray Foley (Willard).

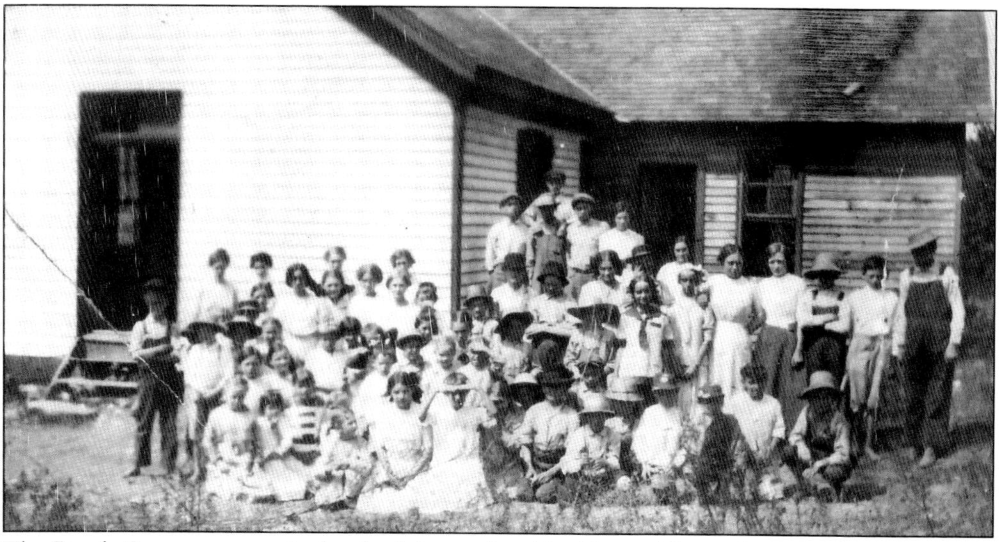

The Beech Grove community has had three school buildings. This is the second one, replaced in 1924. That building ceased use as a school in 1957. Today it is used as a voting precinct. In this photograph, made early in the century, it appears every young man had to have a good, wide-brimmed straw hat.

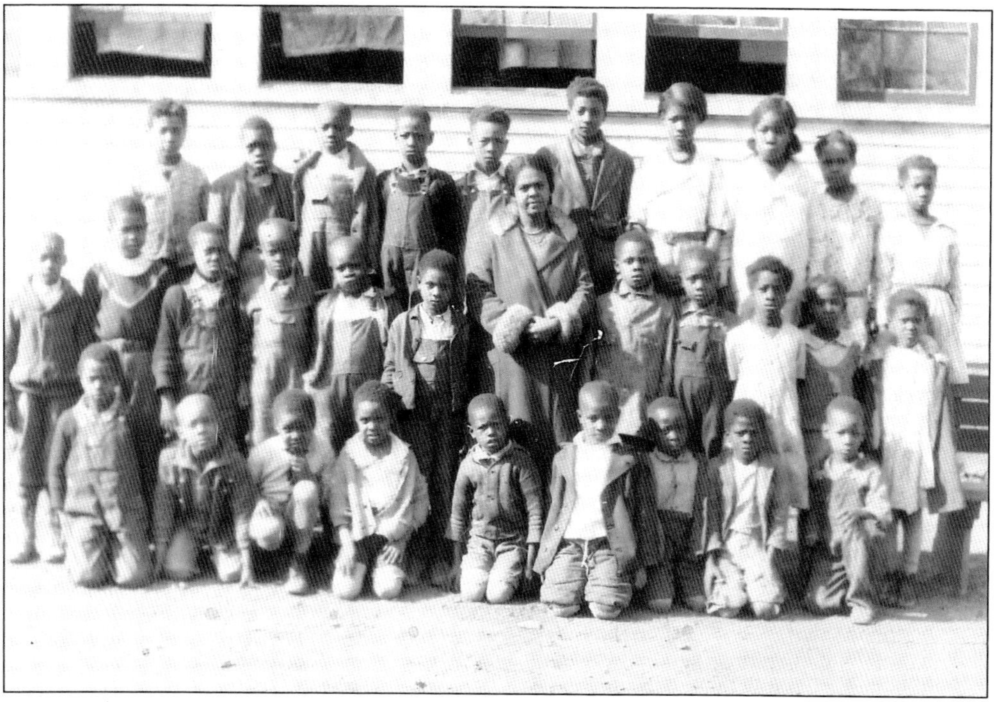

In 1921 after the School In the Woods began to show its age, members of the black community united in efforts to build a new school. They were led by Walter Ward, a Baptist minister in town. The school was built on Morrison Street and named after Rev. Ward. This 1929 photograph shows one of the classes with teacher Deannie Green. The school burned in 1944 and a new Ward School was finished in 1948 on Hall Street.

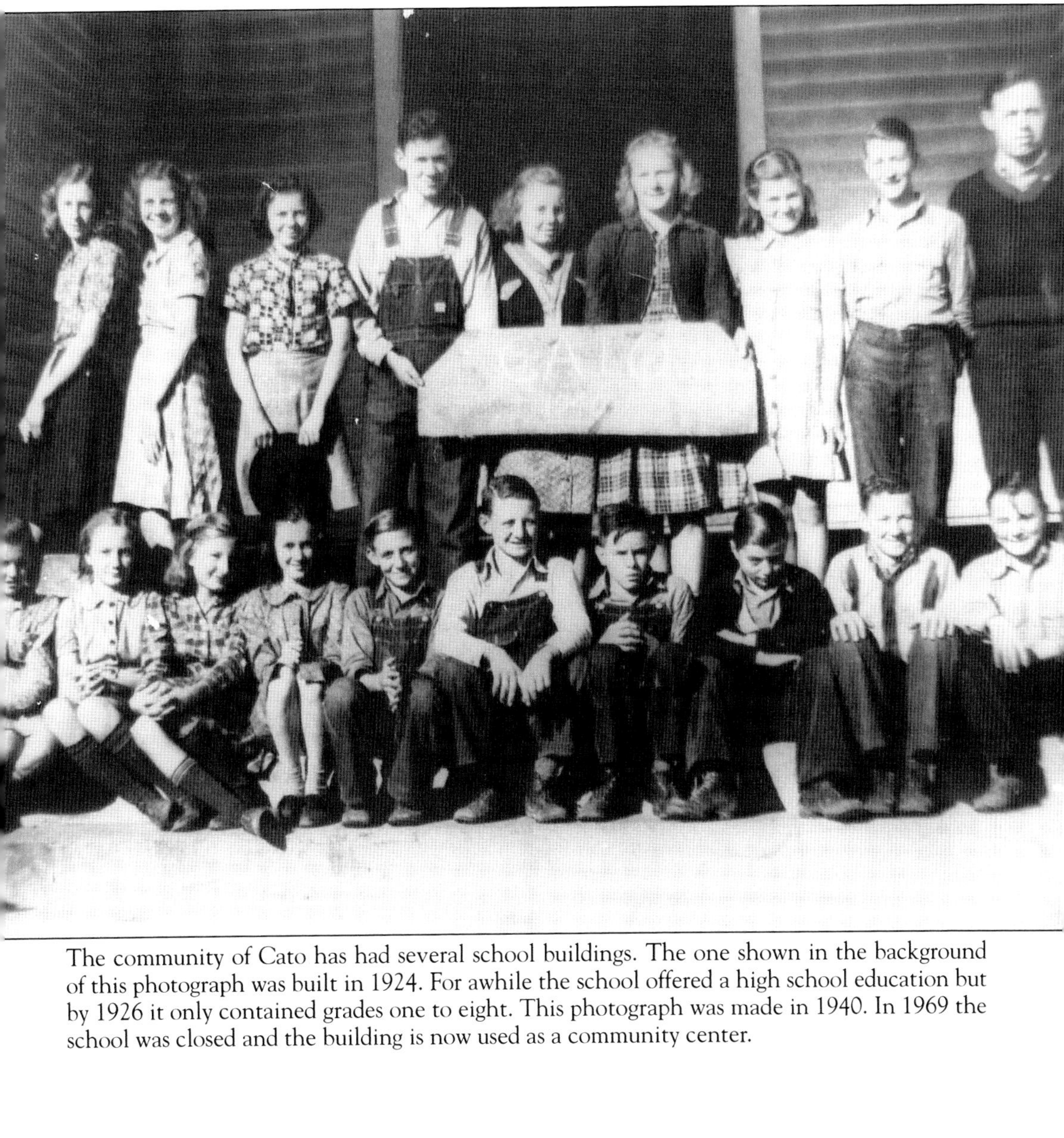

The community of Cato has had several school buildings. The one shown in the background of this photograph was built in 1924. For awhile the school offered a high school education but by 1926 it only contained grades one to eight. This photograph was made in 1940. In 1969 the school was closed and the building is now used as a community center.

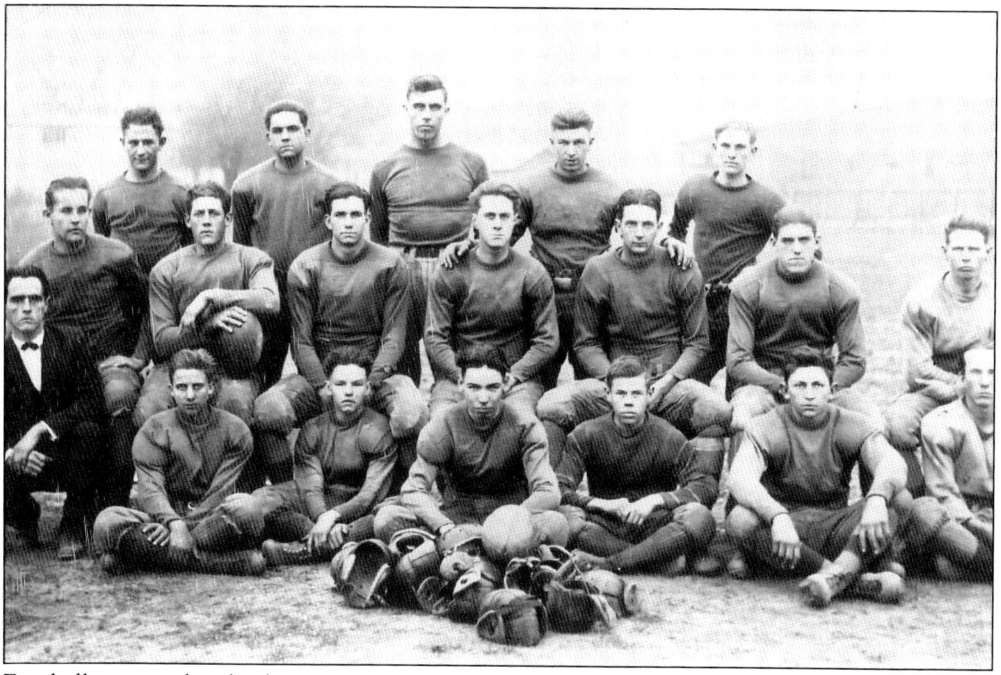

Football is considered a basic part of the high school experience today, but it hasn't always been so. Trousdale County was one of the first schools in this area to field a team. Its first team played under the old Hartsville Masonic Institute name. Teams locally were scarce and Hartsville was forced to play as far away as Bowling Green—against the Ogden College team. They occasionally traveled by wagon. The team pictured here is the 1924 team.

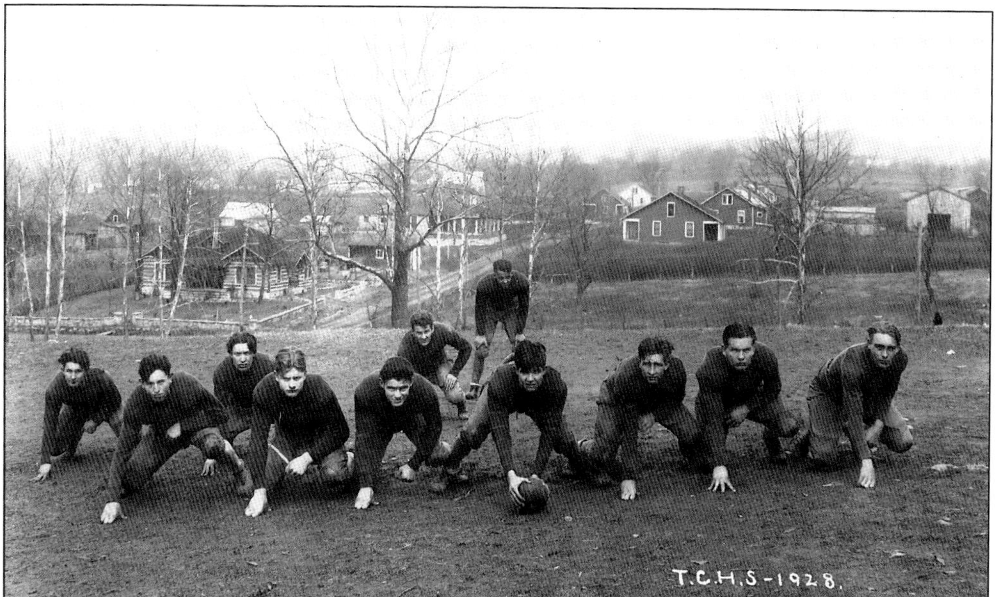

In those early years the team had one football to their name and it lasted several seasons. The 1928 team is in this photograph made in the old, high school yard. In the background is what was then referred to as "New Town." The log cabin was the home of school principal R. N. Chenault. Later the Vaught home, it is the site today of the Vaught Public Library.

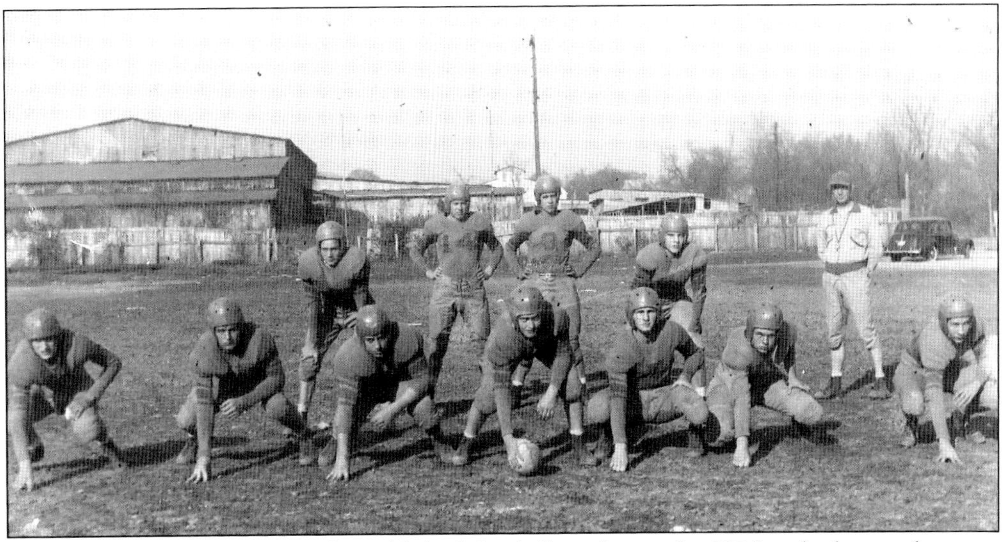

By 1947 Hartsville had a well-established football tradition. In 1922 it had won the state championship with an undefeated season, scoring 392 points against only 13 by all their opponents. In this photograph, made at the practice field, tobacco warehouses can be seen in the background. Players are, from left to right, as follows: (back row) Bill Linville, George Purnell, Leonard Hardee, Cecil Harper Jr., Joe Smith (coach); (front row) Forest Nunley, Jack Wright, Herman Thompson, Jerral Cregory, Clifford Perkins, Douglas Thompson, Jim Satterfield.

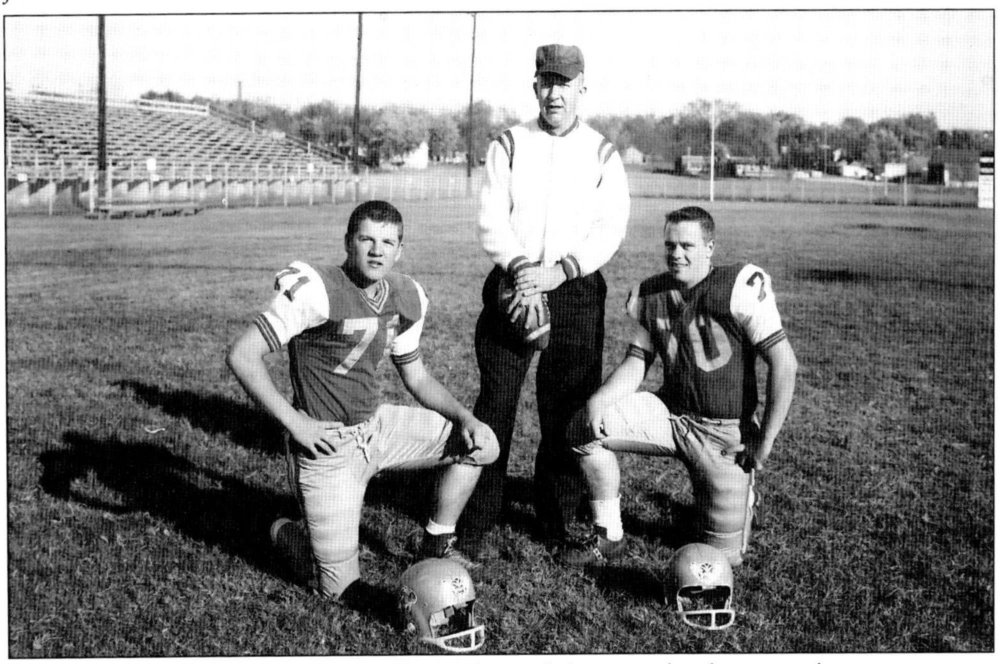

Hartsville's uniforms and equipment have changed, but not the desire to play a great game. In this 1963 photograph, coach Jim Satterfield, who was a player on the 1948 team, stands by players Bobby Towns and Robert Wright. Satterfield went on to become superintendent of schools for twenty-six years, coaching part-time up to his death. Under Satterfield the school won two more state championships.

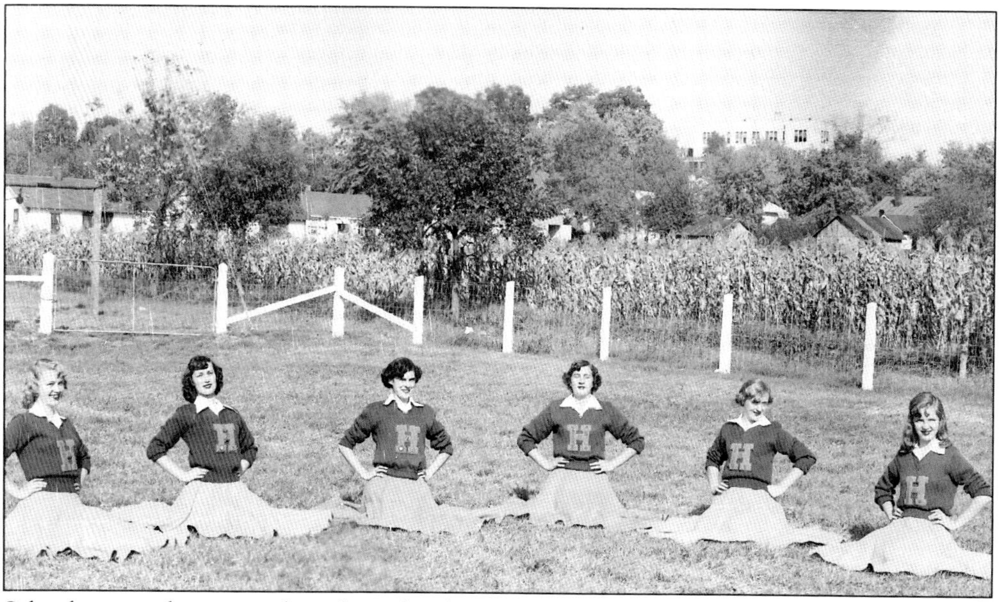

School is more than sports, but what other facet of academic life can boast cheerleaders? In 1952 these cheerleaders posed on the practice field with the old high school, which was stuccoed and painted white by this time, in the background. They are: Robbie Jean Gregory, Clara Bille Long, Wylma Marshall, Shirley Faye Turner, June Beal, and Frankie Fay Gregory.

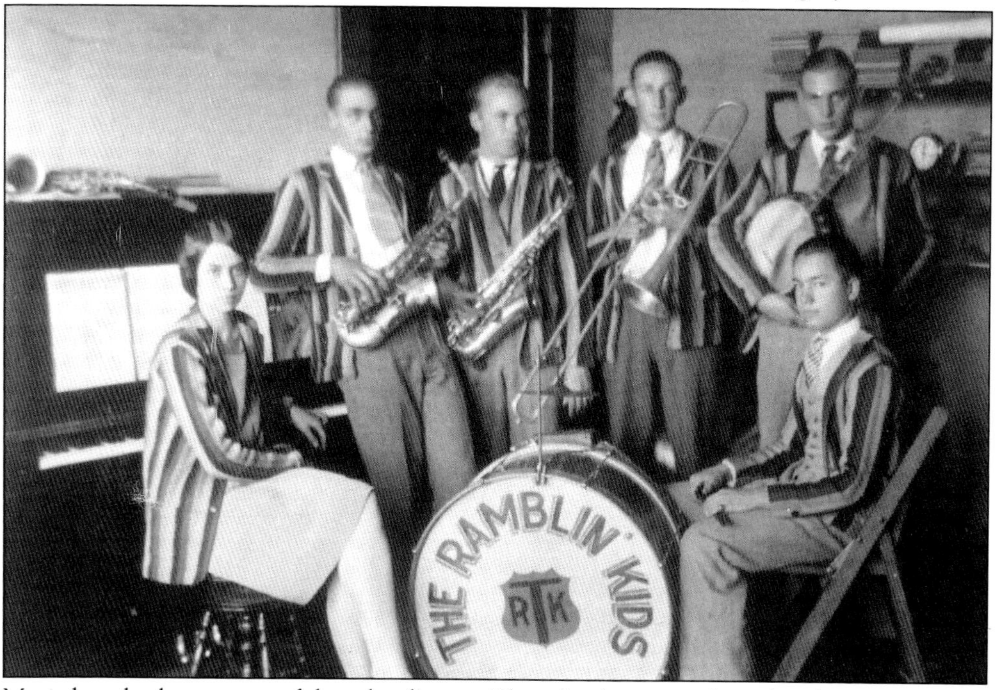

Music has also been a part of the school's past. The school put together a band program briefly in the early 1950s. Again in the 1980s a band was organized that continues today. Before either of those the Ramblin' Kids played locally. The group was put together by Mrs. Gladys Stafford in 1920. They are, from left to right: Leonora Bratton, Albert Becker, Price Womack, Mont Hagen, Nat Becker, and Claude Beasley.

Six

HOMES

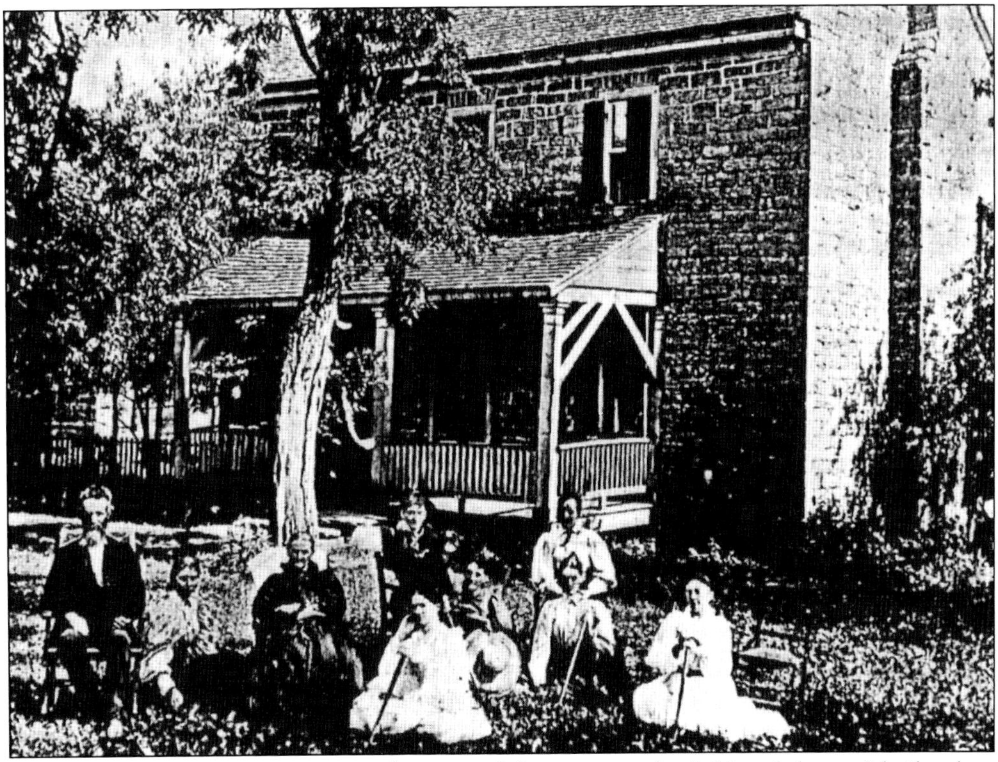

One of the most unique homes in the county's history was the "old rock house," built when this area was still a part of North Carolina. The home stood east of Hartsville facing the old Immigrant Trail, today's Carthage Highway. It was built in 1792 of cut stone quarried close by. The walls were 22 inches thick. It was used as an inn and tavern and a home for over 150 years before crumbling walls forced its demolition in 1935. It was built by John Shelton. The people in the photograph are unidentified.

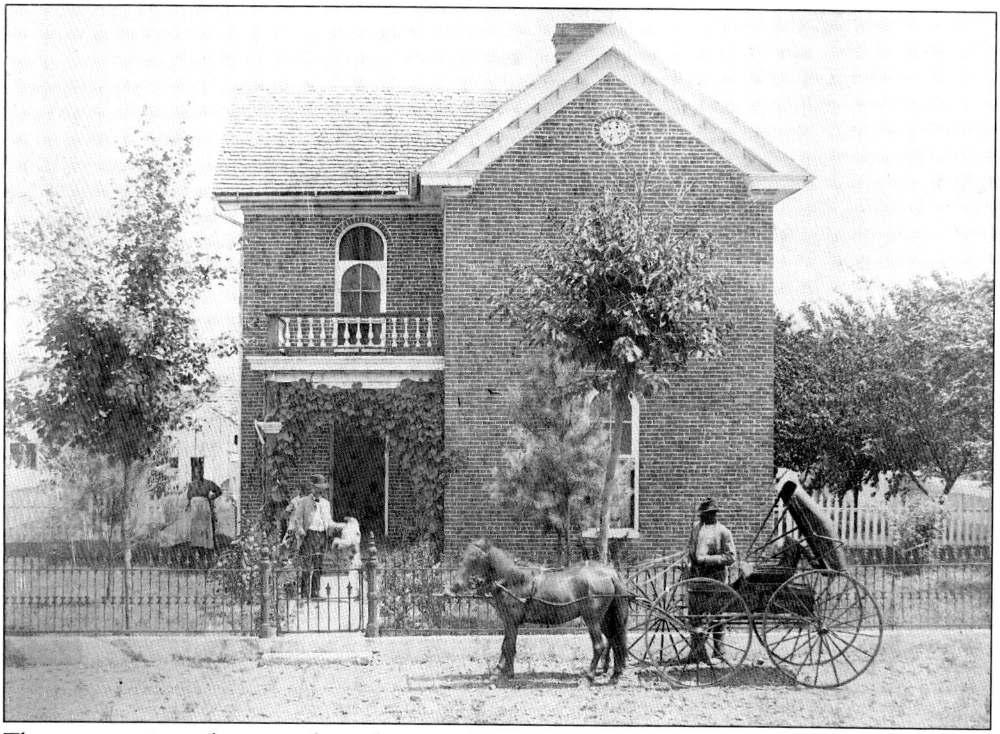

There was a time when traveling photographers would visit small towns and take pictures of people and their homes. These photographs are cherished momentos of the past. Here, Mr. White Hager stands in front of his home on River Street in Hartsville. Built in 1856, today it is the home of James and Marjorie Cunningham.

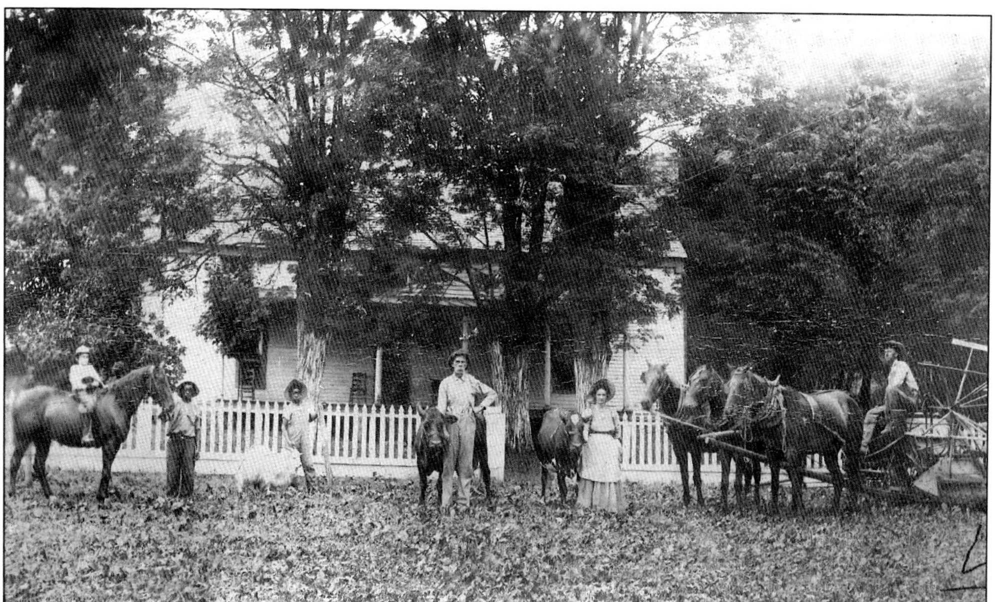

In 1919 the Jim Jones family posed for the photographer. Prize animals were included as well as a newly purchased piece of modern farm equipment, all signs of a prosperous farm.

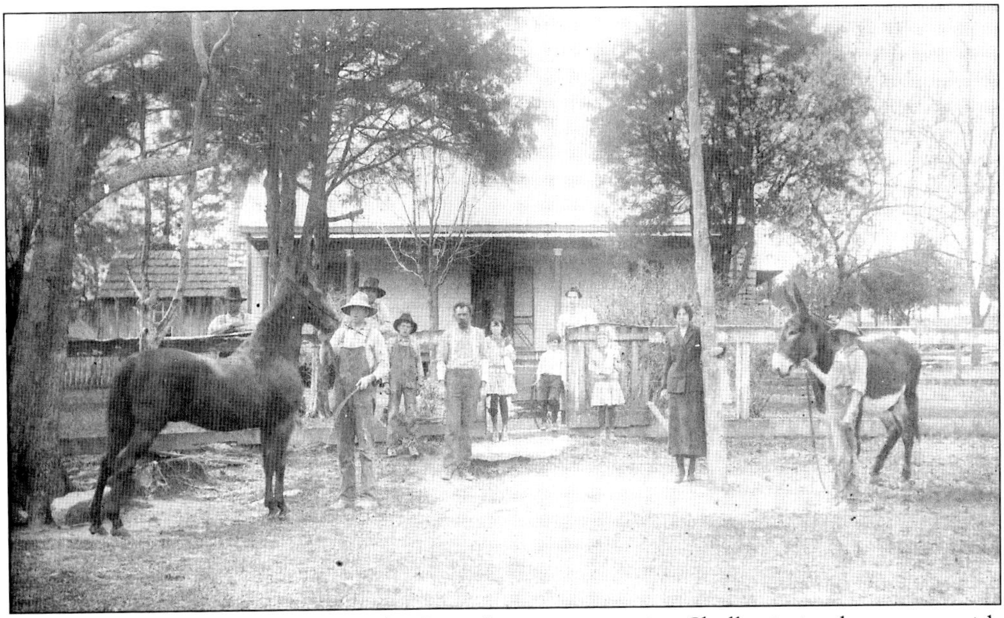

The Shelby Bass home stood in the Providence community. Shelby is in the center with members of his family and several farm hands, around 1910. Mr. Bass raised prize horses and mules, a couple of which are shown here. He once delivered a prize mule to Dallas, Texas, for one thousand dollars.

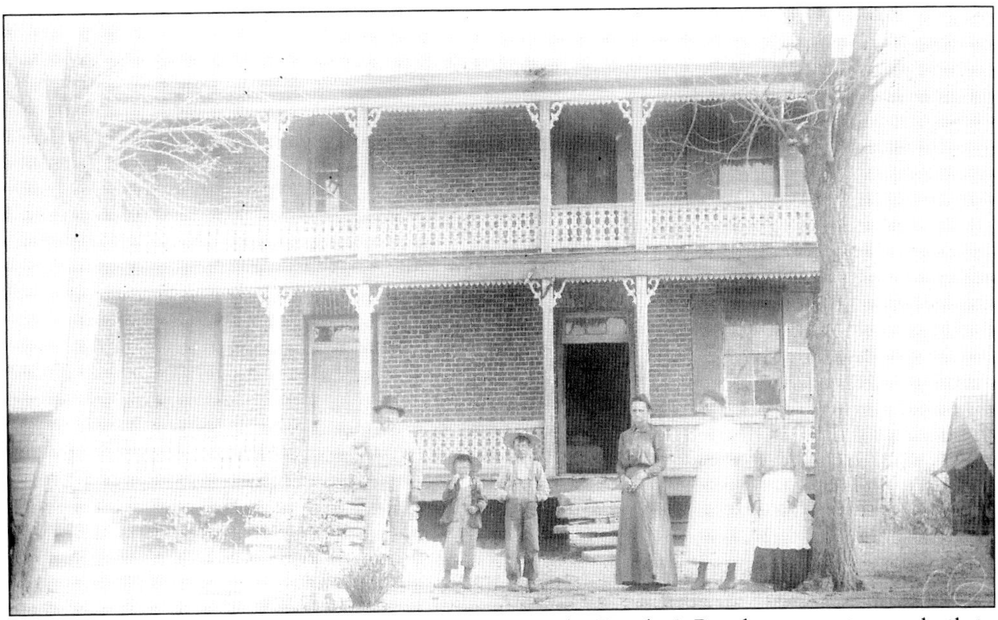

Made from bricks fired on the property, this home in the Beasley's Bend community was built in the early 1800s. The home overlooked the Cumberland River. Mr. Dennis King and family are shown here around 1910. The home is no longer standing.

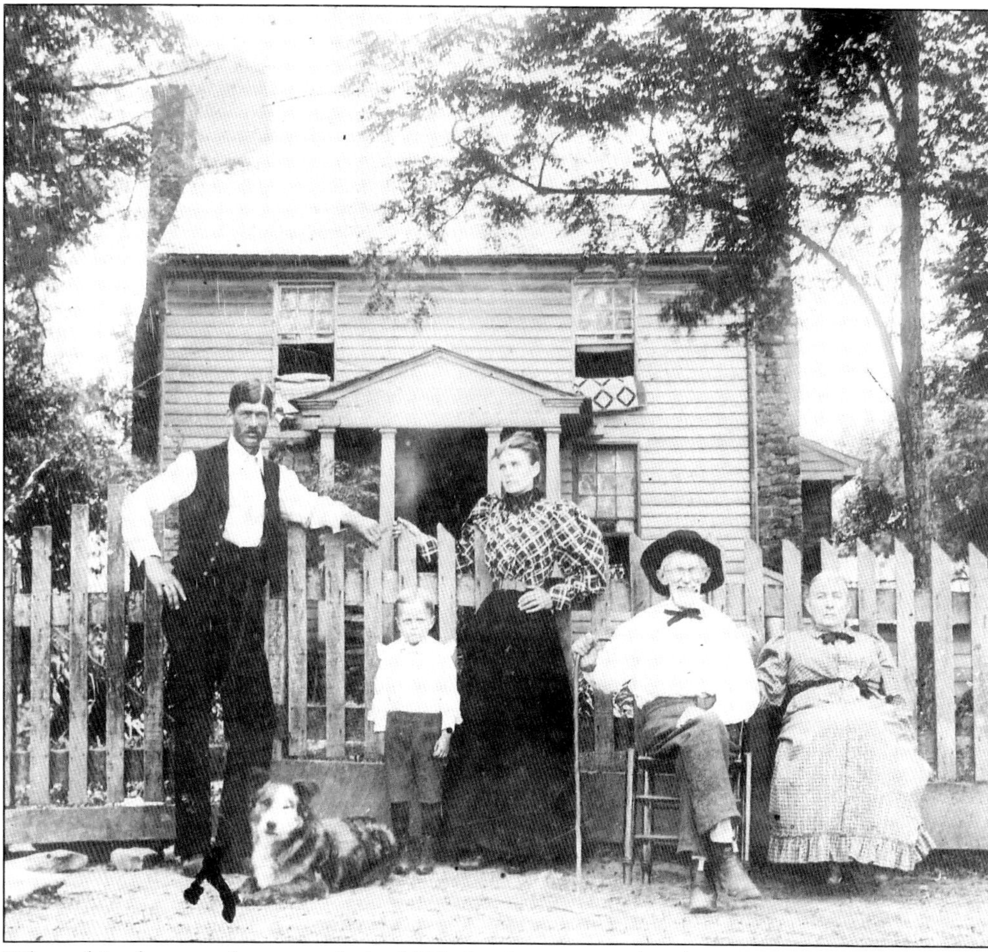

When this photograph was made in 1897 this house was already over a century old. In the Puryear's Bend community this weatherboarded log cabin belonged to the Winn family. From left to right are: "Dock" Winn, along with his son Hubert Winn, his wife Mittie Puryear Winn, his father William R. Winn, and his stepmother L. E. McKinny Winn. The house is still standing and in the Winn family today.

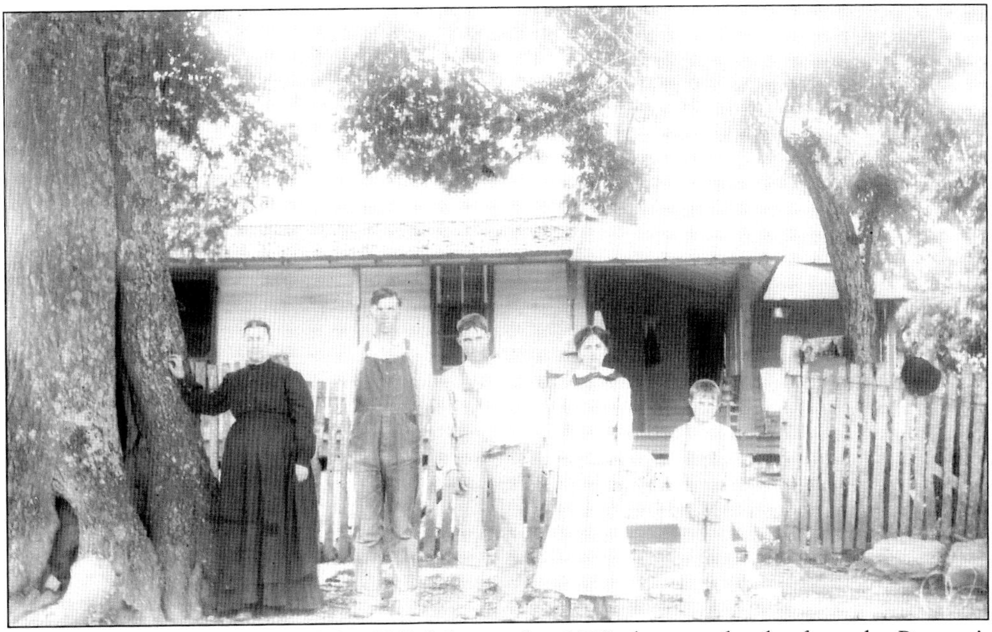

Russell Belcher holds his son John T. Belcher in this 1912 photograph, also from the Puryear's Bend community. From left to right are: Lucy Thomas (from whom Russell bought the home and farm), an unknown hired hand, Russell, his wife Etta, and his brother Lilland. The home and farm are still in the Belcher family today.

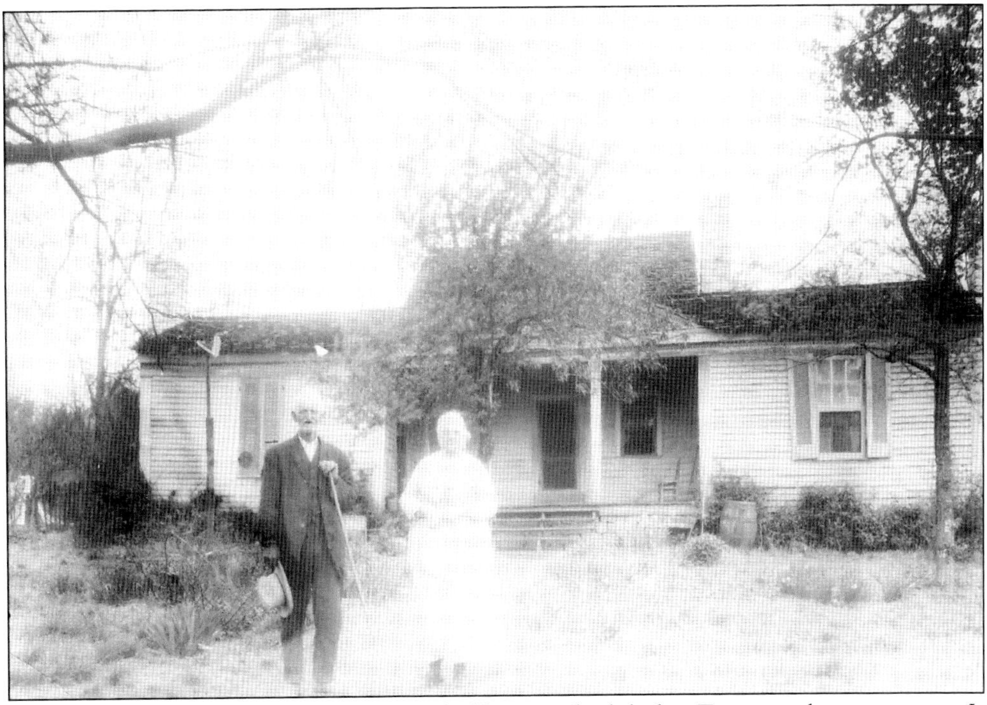

This home, the central portion constructed of logs, was built before Tennessee became a state. It stood on Old Gallatin Road, now Highway 25. Owners Robert Pursley Hall and his wife Sallie Lipscomb Hall stand before the house around 1910. The home burned in the early 1930s.

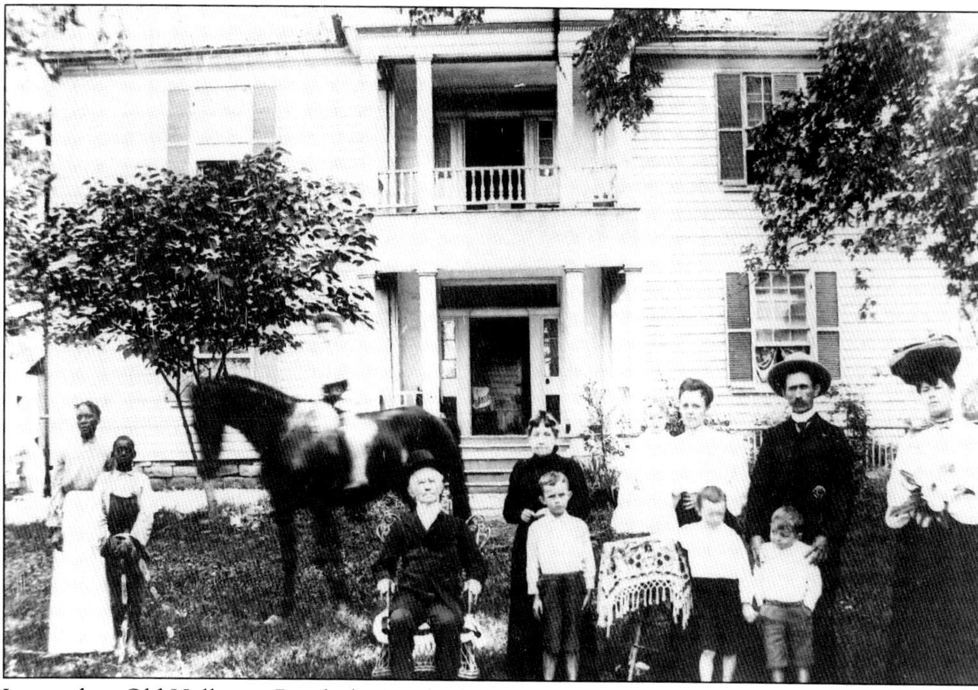

Located on Old Halltown Road, the Lauderdale home was built in the 1840s. This photograph, from the turn of the century, shows the Lauderdale family. Mittie Valentine and her son Emanuel are on the far left. Seated is James Hart Lauderdale, the head of the Lauderdale family. Ft. Lauderdale, Florida, is named for a member of this family. The home is still standing.

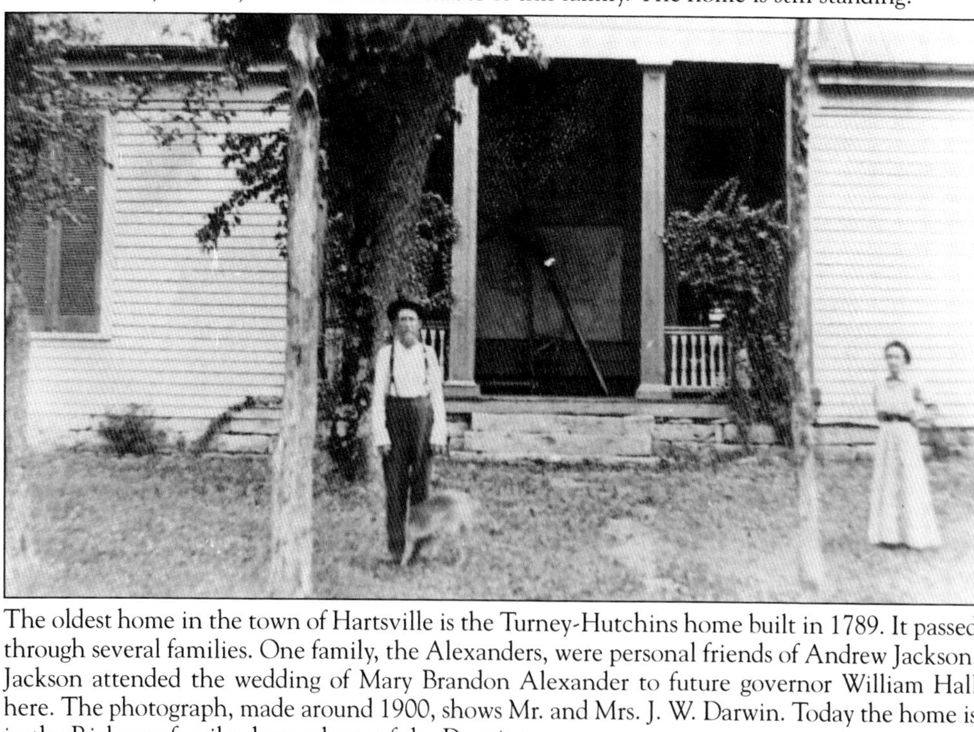

The oldest home in the town of Hartsville is the Turney-Hutchins home built in 1789. It passed through several families. One family, the Alexanders, were personal friends of Andrew Jackson. Jackson attended the wedding of Mary Brandon Alexander to future governor William Hall here. The photograph, made around 1900, shows Mr. and Mrs. J. W. Darwin. Today the home is in the Rickman family, descendants of the Darwins.

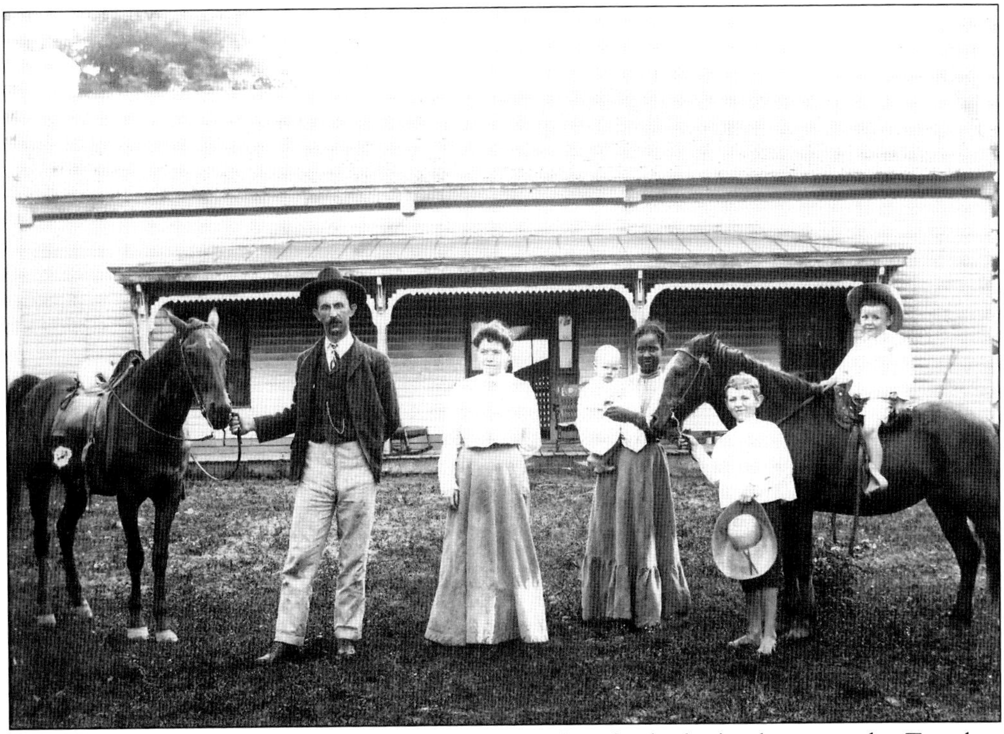

Mark Rickman was a revolutionary war veteran when he built this home in the Templow community in 1798. It is the oldest home in the county still standing. Shown in 1903 are: William Rickman, his wife Lucy Wood Rickman, son N.B. Ricknan, the family maid, and sons Wood Rickman and Sam Rickman. The home is still in the Rickman family today.

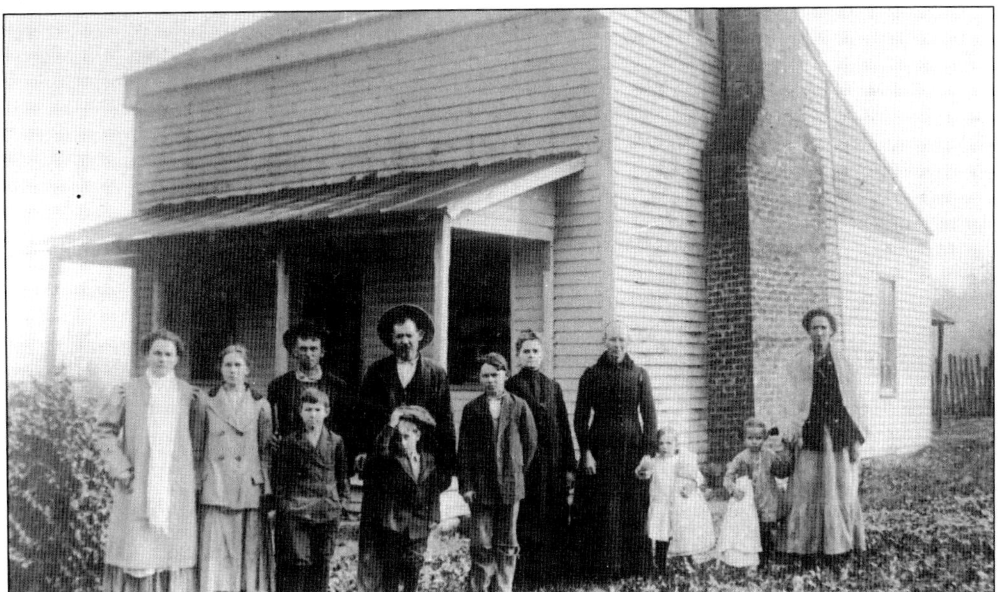

The Providence community was settled early in the county's history. This weather-boarded log home was built in the early 1800s. Mr. Cato Dies and his family stand in front of their home in 1877. The home is still standing today.

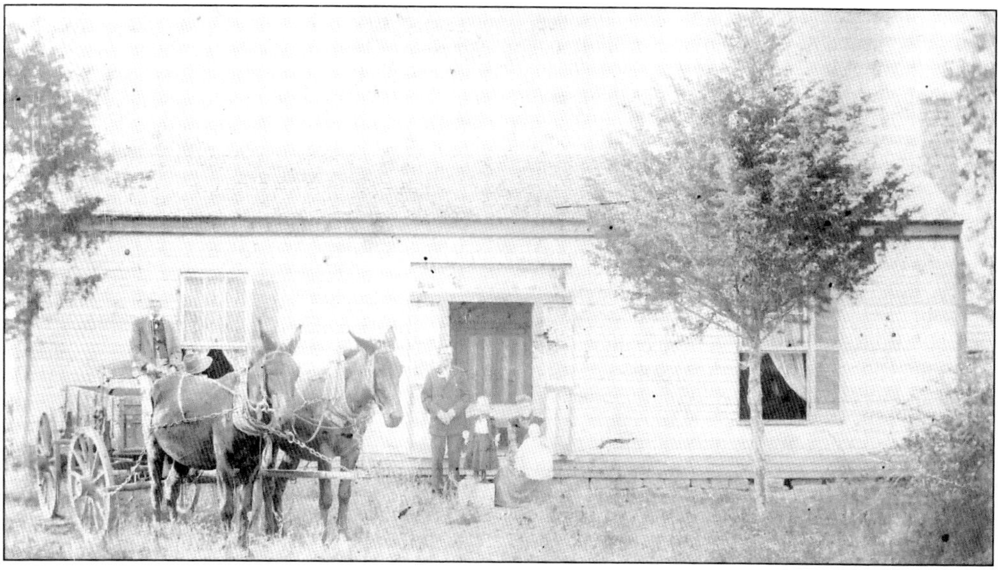

This home in the Payne's Store vicinity was built in 1840 by William Lockett. In 1892 James McMurtry bought the house and farm. He is shown here on the wagon. Sam Bryant McMurtry, his wife Effie, and children Will and Lewis are next. The photograph was made in 1894. The home was torn down in 1948 and a new one built. The McMurtry family have lived on the farm over a hundred years.

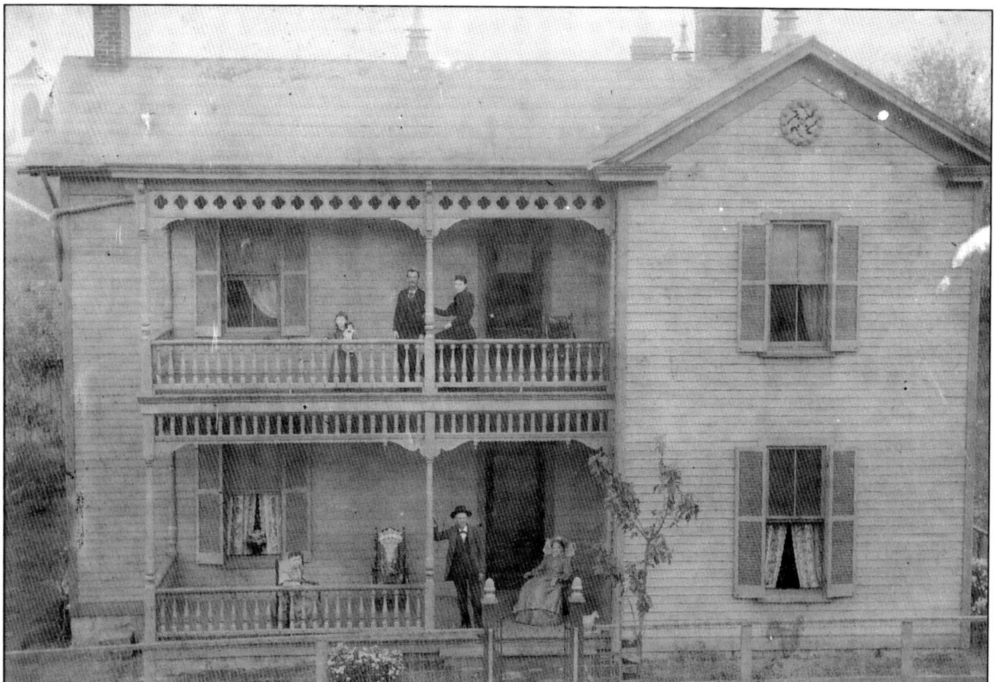

Built around 1870 for the Throp family, this home on Church Street is still in use today. In this 1893 photograph, the Franklin Throp family is downstairs and the John Throp family is upstairs. The Throps were cabinet makers who went on to become Hartsville's first undertakers. The home doubled as a funeral home for many years.

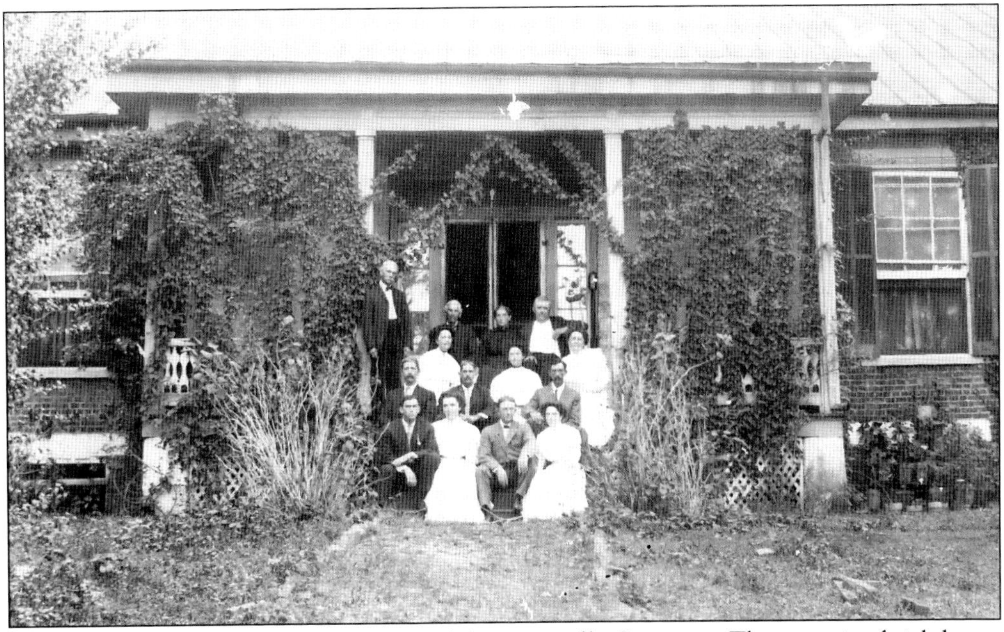

The Thomas Stalker home stood south of the Hartsville Cemetery. The imposing brick home was built in the early 1800s. The Stalker family is shown in this photograph made after 1900. Later the Upshaw family lived here. The home was demolished some time ago.

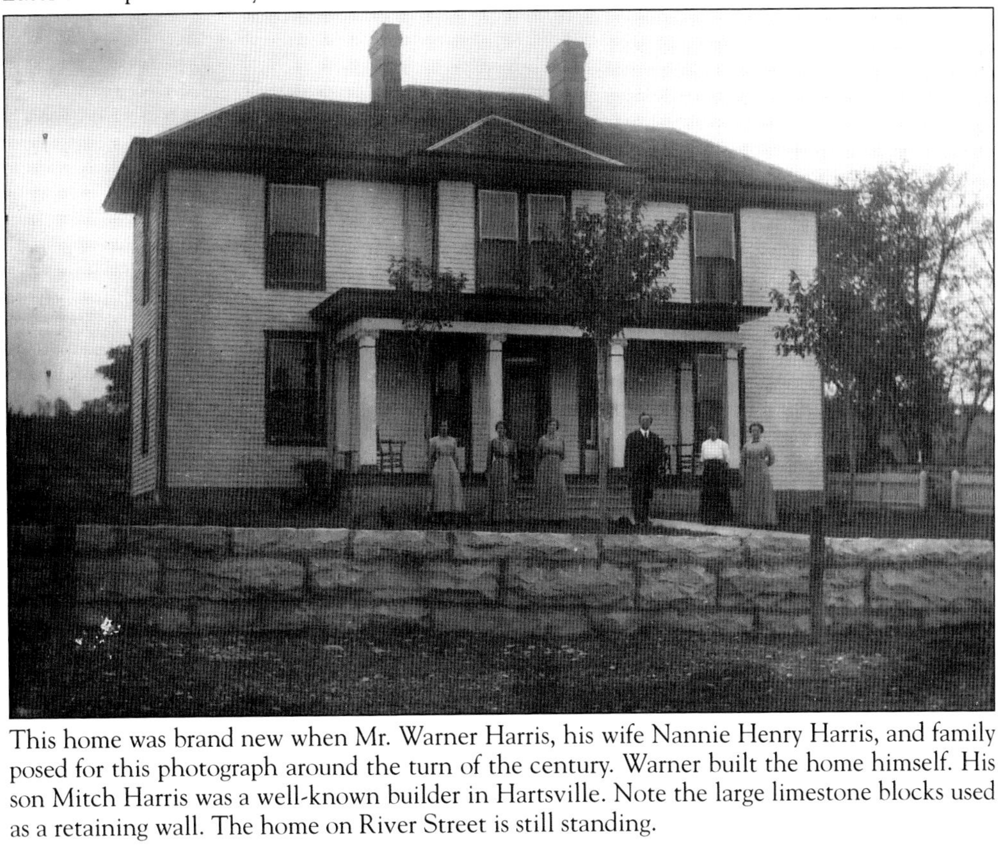

This home was brand new when Mr. Warner Harris, his wife Nannie Henry Harris, and family posed for this photograph around the turn of the century. Warner built the home himself. His son Mitch Harris was a well-known builder in Hartsville. Note the large limestone blocks used as a retaining wall. The home on River Street is still standing.

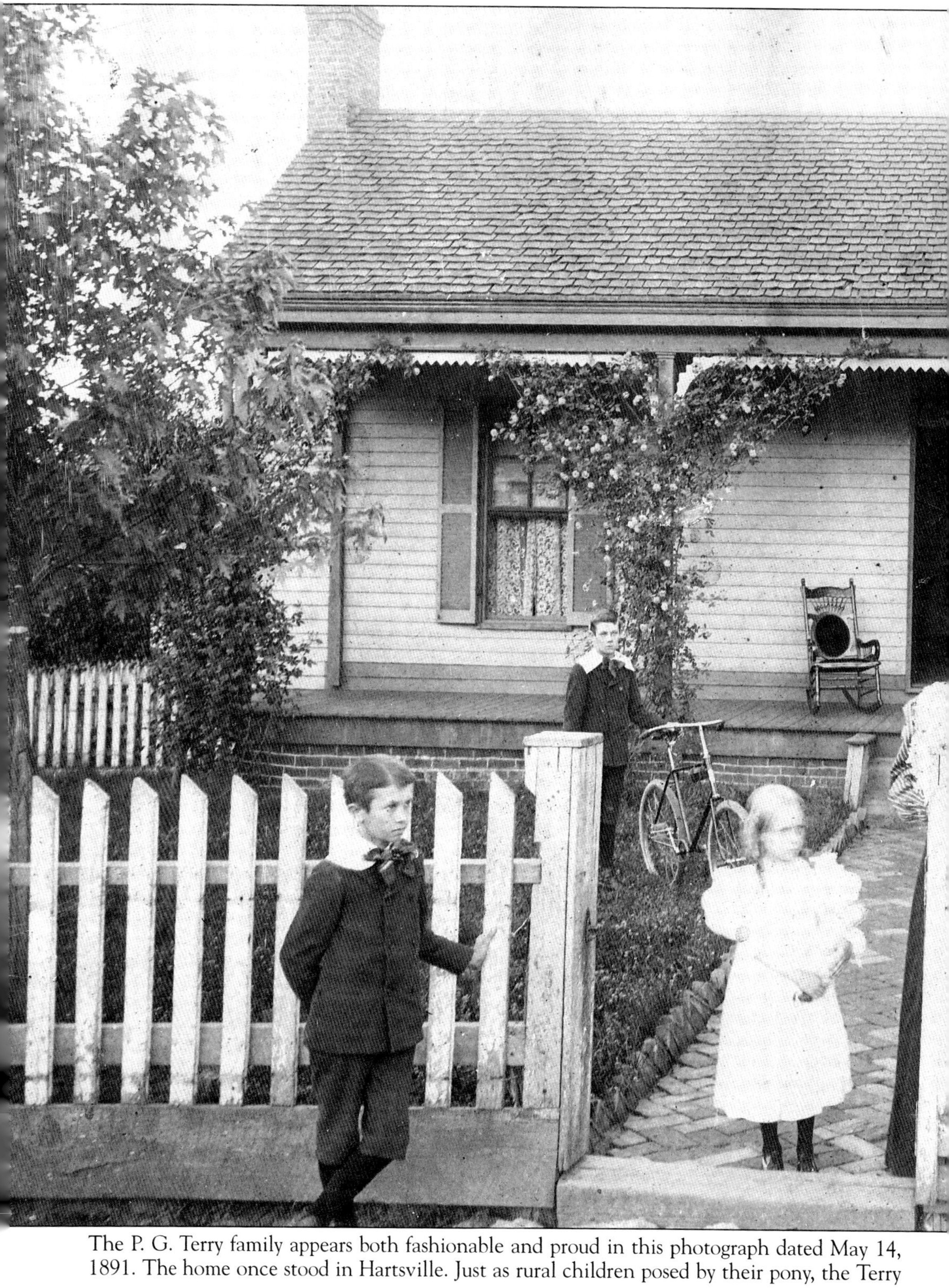

The P. G. Terry family appears both fashionable and proud in this photograph dated May 14, 1891. The home once stood in Hartsville. Just as rural children posed by their pony, the Terry

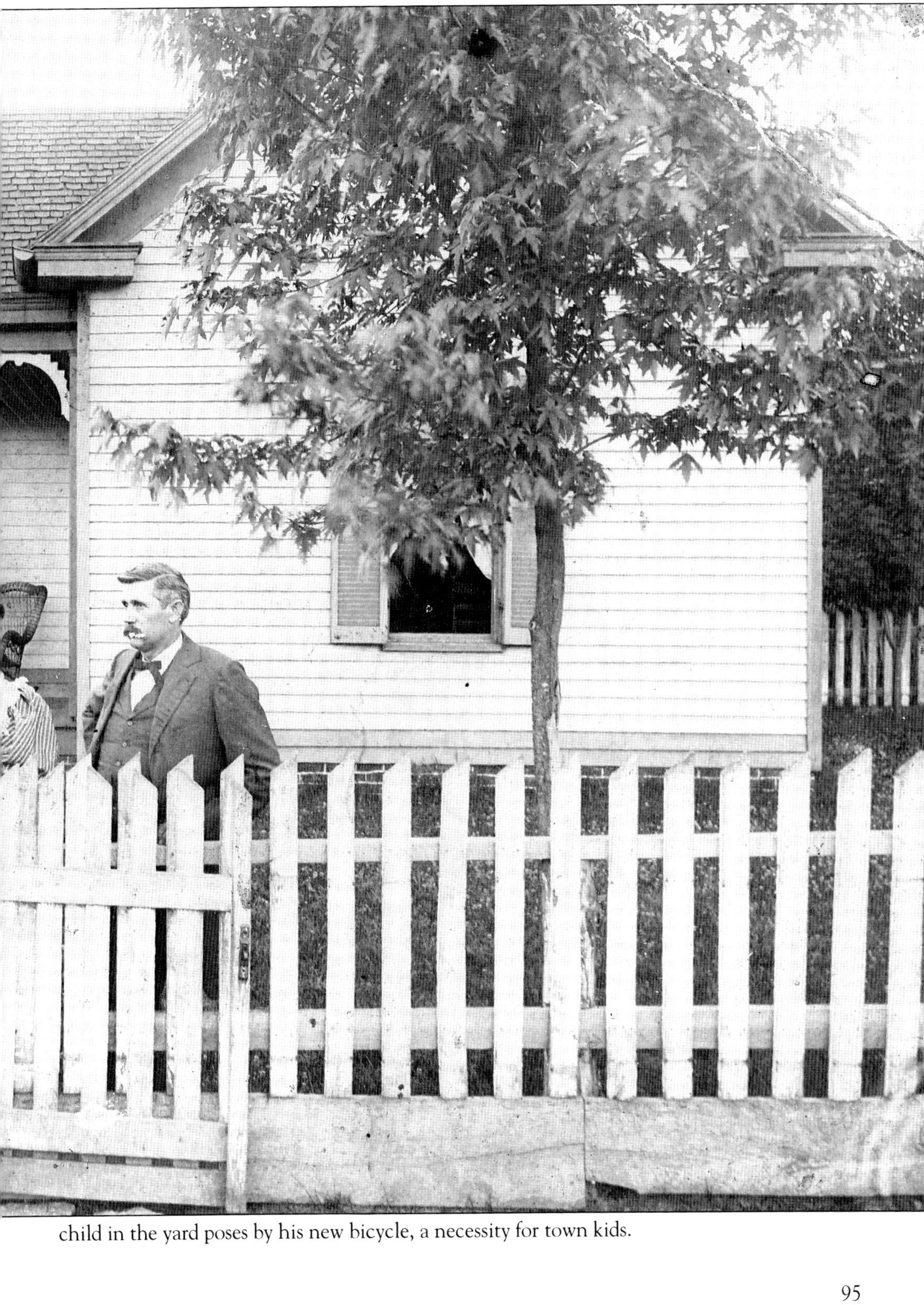

child in the yard poses by his new bicycle, a necessity for town kids.

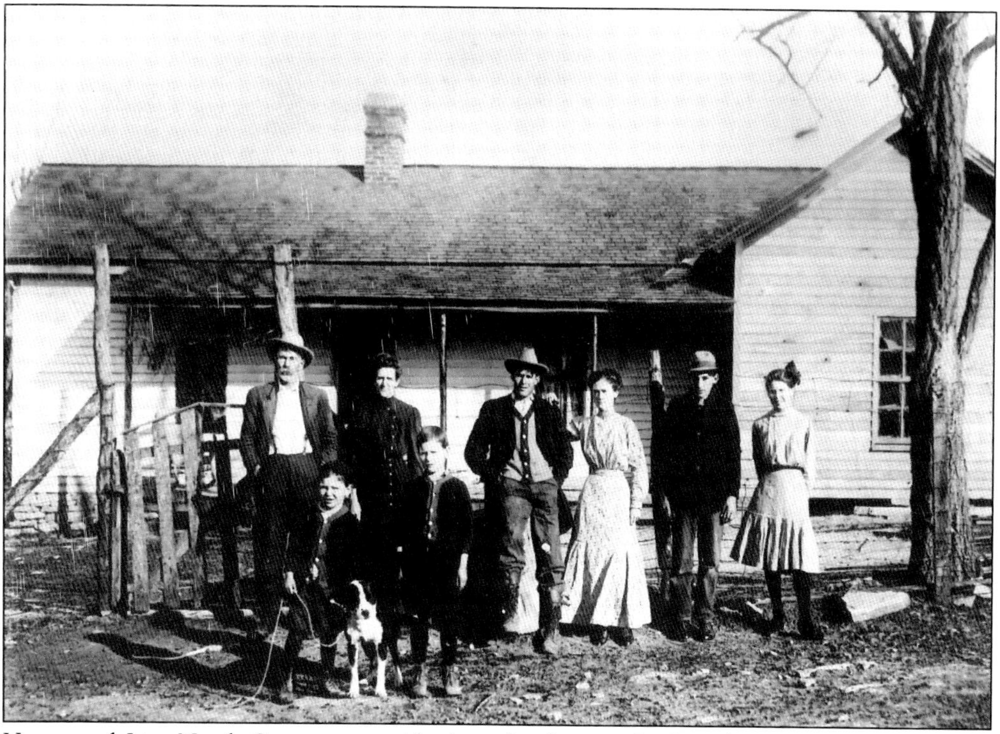

Henry and Liza North Stone pose with their family outside their home in the Providence community. The photograph was made after 1900. In 1974 a tornado ripped through parts of Trousdale County and destroyed this house.

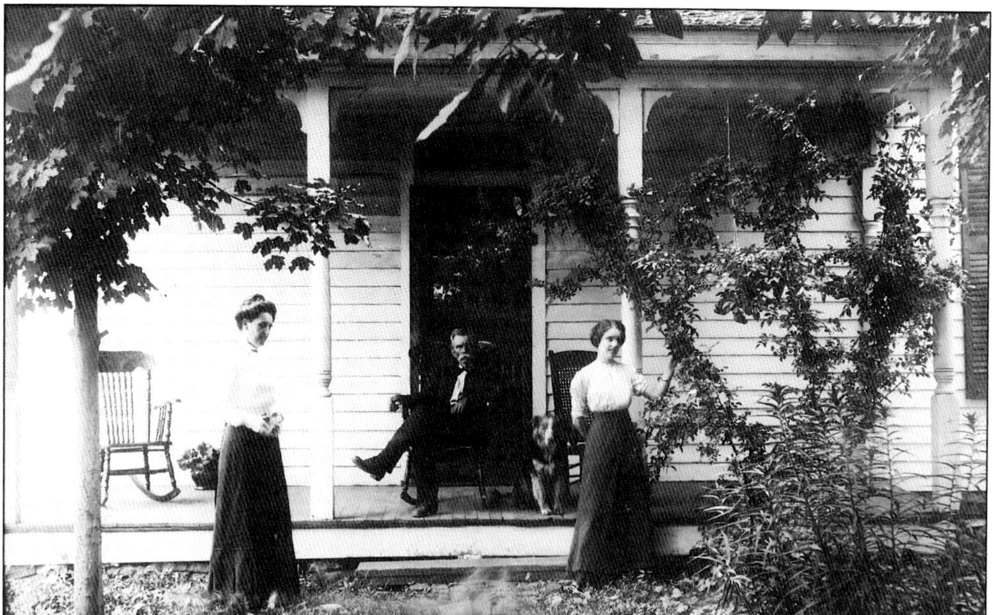

The Puryear family, for whom Puryear's Bend is named, is shown in this photograph. Fate Puryear is the gentleman on the porch. His wife and daughter are shown with him. The photograph was made around 1900. The home is no longer standing.

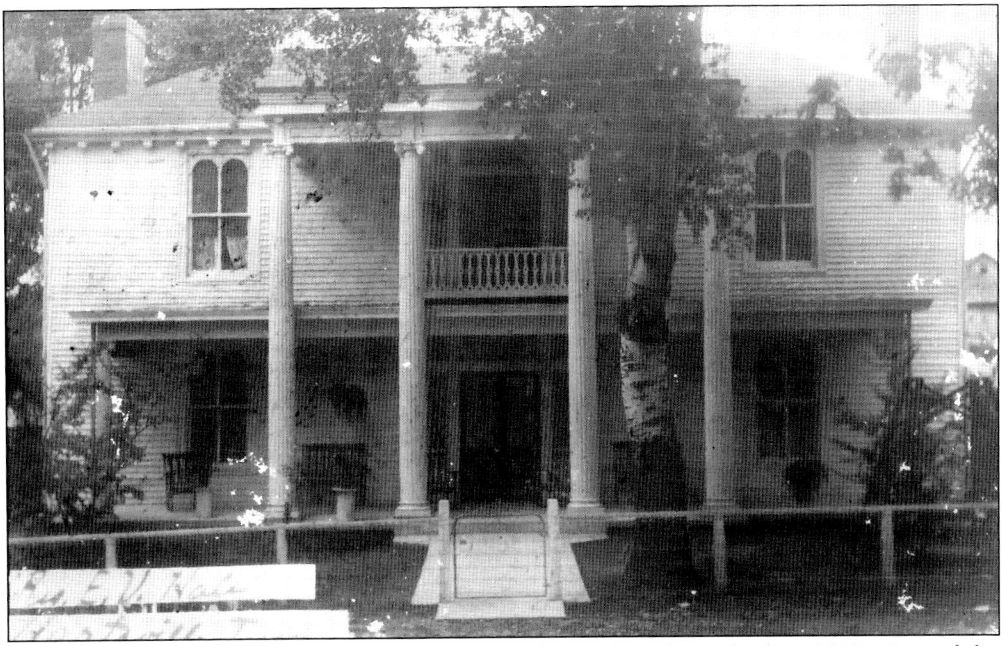

This stately home on East Main Street was built for W. J. Hale in the late 1800s. Part of the framework is log. For many years it was the home of Miss Will Hale and her sister Virginia Hale Gregory. Today, still stately, it remains in the Hale family. The photograph was made in the 1920s.

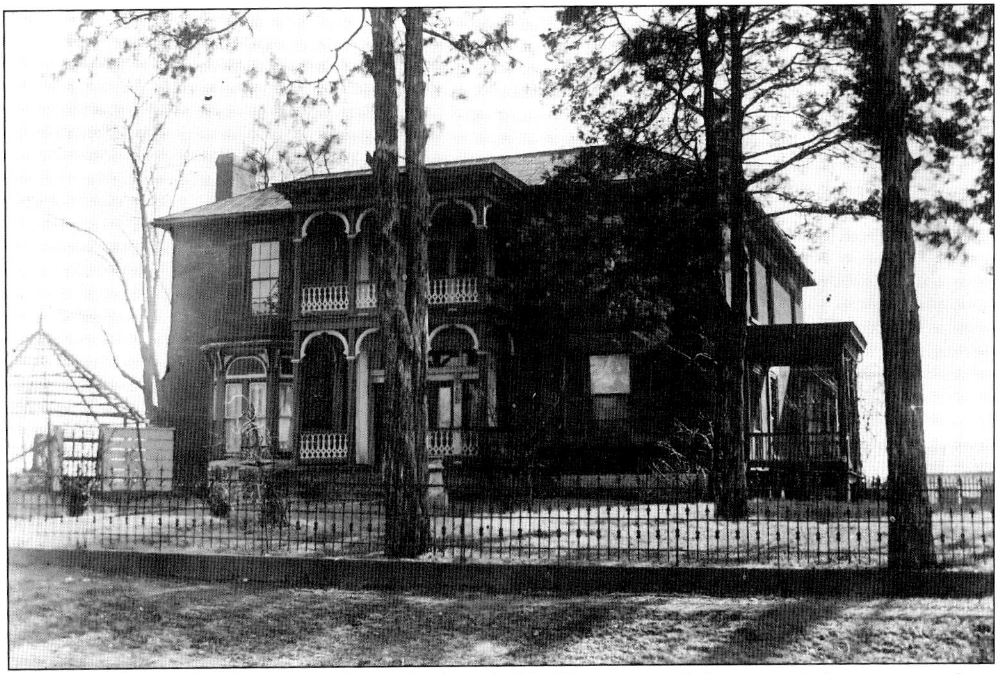

Also on East Main Street is this home built by F. M. Winn around the turn of the century when this photograph was made. It was later the home of R. C. Owen, who changed the facade by applying stucco and adding a pair of tall white columns. Today it is the home of Mr. and Mrs. Andy Vaught.

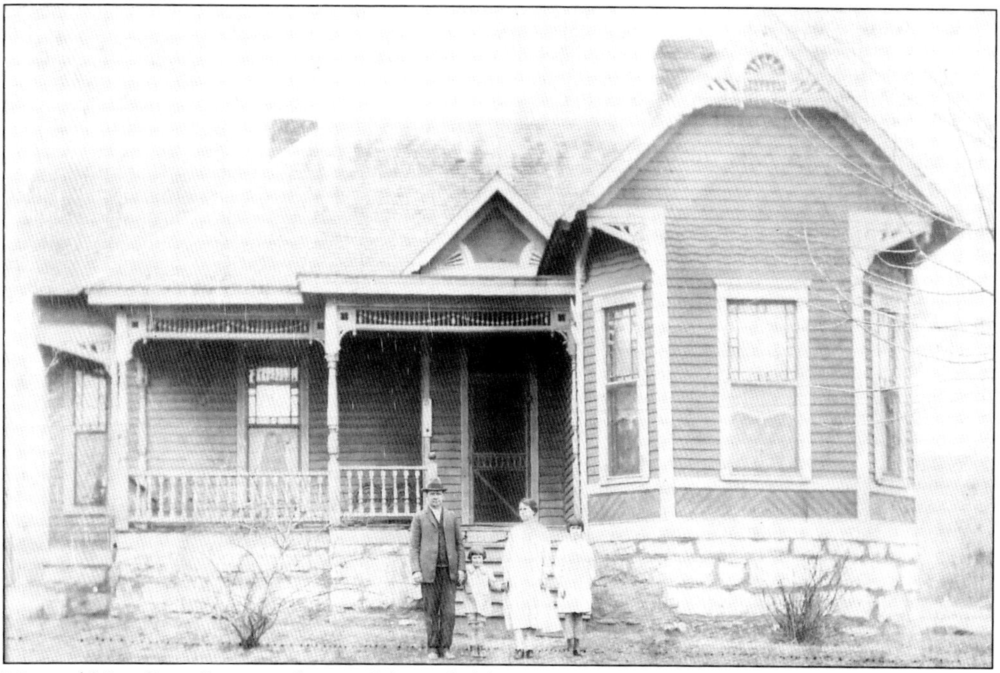

Mr. and Mrs. Sam Owen and two of their children stand in front of their home on old Gallatin Pike. The home was built with lumber and millwork from the Welch Mill. Mr. and Mrs. Owen lived in the home, which is still standing today, for seventy-six years. The picture was made in the 1920s.

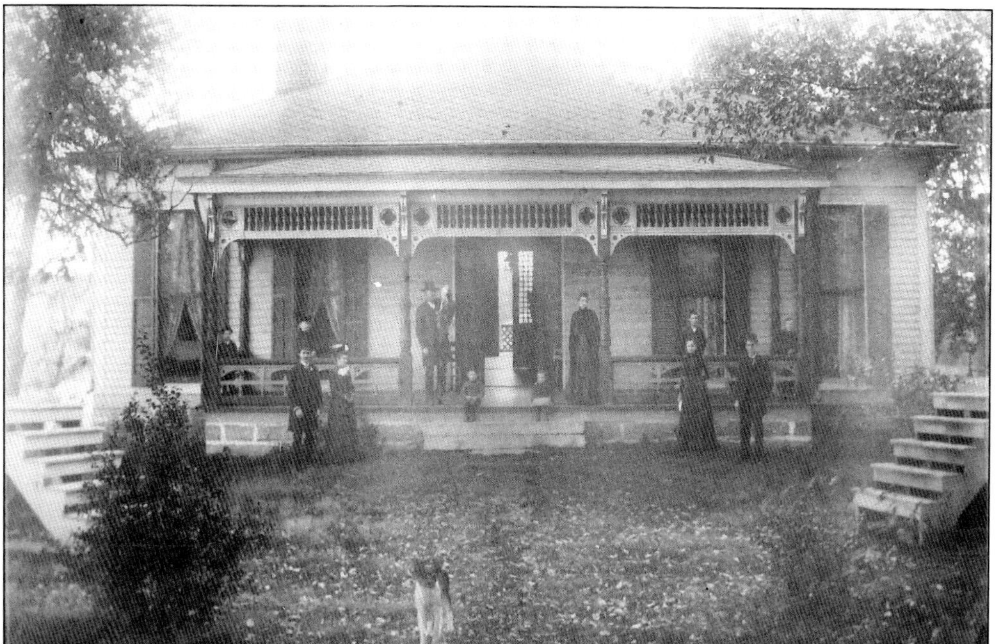

This home stood outside the city. It was the home of F. M.Winn and family before he moved to town. His daughter Maye and her husband Leslie Foley lived in the home after he moved. The home is no longer standing.

Seven

PEOPLE

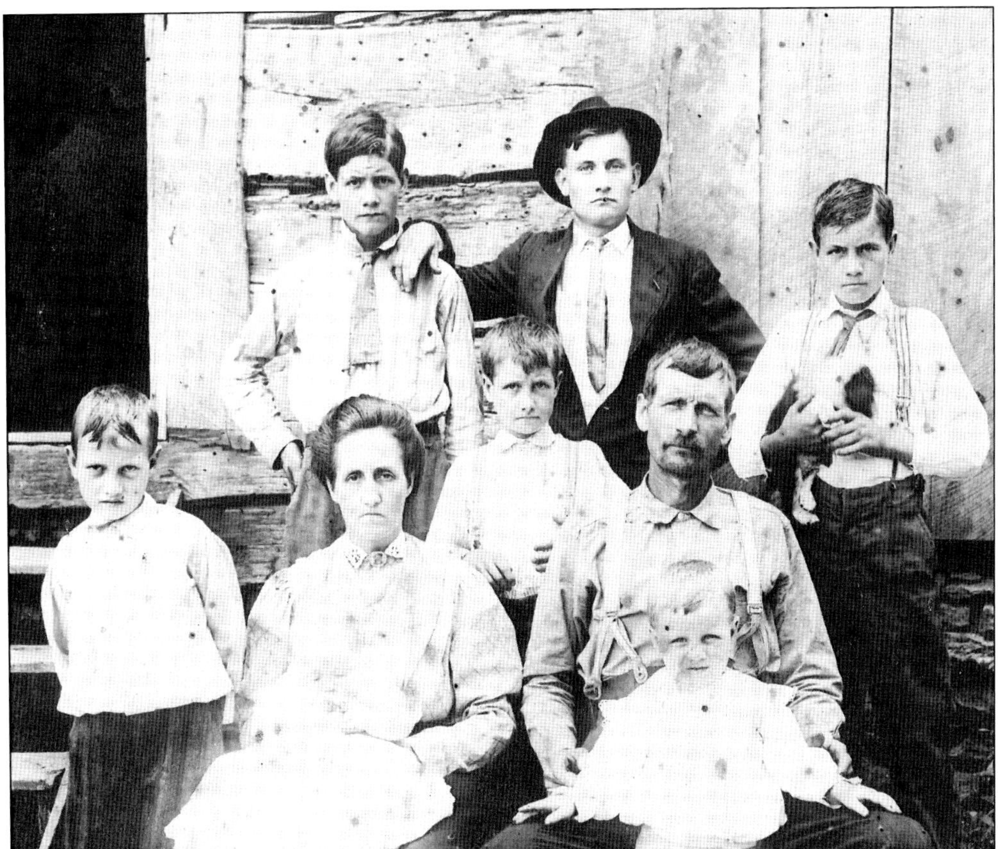

Seven children was the average when large families were the rule. Mr. and Mrs. "Spud" Gregory of the Cato community had their hands full when this photograph was made around the turn of the century.

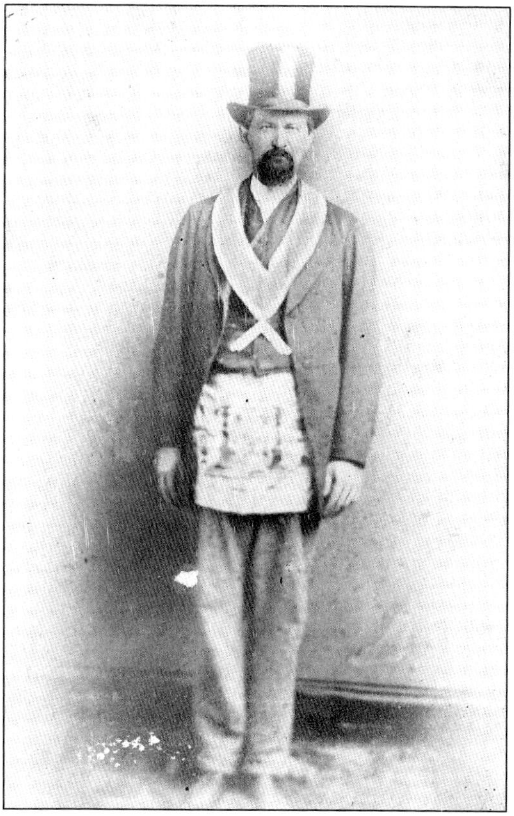

Captain Christopher Lynch Bennett fought with General John Hunt Morgan in the Civil War. After the war, like many others, he continued to use "Captain" as part of his name. He was a member of the Hartsville Masonic Lodge. From 1851 to 1852 he served as Worshipful Master. Here he is shown in his uniform.

Robert Allen Robertson sits beside his wife Mirinda Badgett Robertson while his children and other relatives stand around in this picture from the 1930s. Behind them are: (second row) Payne Robertson, Fanny Byrd, Virginia Robertson; (back row) Emma Robertson Byrd, Fanny Robertson Pruitt, Edd Robertson, Daisy Mae Robertson, Nanny Robertson, and Alta Byrd.

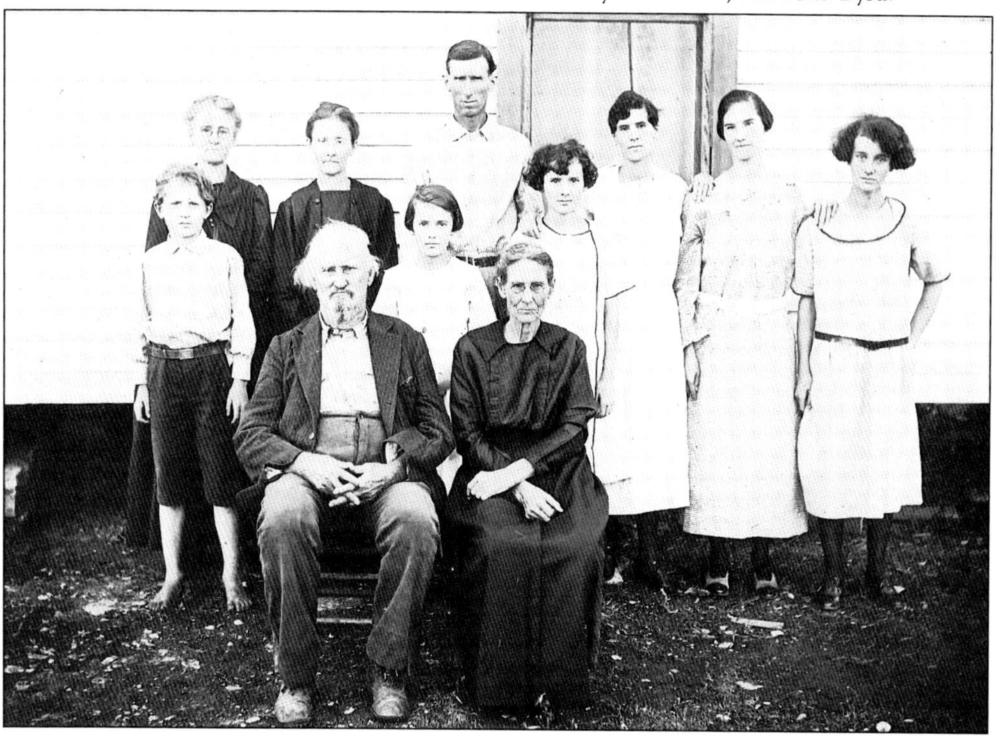

Brice Gregory was a widower when this photograph was made in Cato in 1903. His wife Mattle Smith had died at age thirty-three, leaving eight children. Brice sits by Billy, Florence, Effie, and Leslie. Behind their father are Thomas, Maggie, Shelby, and Ruthie. He later remarried and had five more children.

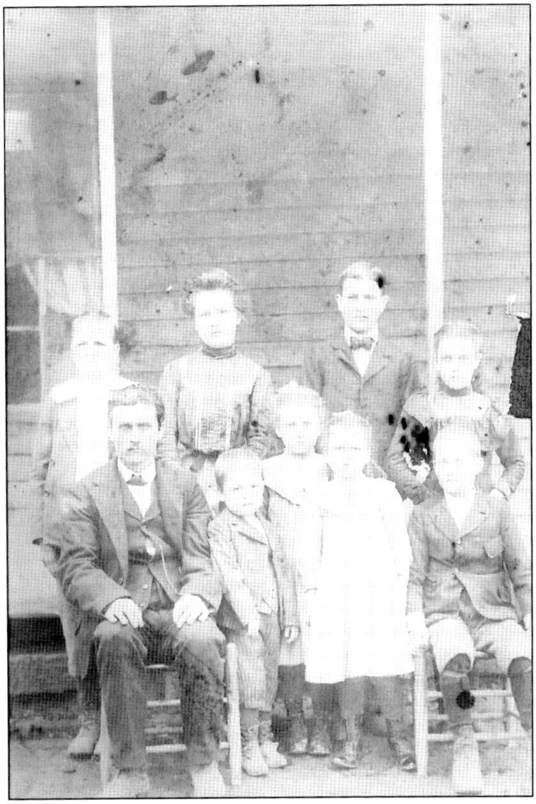

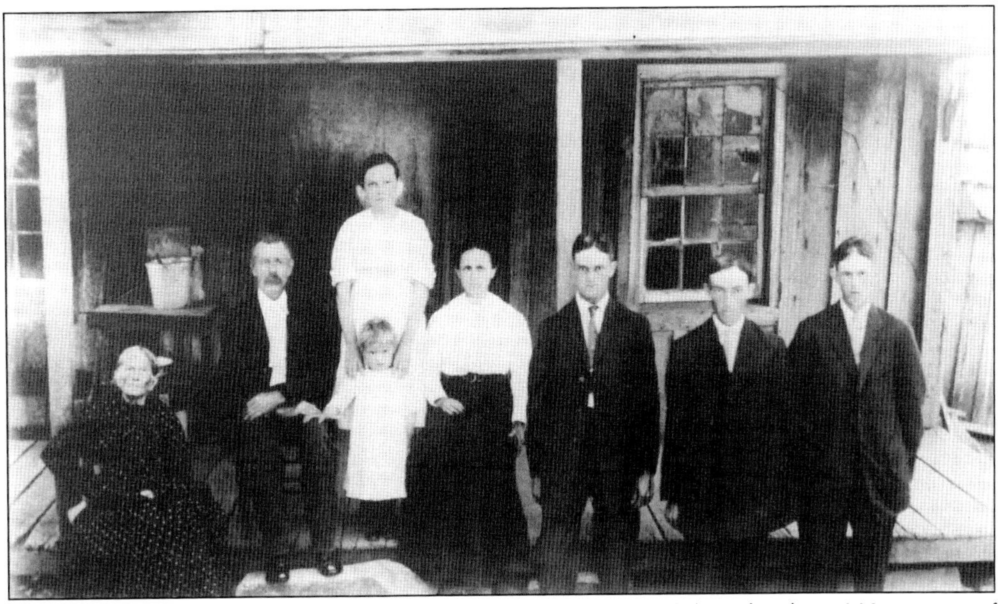

The house in the county Living History Museum was the backdrop for this 1909 portrait of the W. N. Nollner family. Mr. Nollner sits beside wife Cora Carman Nollner, with children Mary and Wilson between. The three boys are Harris, Bill, and Jim Nollner. The woman is an unidentified relative.

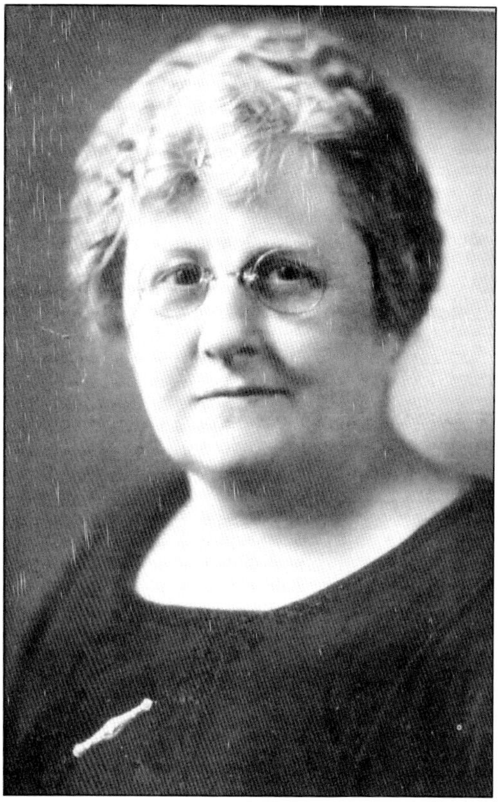

In 1936 the county built a separate elementary school for grades one to six. Previously all grades jointly used the old high school, except for those students in the rural schools. This new school was named for "Miss" Kate Wilson, shown here. She was a beloved teacher for many years. The old Kate Wilson Gym is still in use today.

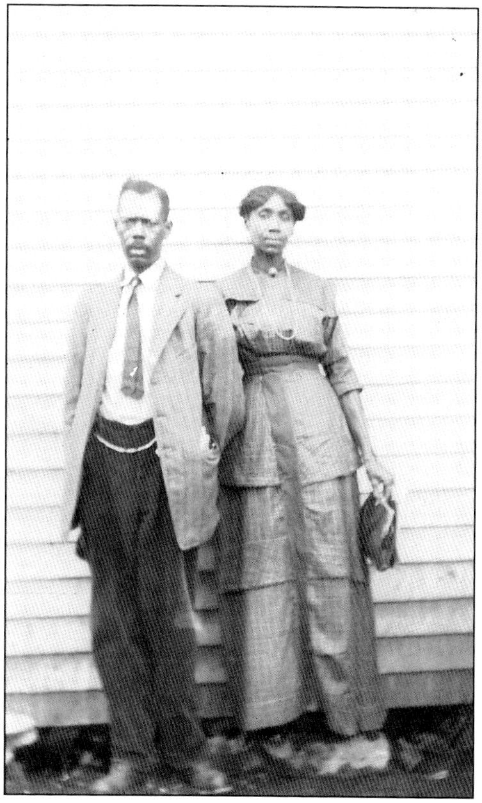

The black community maintained separate schools until 1967 when all county schools were consolidated. Hester Foley was a teacher at the old Ward School. She is shown here with her husband James in a 1916 photograph.

Another well-known and respected teacher was "Miss Annie" Stalcup. Mrs. James Stalcup began teaching at age seventeen and despite raising two daughters, taught school for forty-one years. She taught at West Point, Walnut Grove, Templow, and Hartsville.

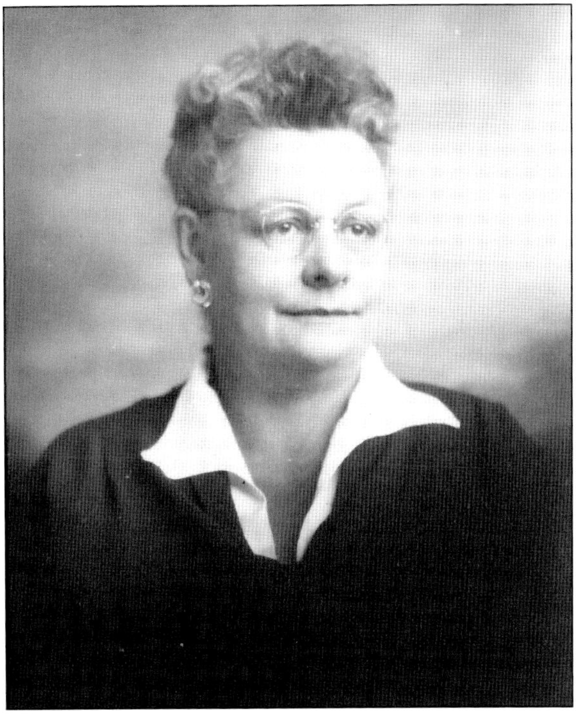

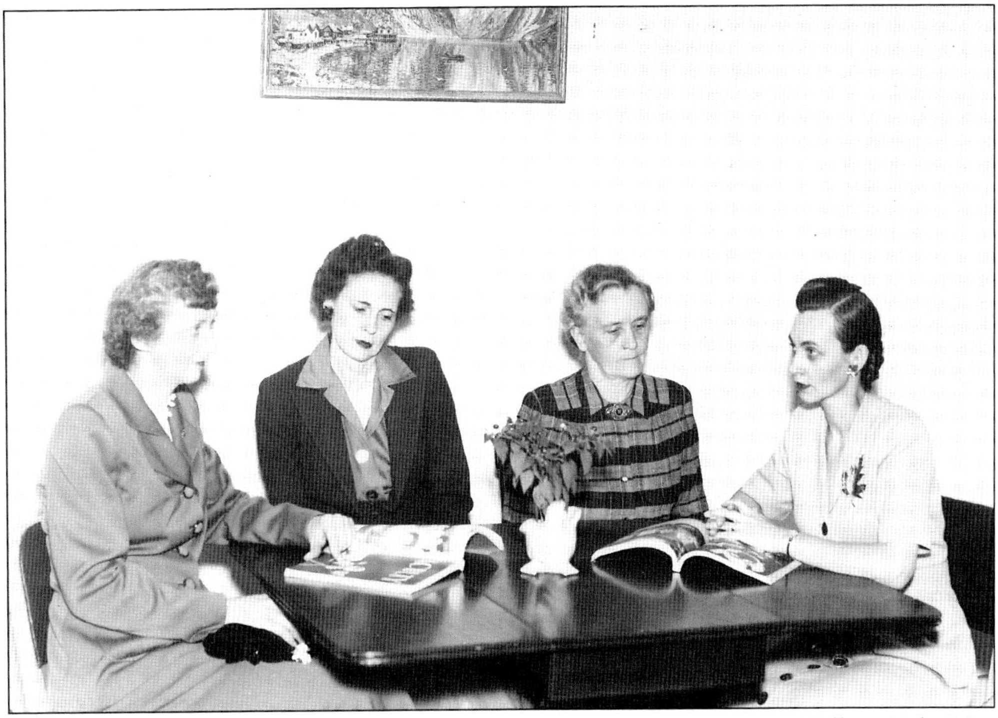

Hartsville had an active PTA for many years. In 1951 the officers were Mrs. William Kyle, Mrs. Robbie Wiley, Mrs. William Horsley, and Mrs. Ray Chitwood. Mrs. Wiley taught elementary school for many years. Mrs. Chitwood is best remembered as the yearbook sponsor, senior English teacher, and senior trip leader. She taught school for thirty-nine years.

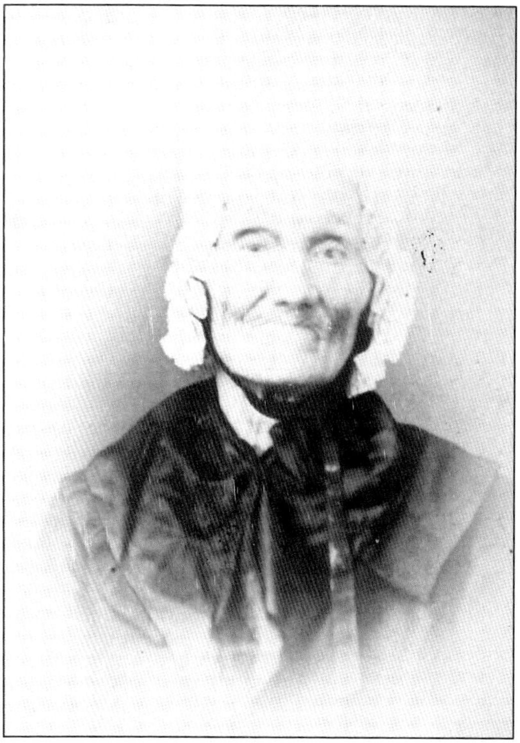

Nancy Rickman was the first white child born in Davidson County (Nashville). She moved with her family to Trousdale County while still a girl. Born in 1797, she married William S. Carter in 1822, and died in 1893. She is buried locally.

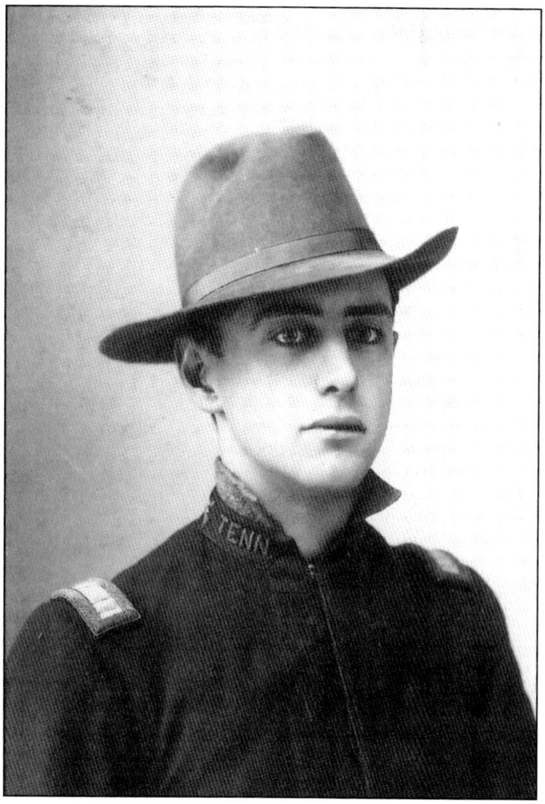

James Fount Hager, of Hartsville, was the youngest commissioned American officer in the Spanish American War. Here he is shown in uniform at age twenty-three. He saw duty in the Philippine Islands and was in the Philippine Insurrection after the war. Hager's uniform is now in the Depot Museum in Hartsville.

Marcus "Mark" Douglass Rickman was born in Trousdale County in 1849. In 1909 and 1912 he served in the Tennessee State Legislature from this area. He was also Worshipful Master in the local Masonic Lodge in 1903 and 1911. A businessman also, he built the old rolling mill.

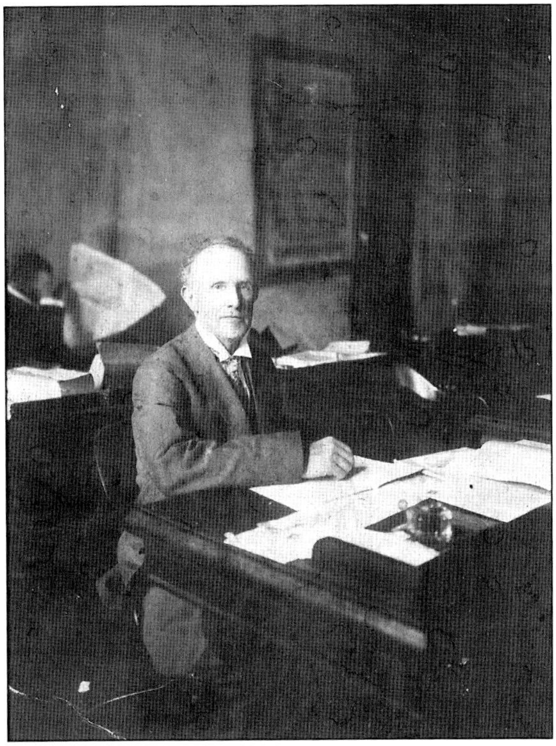

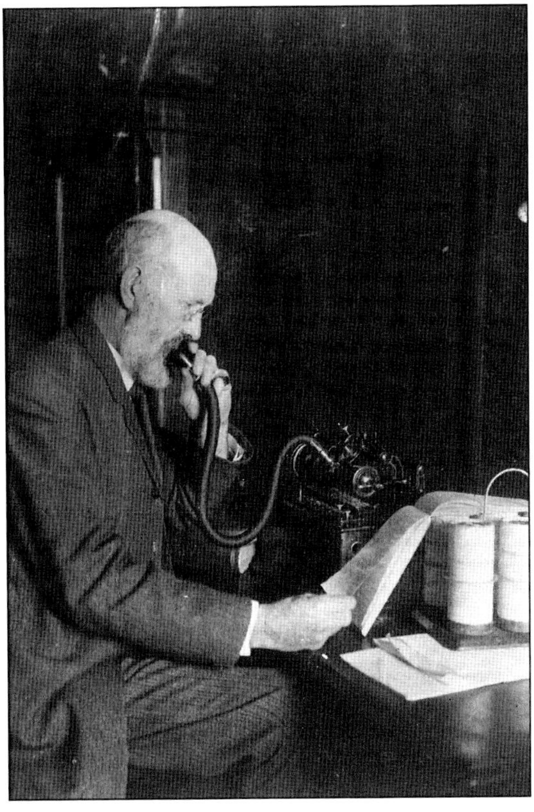

Mr. A. C. Welch was originally from Bristol, England. He moved to the U. S. In 1871 and a few years later moved to Hartsville where he purchased and ran the Hartsville *Vidette*. He was also a founder of Citizen's Bank. For twenty-five years he traveled to Washington, DC, and served seasonally as a congressional reporter. He is shown here using an early dictaphone.

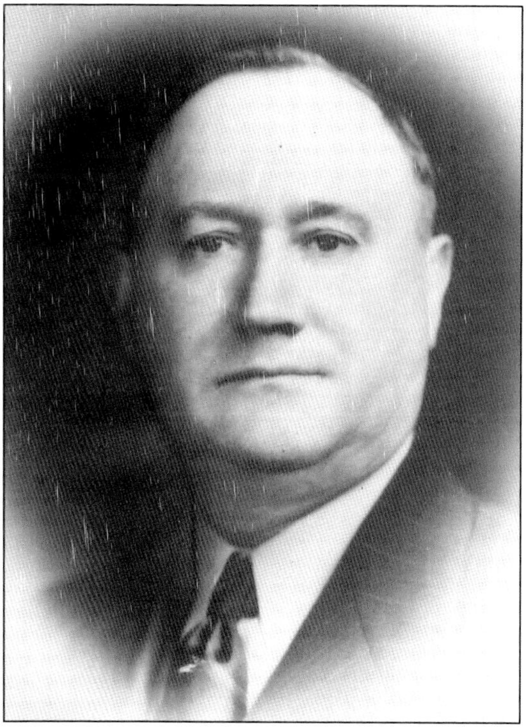

Mr. Jim Tom "J. T." Cunningham was a state representative from this area. He also served as the county court judge and was the county road commissioner for twenty-seven years. He and his wife, Willie Mae Brummett, had thirteen children. Many county residents today are descendants of Mr. and Mrs. Cunningham.

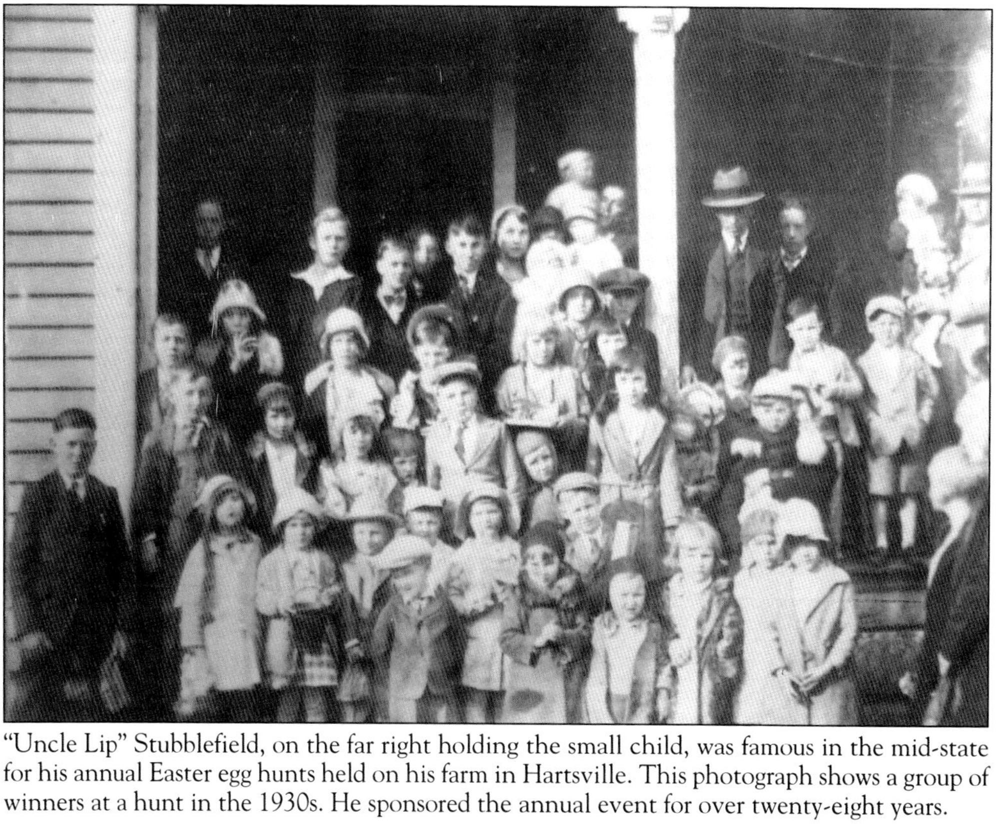

"Uncle Lip" Stubblefield, on the far right holding the small child, was famous in the mid-state for his annual Easter egg hunts held on his farm in Hartsville. This photograph shows a group of winners at a hunt in the 1930s. He sponsored the annual event for over twenty-eight years.

Long a Hartsville fixture was barber Dewey Frye. Mr. Frye cut hair in town for over fifty years. He was especially good with children and many men had their first haircut in Dewey's chair. At one time he had a small shop off the lobby of the old hotel but later worked in a shop behind the old Bank of Hartsville.

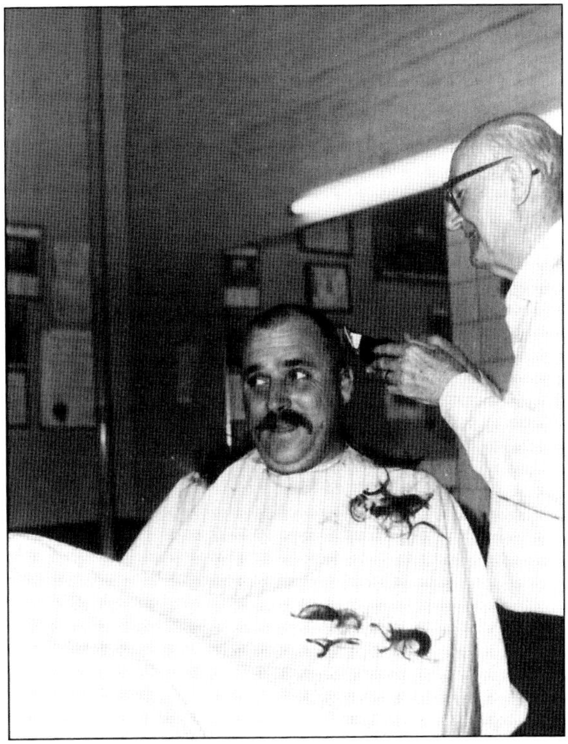

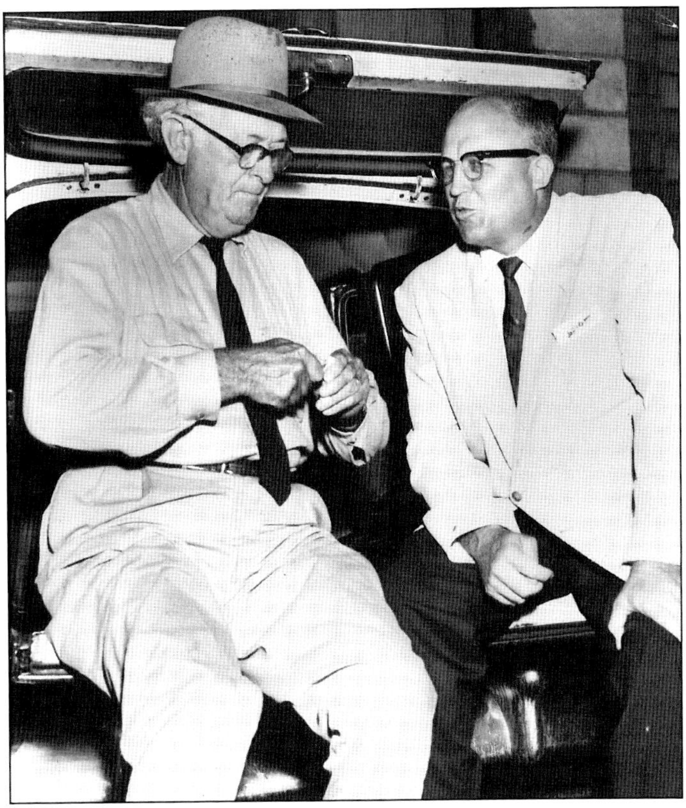

Mitch Harris (left) and Phil Dickens (right) both played football for Hartsville. Mitch was a local contractor and was famous for carving tiny working pairs of pliers from small pieces of wood. Phil played football at the University of Tennessee and went on to coach college football at the University of Wyoming and the University of Indiana.

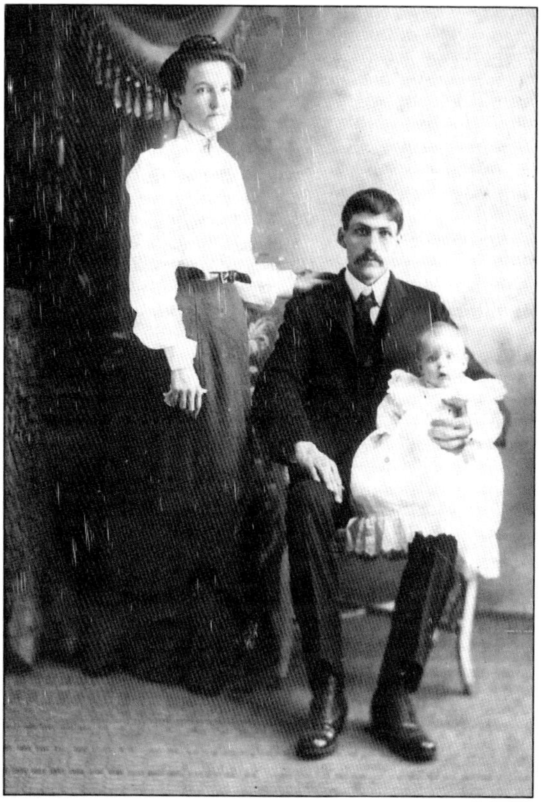

Of the county's many elected officials, the office of sheriff often commands the most respect. Albert Parkhurst, shown here with his wife Lucrettia, and son Cedric, was sheriff of Trousdale County for eighteen years in the early part of the twentieth century.

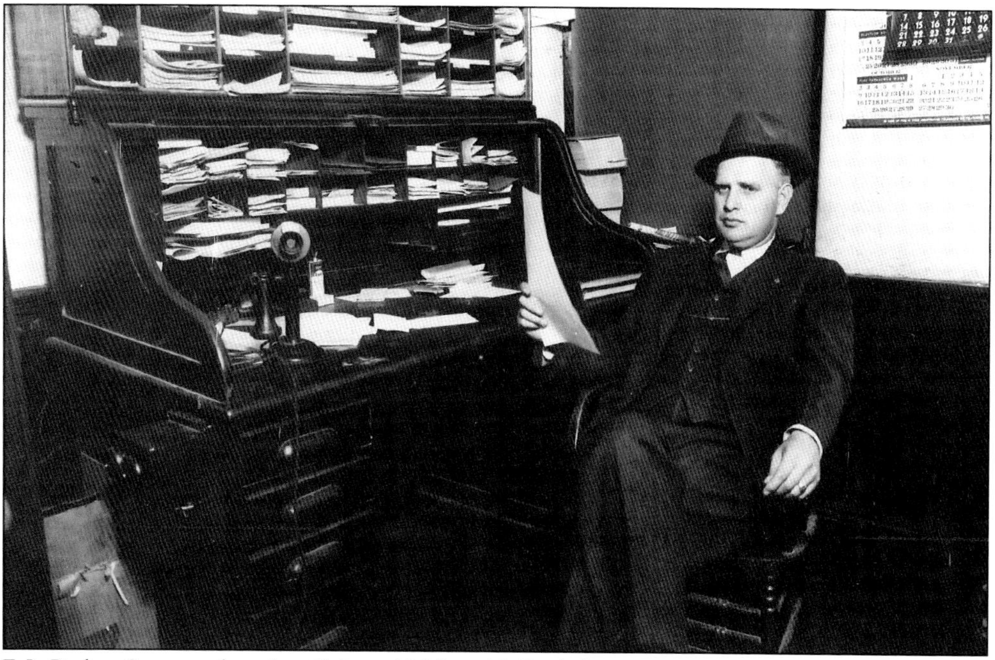

E J. Parker Sr. served as sheriff from 1936 to 1942. A businessman as well, he sold clothing, owned a gas distributorship, and served as county court judge for several terms. He is shown here at his desk in the old jail in 1939.

T. A. "Tommy" Jones was known as the county's "singing sheriff." He is shown here in 1966 with J. W. Gregory, the county court clerk for many years. Tommy sang with his group, The Blue Sky Boys, at local events, on regular radio shows, and most familiar to locals, at "cake walks" held on the town square.

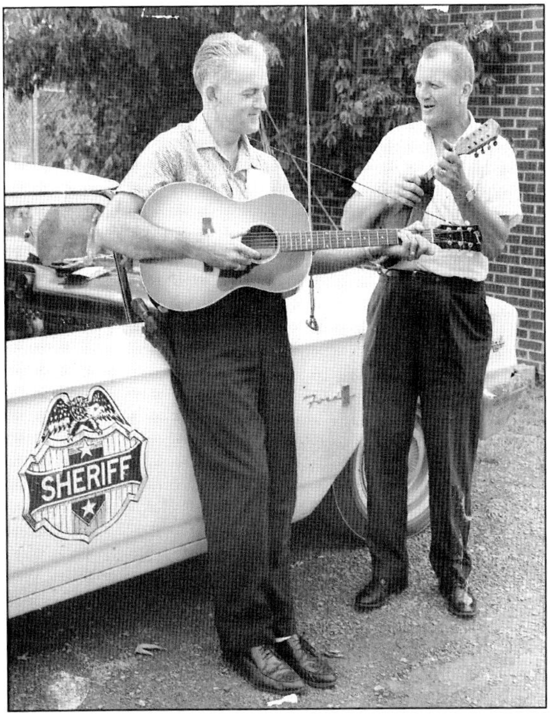

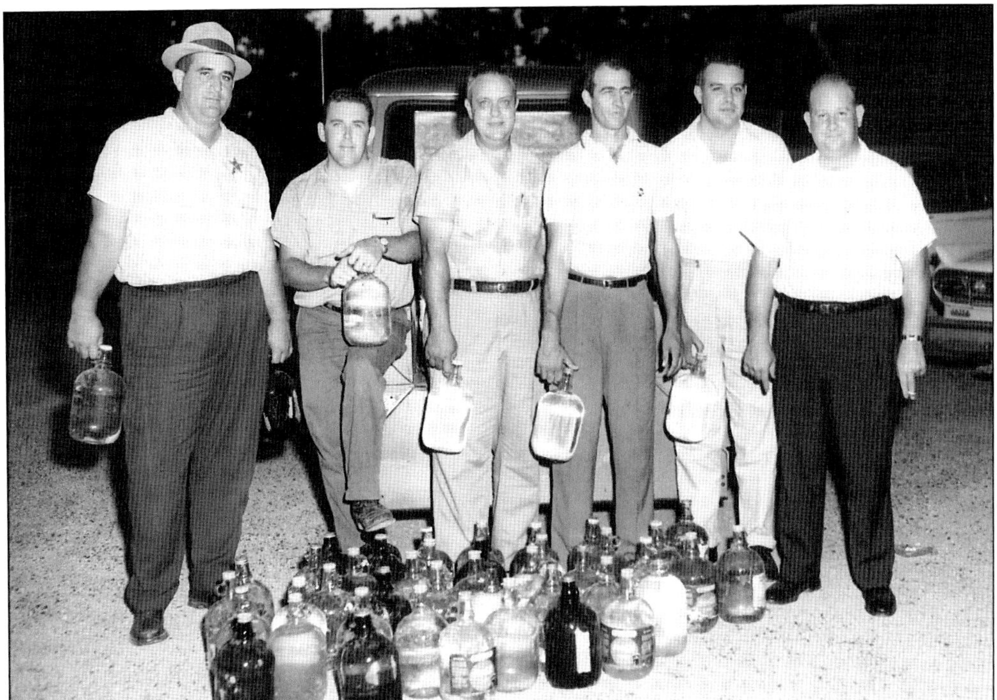

Another well-known sheriff was Claude Kerr. Claude was an outstanding athlete for the local high school and, later, at Cumberland University. He was chief of Hartsville police before becoming sheriff in 1958. He died in office from an illness, his wife Rosie Lee finishing his term. Mr. Kerr, on the far left, is shown with some confiscated "moonshine."

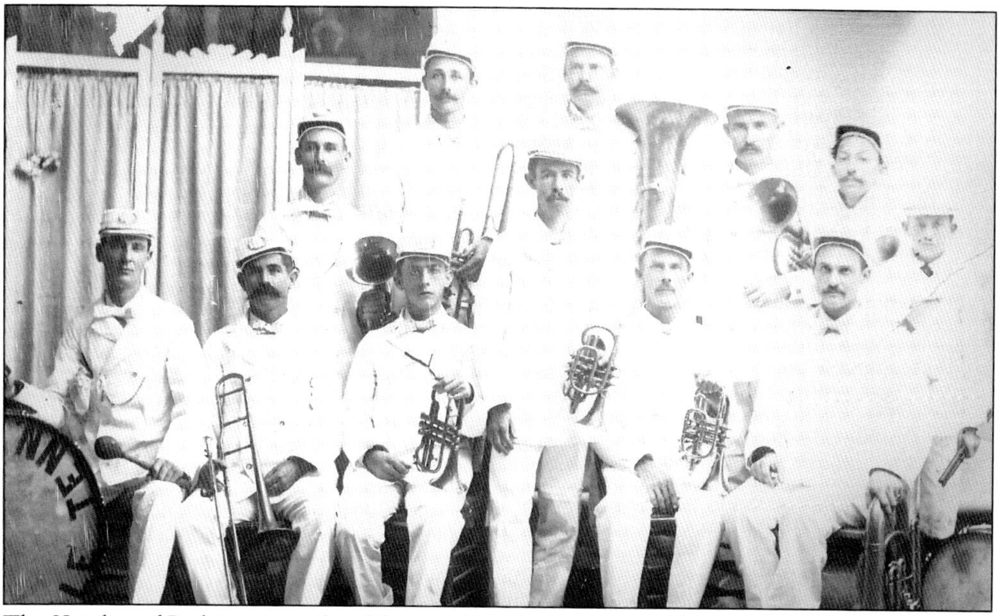

The Knights of Pythias were a local fraternal organization around the turn of the century. This band was organized by the group and played locally as well as at the nearby Dixon Springs Fair. Included in the photograph are: E. V. Hale, J. W. Throp, J. Fromme, C. V. Gwin, M. T. Hall, E. P. Freedle, Fletch Marshall, and Walter Andrews.

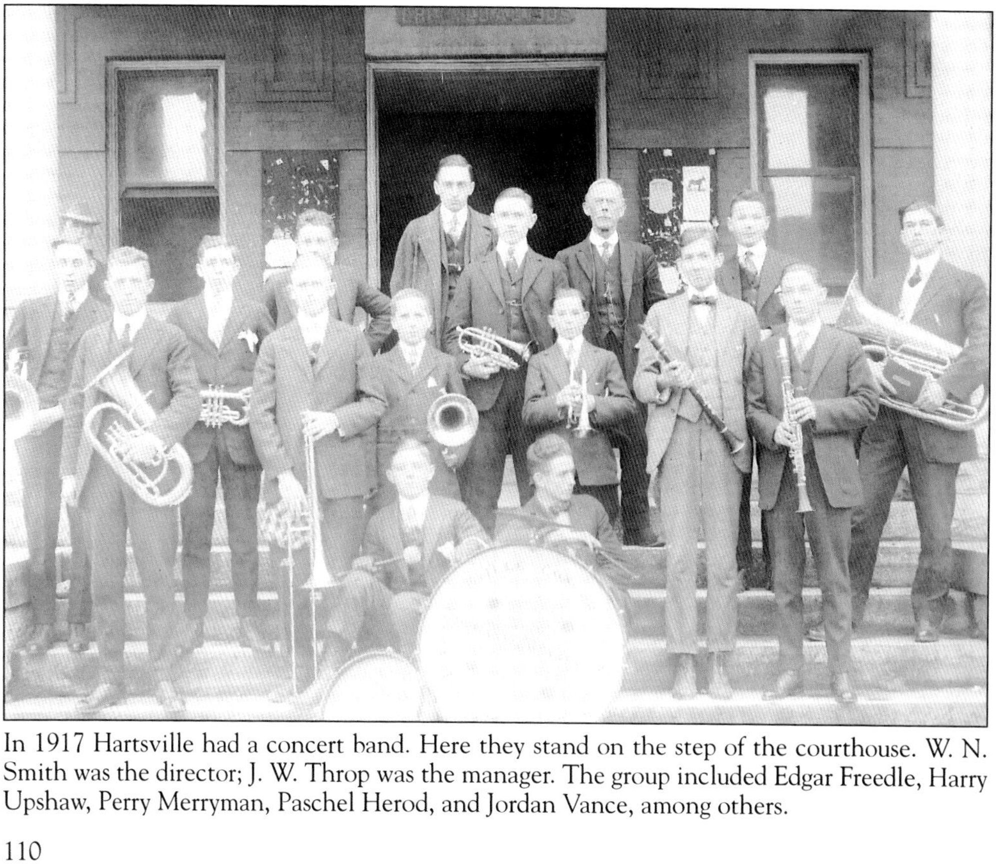

In 1917 Hartsville had a concert band. Here they stand on the step of the courthouse. W. N. Smith was the director; J. W. Throp was the manager. The group included Edgar Freedle, Harry Upshaw, Perry Merryman, Paschel Herod, and Jordan Vance, among others.

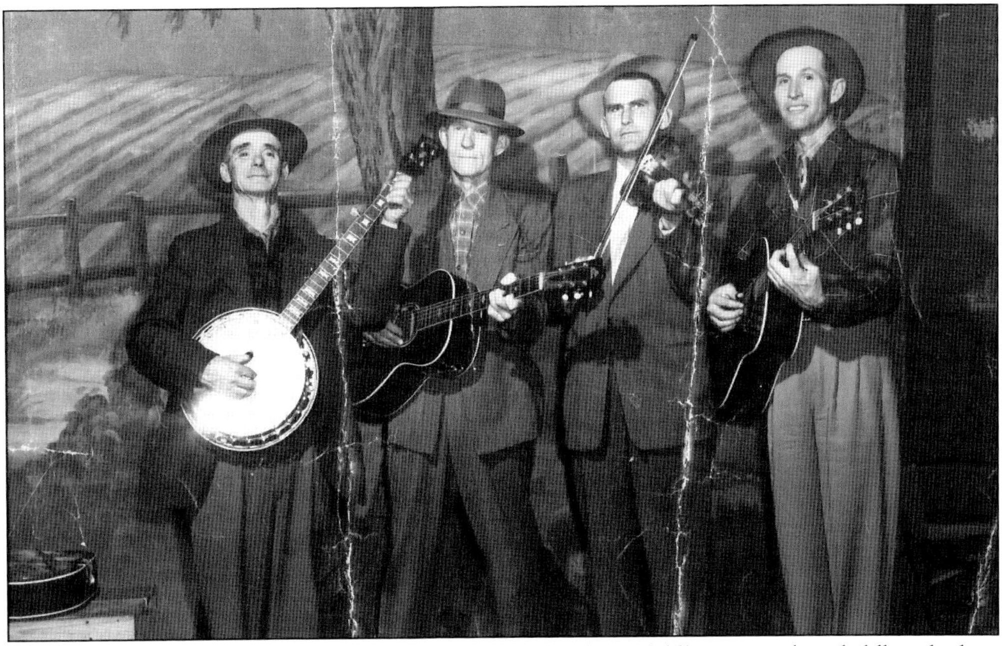

"Monk" Scruggs, from the Lick Creek community, has been fiddling since his childhood when he and his brothers Carl, Risey, and Arnett would sneak and play their father's Sears and Roebuck fiddle. From 1949 to 1959 he played on the Grand Old Opry as a member of the Possum Hunters Band. In the photograph he is the second from the right.

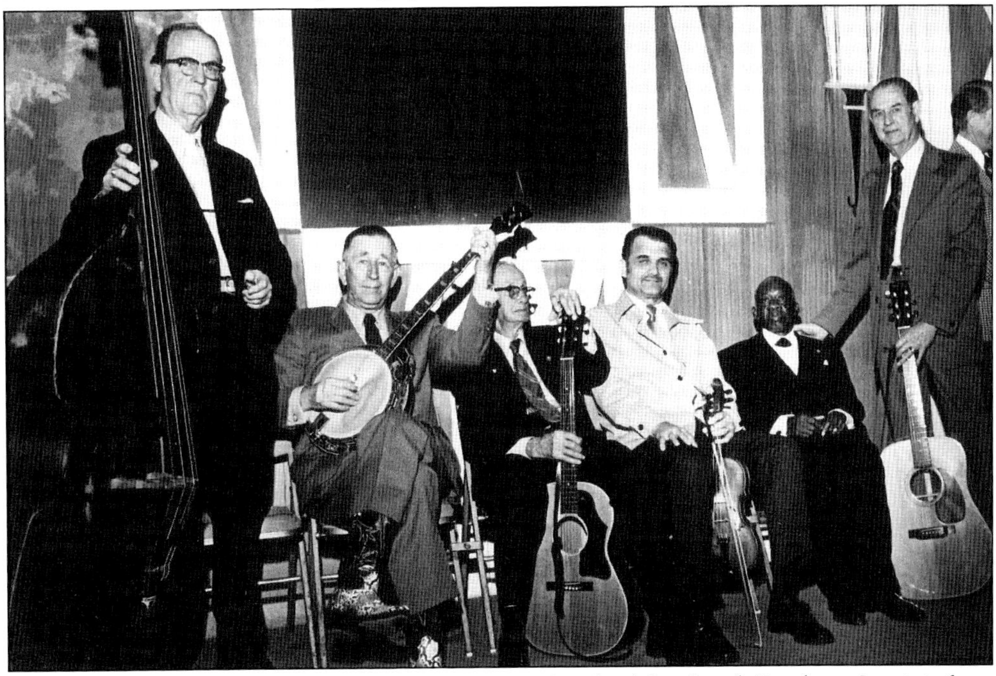

Another musician from Trousdale County is Lewis Crook of the Crook Brothers. Lewis is from the Rocky Creek community. Lewis joined the group in the 1930s. The Crook Brothers were regulars on the Grand Old Opry. Herman Crook is on the far left, Lewis Crook is next. Second from the right is the well-known Deford Bailey.

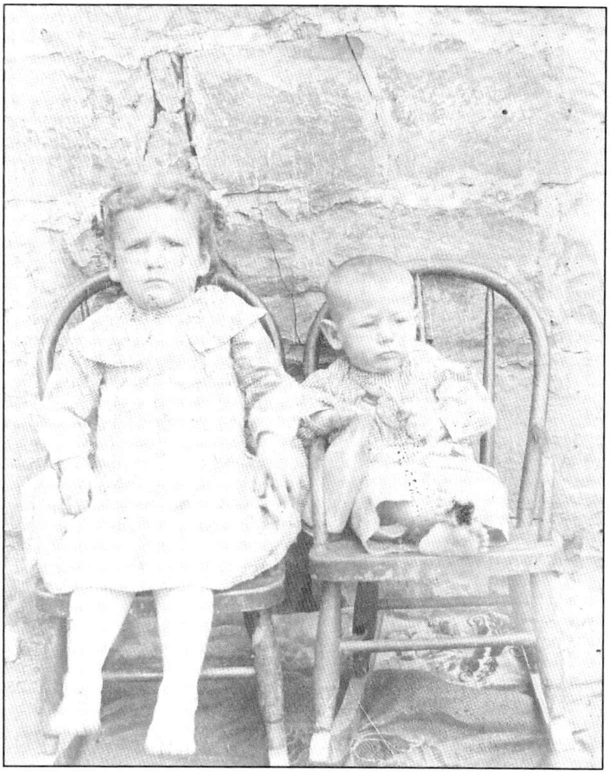

Parents are always eager to have their children dress up and pose for the photographer. In this photograph, a baby Harry Leath and his older sister Addie sit for their pictures in 1909. As an adult, Harry worked for the city for many years as building inspector.

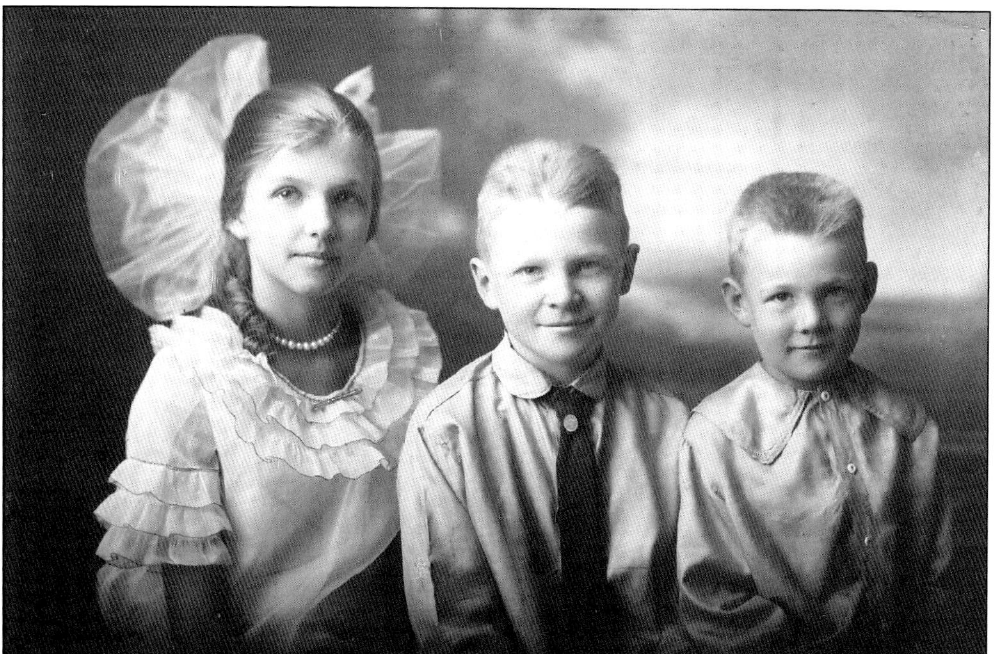

Around 1920 the children of Mr. and Mrs. T. J. Thompson had their picture made. Lavelle is pictured on the far left, next is Tom, and then Lawrence. Tom grew up to practice law in Hartsville; Lawrence ran a hardware store on the square for a number of years.

White lace and large bows make this pair look angelic. In 1910 Miss Will Hale and her brother Randolph stood still long enough to have their portraits made. The Hales lived on East Main Street in Hartsville. Will stayed in the family home for ninety-four years, until her death.

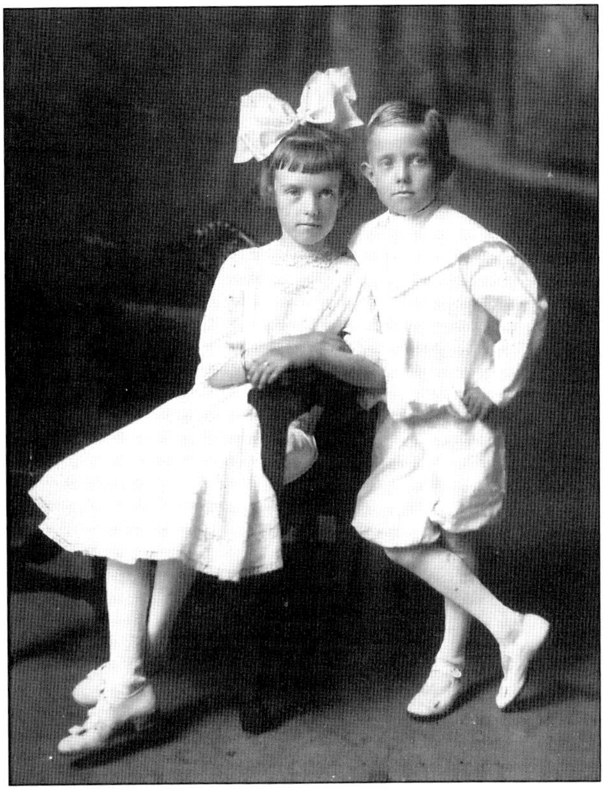

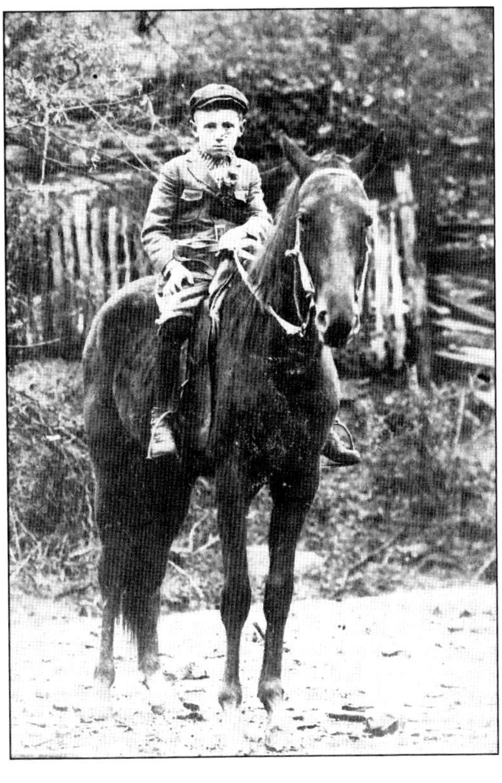

Jeff Oldham of the Cato community looked serious for this photograph made in the 1920s. His horse looks no less serious. The legs of his britches only go to the knees where they meet a pair of high stockings. Called "knickers," they were proper wear for the time.

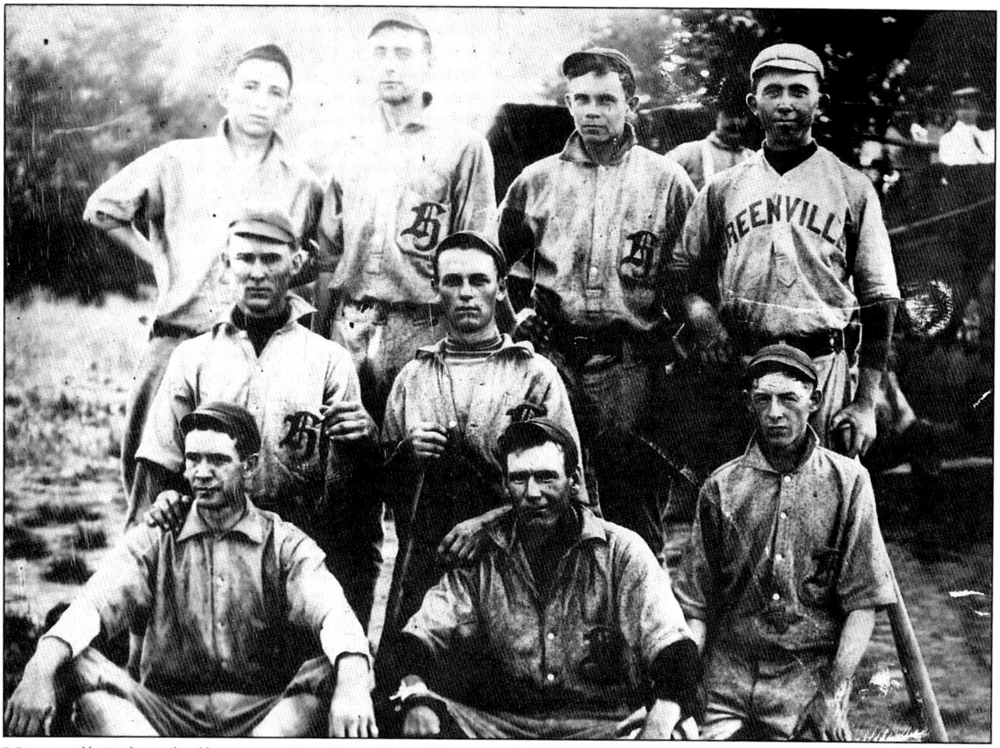

Hartsville's baseball team shortly after the turn of the century are a classic looking group. Although one player's suit is from Greenville, most sport a big *h* on their jerseys. They are: (first row) Bob Owen, Bressie Woods, Roy Rickman; (second row) Henderson Head, unknown; (third row) Ed Payne, Jim Hager, Reagan Collinsworth, and Bud Howell.

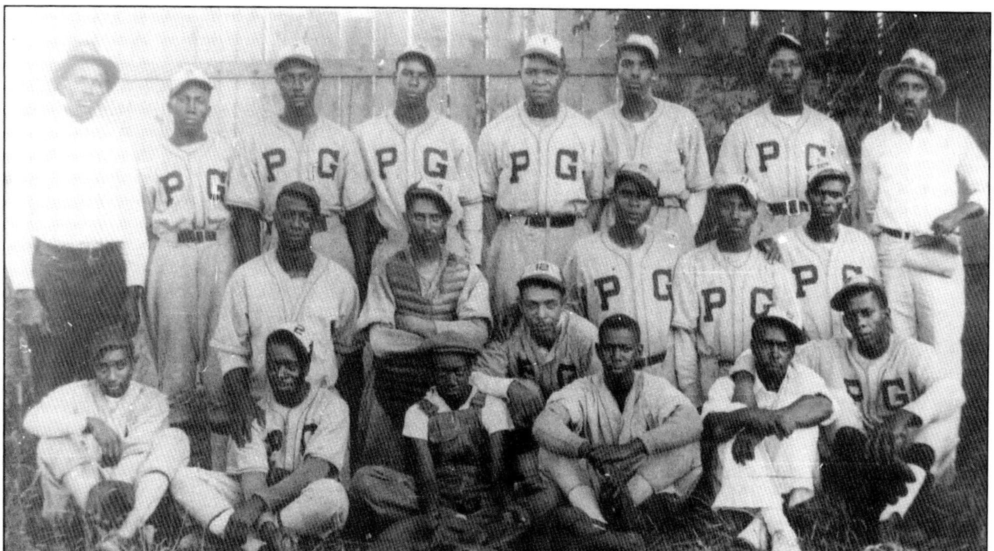

In 1924 the Peerless Giants were a local team that played regionally in the old Negro League. The team traveled out of state, as far as Ohio, Kentucky, Georgia, and Missouri. They disbanded in the 1960s. The group includes: Richard Hogg, Willie Dalton, R. J. Young, Erby Luster, and William Beasley.

Eight

Farming and Tobacco

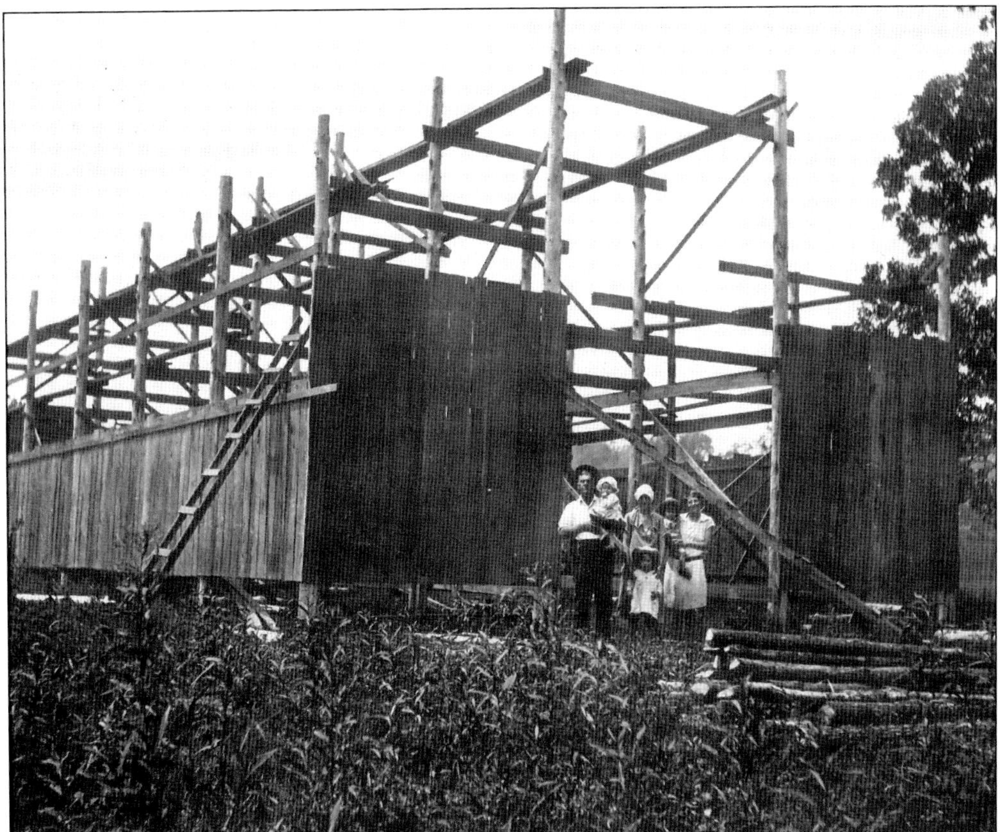

Farming, particularly tobacco farming, has been the backbone of Trousdale County's economy. A good farm must have a good barn. In 1928, Hubert Ward Sr. had this barn built on his farm in the Providence community. Mr. and Mrs. Ward stand by the barn with their children. The barn is still in use today.

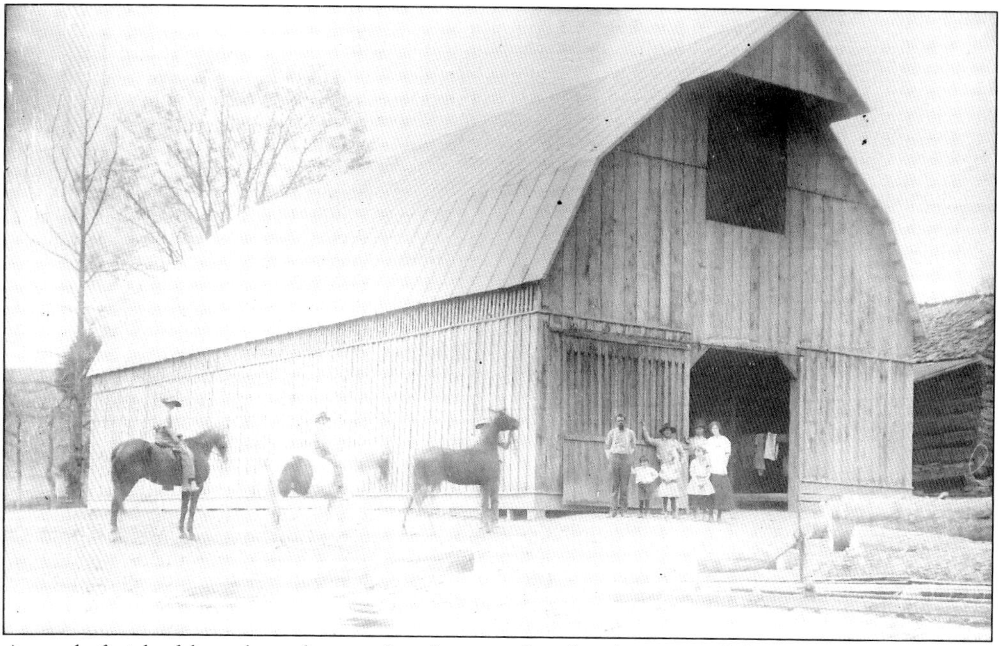

A newly finished barn brought out the photographer for this turn-of-the-century photograph. The barn was built on the farm of Shelby Bass in the Beasley's Bend community. Mr. Bass raised horses and mules. The barn is still in use today on the farm of Mrs. Allen Bass.

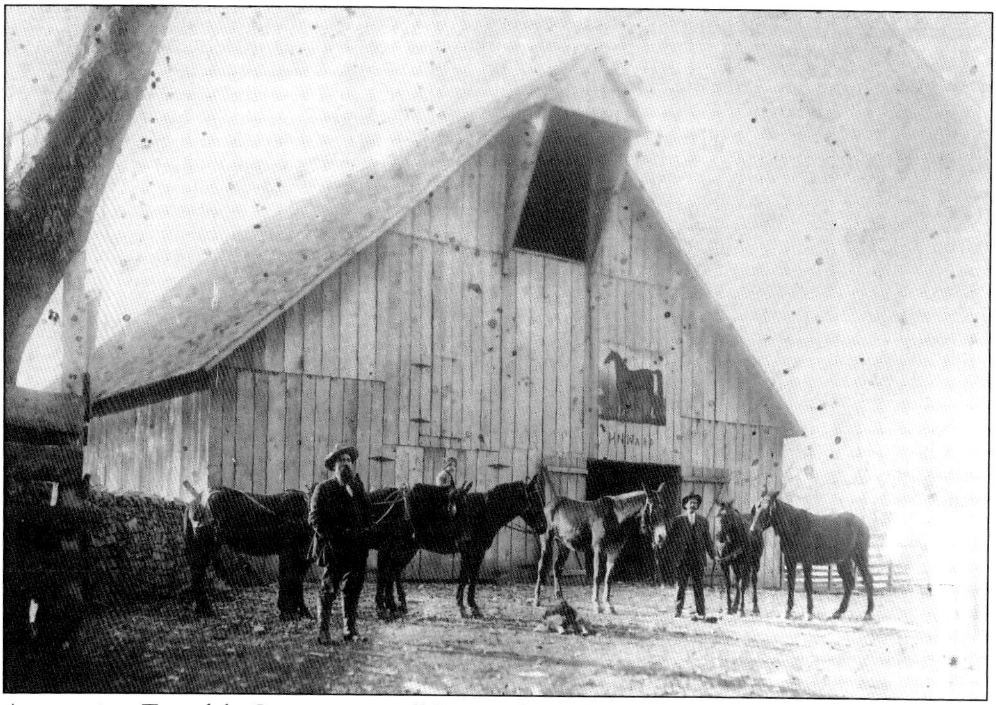

At one time Trousdale County was well known for its breeders of horses and mules. A good mule was like a valuable tractor today. In 1902 Andrew and Hubert Ward showed off their prize stock. This barn is also still standing today.

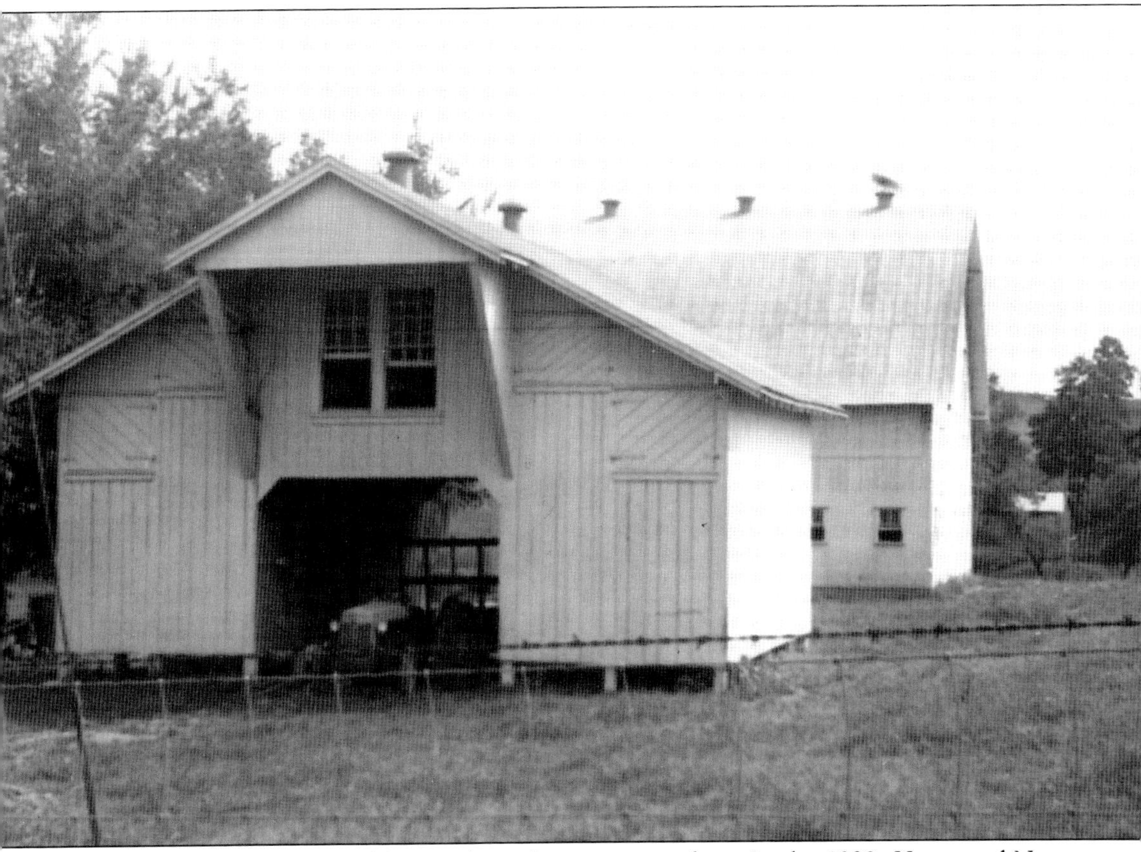

A well built and maintained barn indicated a prosperous farm. In the 1930s Henry and Nan Haynie had this grainery and barn built on their farm in East Hartsville. The two buildings are as solid today as the day they were built. They can be seen just off Highway 25 on the farm of H. B. Cunningham.

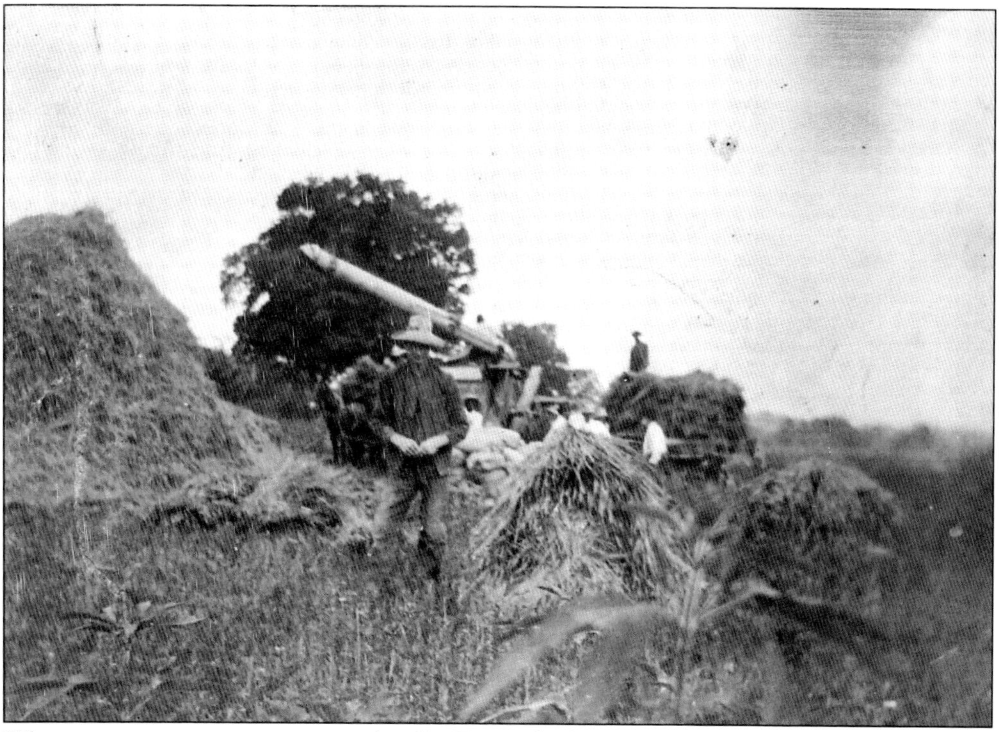

Wheat was once an important crop locally. To get the harvest in, steam threshers were used. In this 1920s photograph, Lewis McMurtry stands in front of his family's steam-powered thresher. After threshing, local people would take the straw and use it to stuff their mattresses.

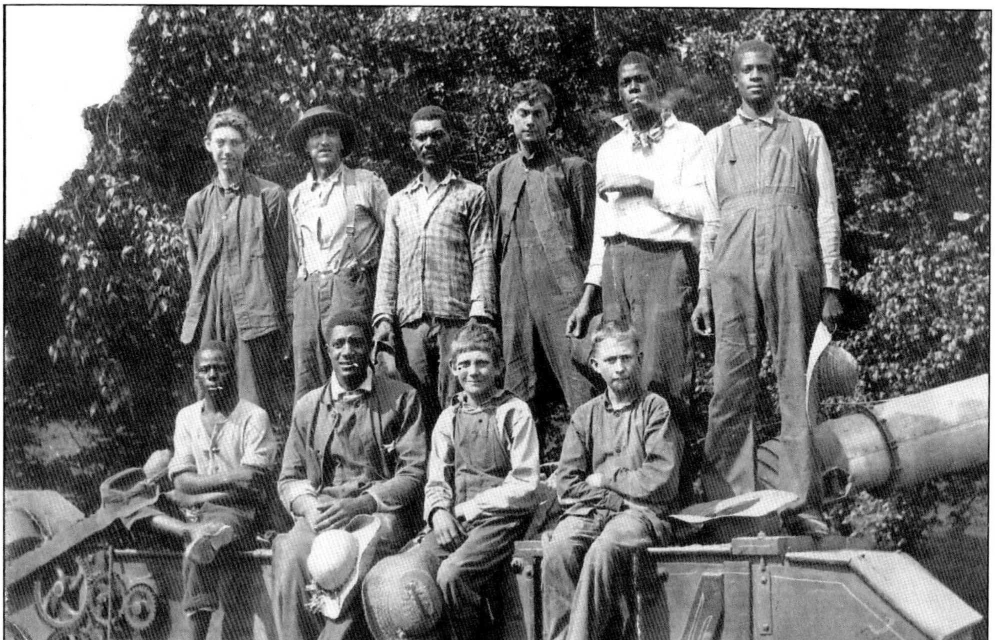

Sam McMurtry's threshing crew got together on top of the steam thresher for this photograph. Not all the men are identified, but the group includes Ed, Lewis, Sam, and Will McMurtry.

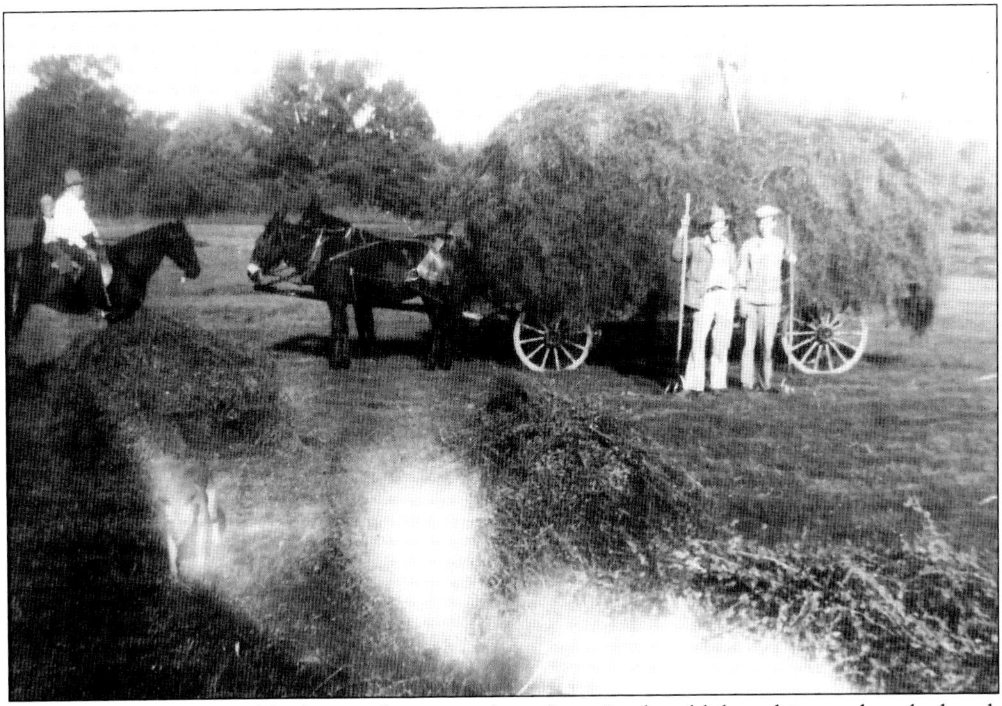

Hay had to be harvested for livestock on a working farm. In the old days this was done by hand. This photograph from the 1940s shows Edgar Waller and Hubert Ward Jr. with pitch forks. Lewis Ward and Hubert Ward Sr. are on the mare. The scene is from the Providence community.

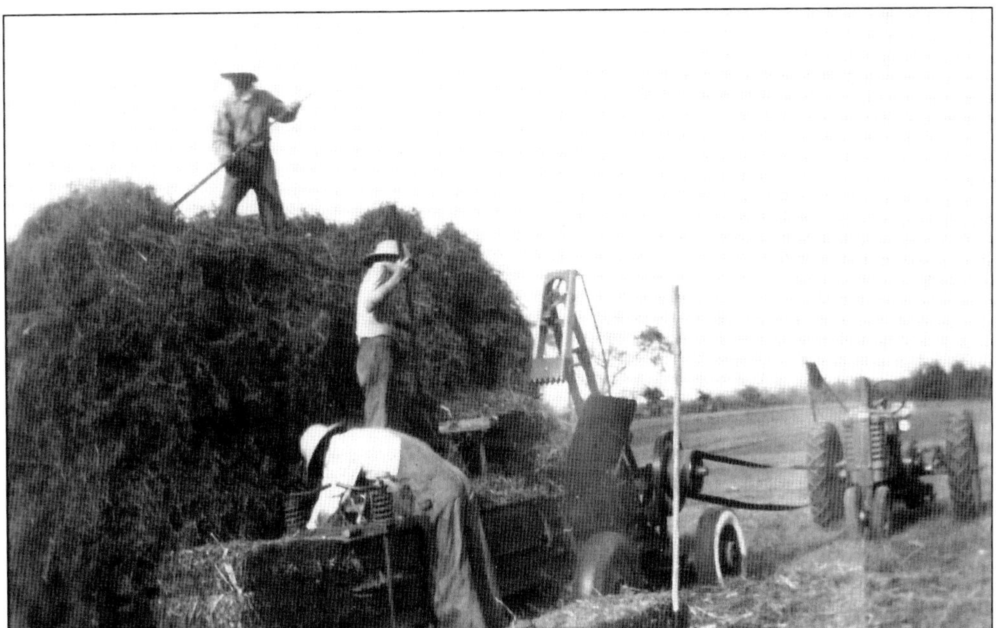

Gone are the days of square hay bales. In the early 1940s when this photograph was made, a portable baler could be hauled to your field and run from a tractor, as shown here. Julius Herod and Norman Herod worked with Hurlin Burns on the Herod farm.

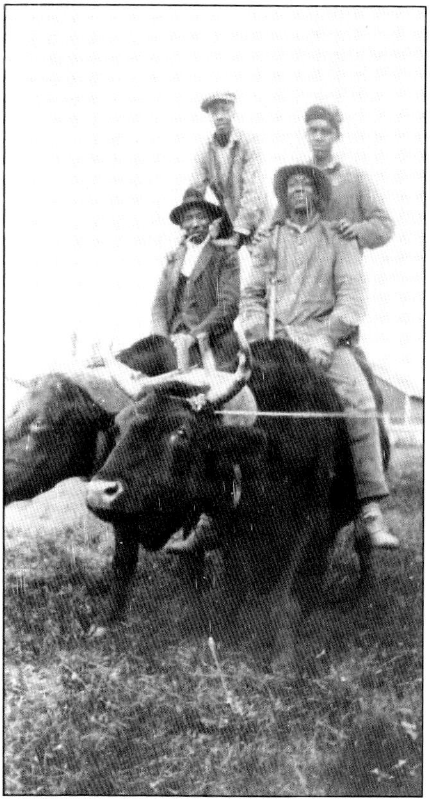

A yoke of oxen is a rare sight today, but the sturdy animals were used in the county up into the 1940s. These unidentified fieldhands proudly show off this matched pair of oxen, complete with heavy wooden yoke.

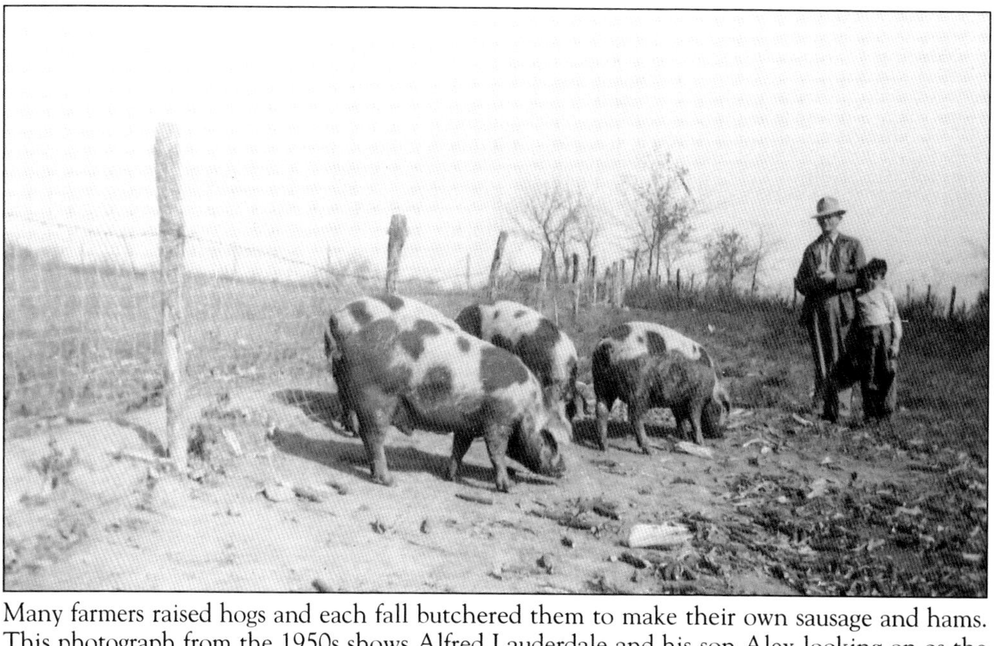

Many farmers raised hogs and each fall butchered them to make their own sausage and hams. This photograph from the 1950s shows Alfred Lauderdale and his son Alex looking on as the animals root in the ground.

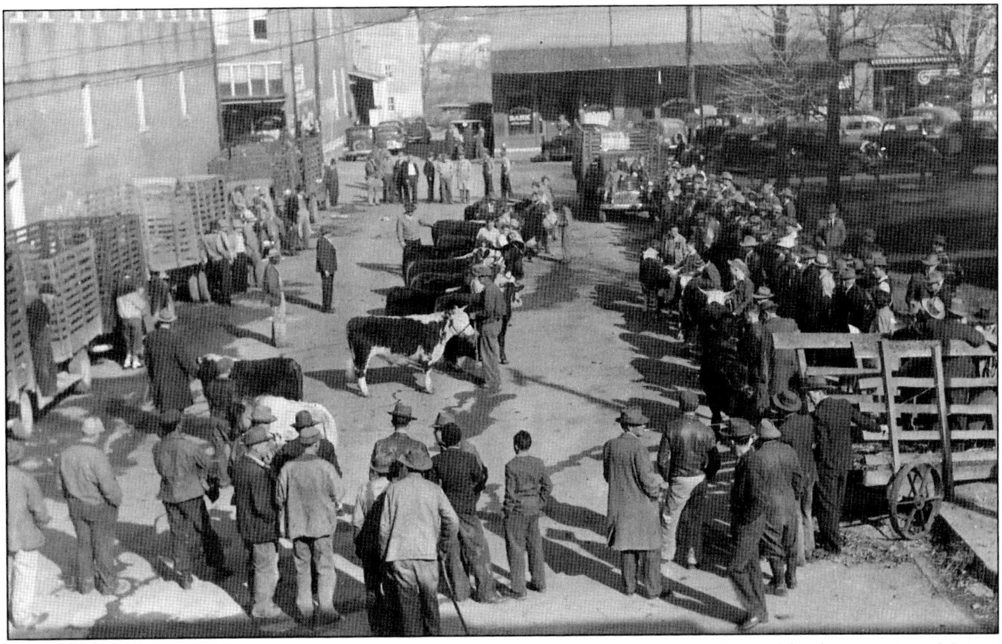

An indication of how important agriculture is to the county is this fat calf sale in 1943. Using the courthouse square as the auction block was a tradition. Mule sales also took place on the square for many years. Although cattle sales are a thing of the past, the square is still the site of many events, particularly cake walks and musical entertainment.

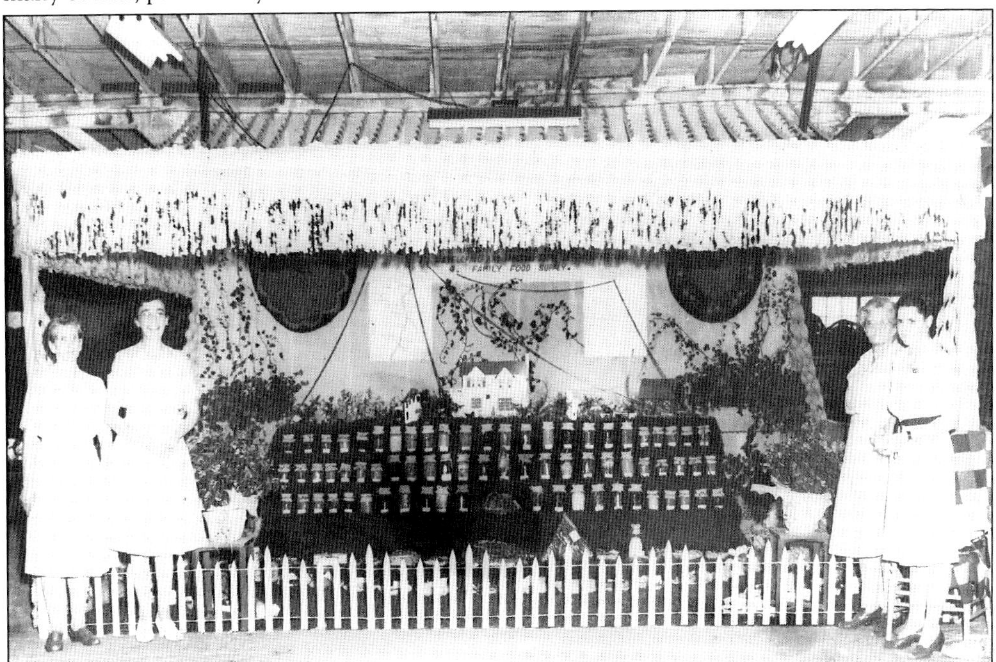

County fairs and 4-H fairs are also a part of the county's history. In 1950 the Halltown Community Club set up this booth for the county fair, which was held in a tobacco warehouse. Prize preserves line the shelves as Agnes Stubblefield, Ida Taylor Duncan, Hazel Perkins, and Ethel Lauderdale look on.

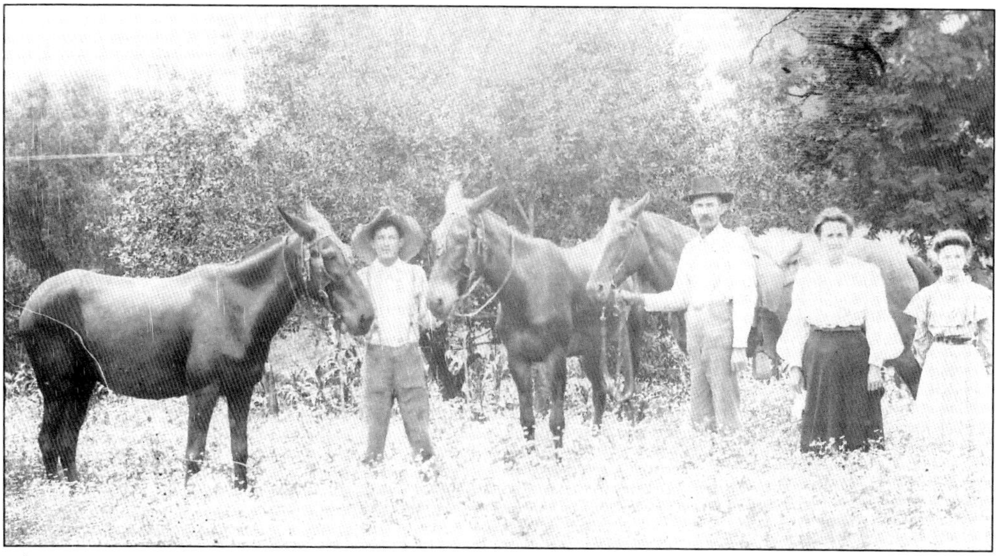

The W. C. Biggers family of the Beech Grove community were farmers, store owners, and, from the looks of this photograph, proud of their livestock. Winston Biggers is on the left, next is his father W. C. Biggers, his mother Fannie Marshall Biggers, and cousin Florence Marshall.

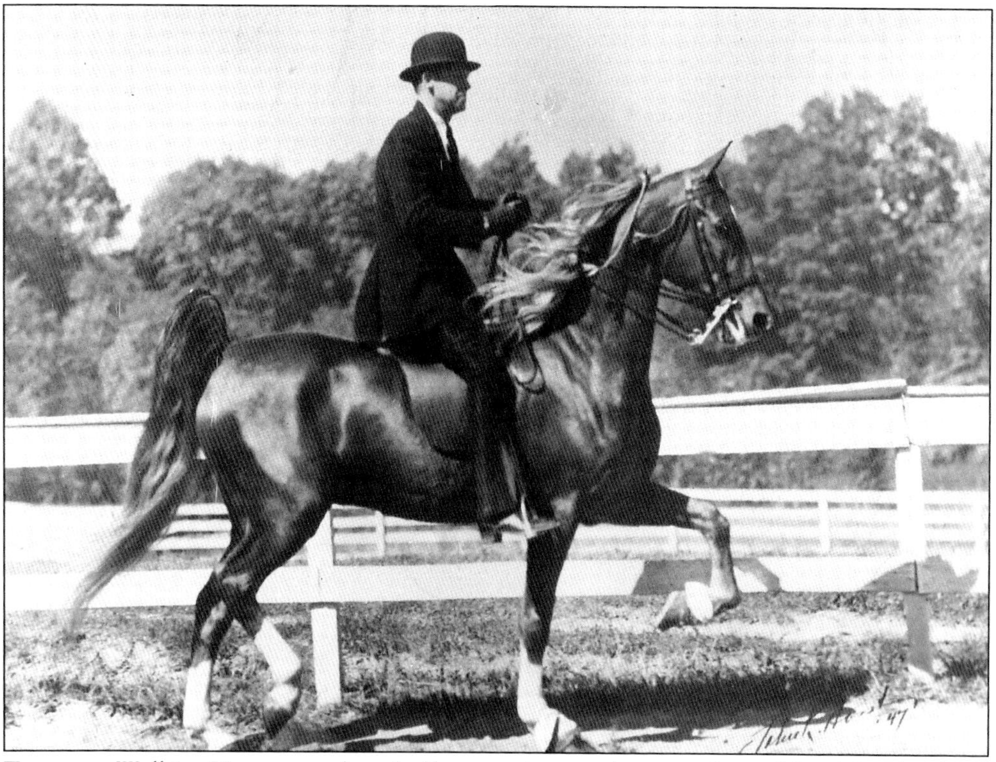

Tennessee Walking Horses are a breed of horse unique to the state. Several local families have bred this horse, known for its peculiar gait. The Crenshaw family raised and sold horses for over a half-century from their farm on Crenshaw Lane. In this photograph Edward Crenshaw rides one of the horses from the family stable in the 1950s. The family has since moved from the county.

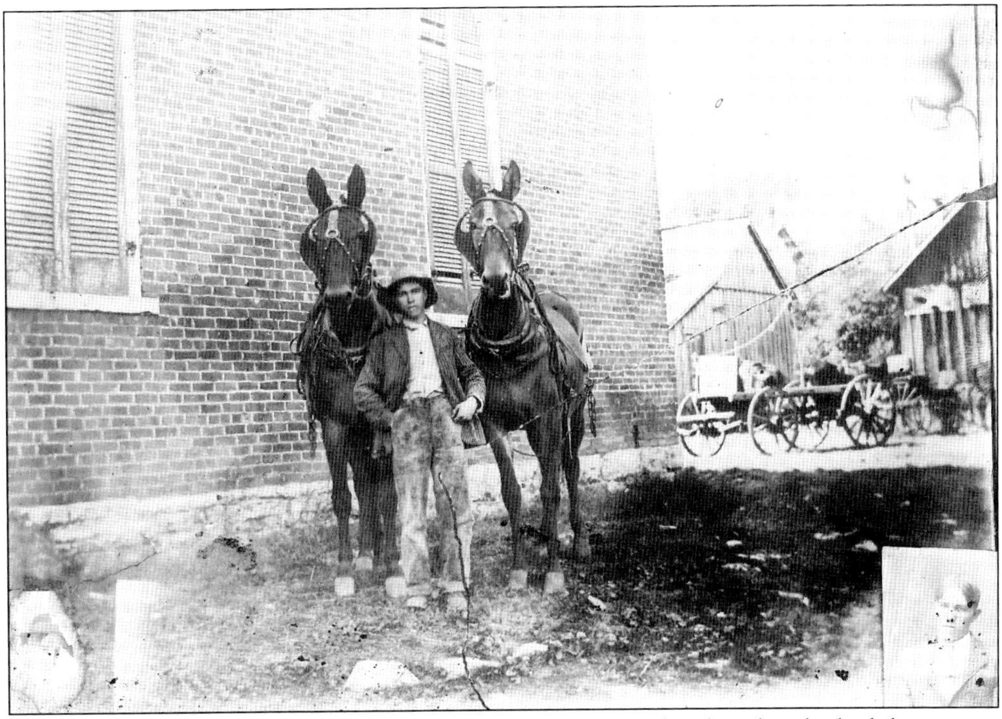

Young farmer Russell Belcher Sr. was proud of this fine team of mules when he had this picture made in 1910. Behind him is the old Presbyterian church in Hartsville. In the background is Jim Andrew's Farm Implement Shop. Russell farmed in the Puryear's Bend community.

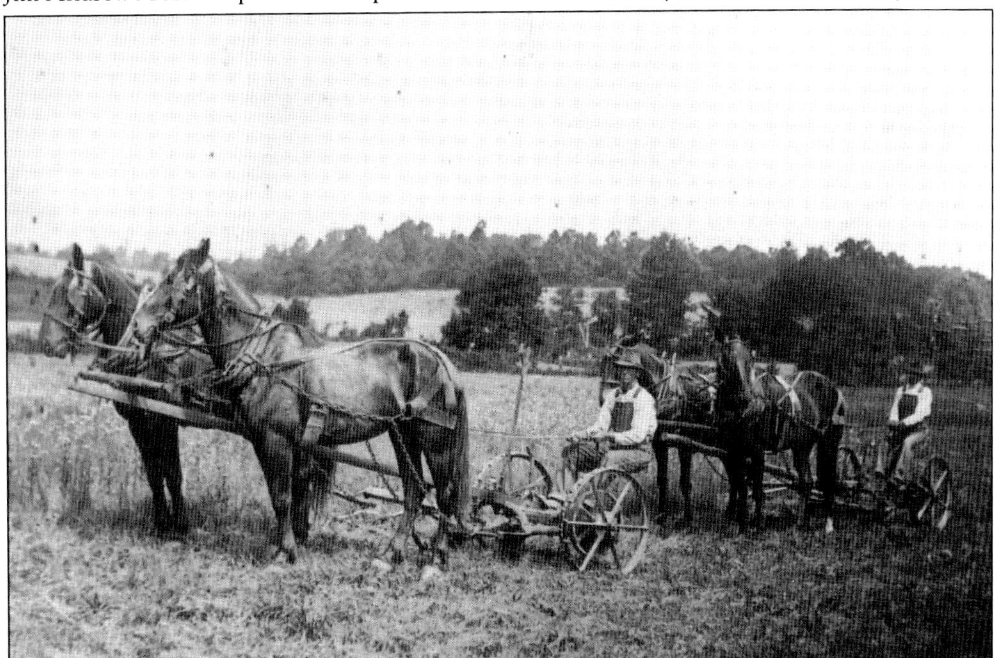

Tractors weren't an option when farmers S. L. Sanford and Ed Akins worked the fields in 1923. This photograph was made in the Cedar Bluff community on the edge of Trousdale County.

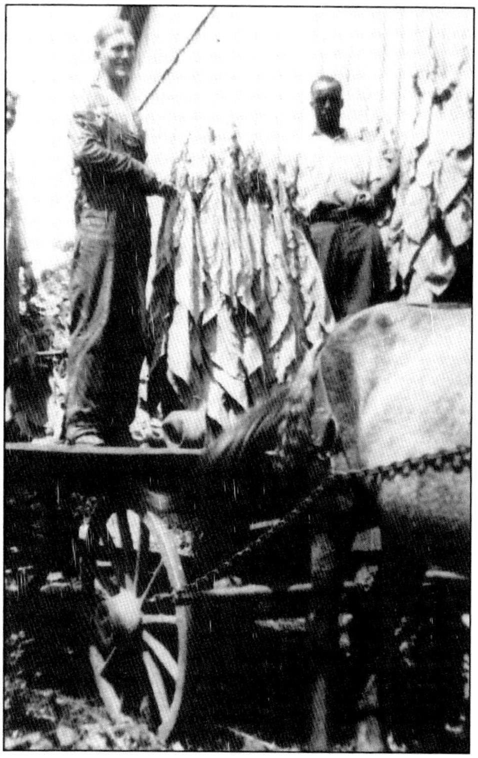

Tobacco is Trousdale County's biggest cash crop. Since its beginning, the county has seen the crop grow annually in importance and revenue, although its future may be clouded. In this photograph from the 1930s, Brown Draper helps an unidentified hired hand prepare to hang tobacco in the barn to cure.

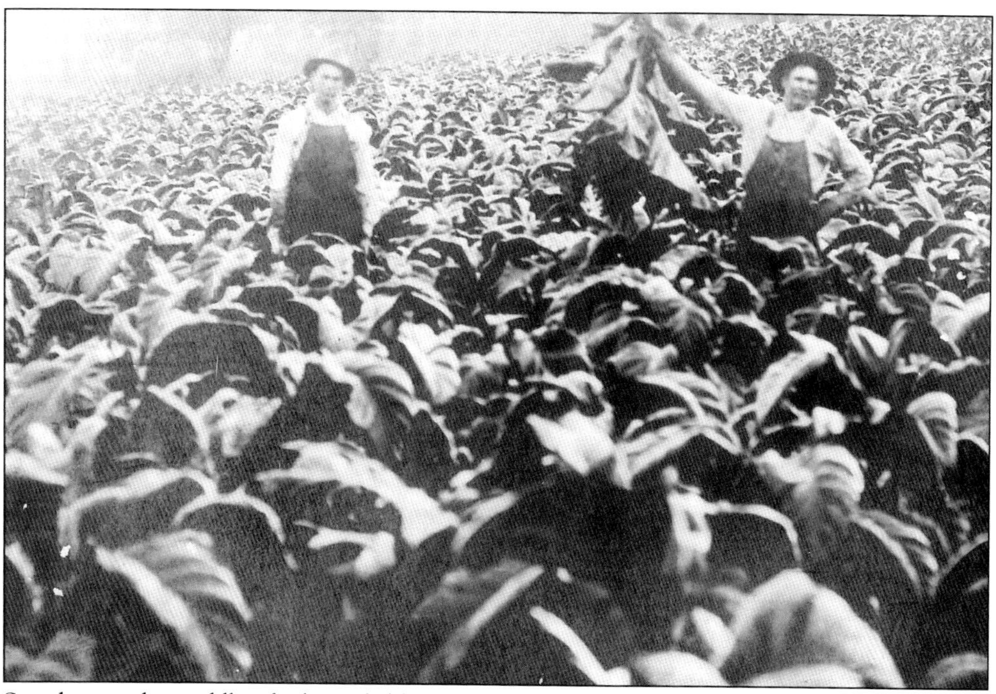

Standing in the middle of a large field of tobacco, these two unidentified men seem proud of their crop. Most tobacco farmers of the past lived from crop to crop, charging for goods, to pay later when their "backer sold." Trousdale County is best known for its Burley crop.

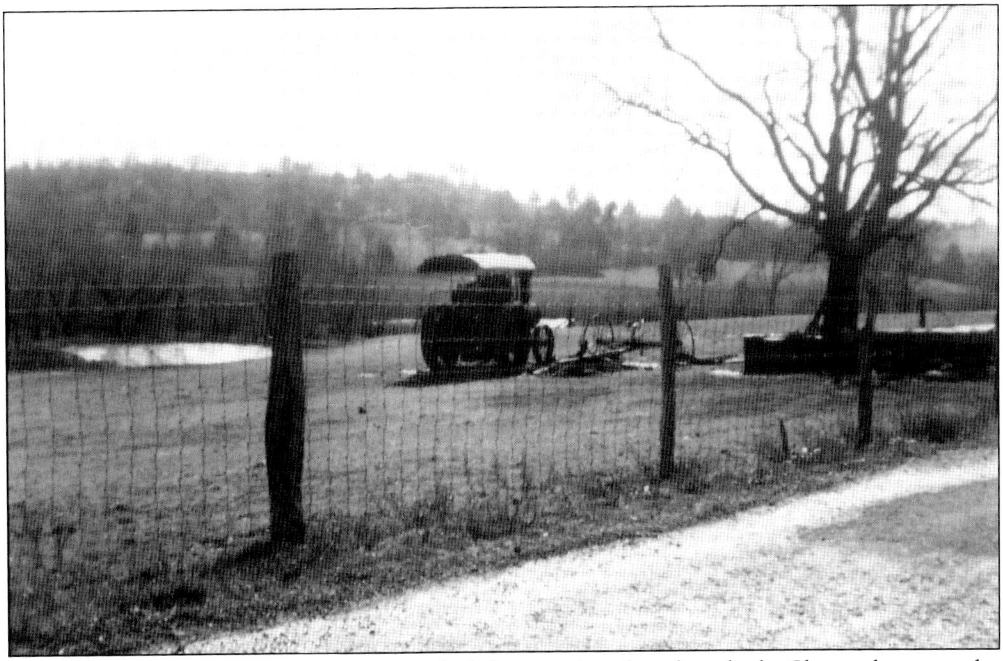

Part of the tobacco-growing process included preparing the plant beds. Shown here on the farm of Richard and Howard Burnley is a steam engine used to steam the plant beds. The steam killed any weeds or grass that might sprout up. The steamer was moved from farm to farm. When finished with a job, Mr. Burnley would pull on the steam whistle for two or three long blasts.

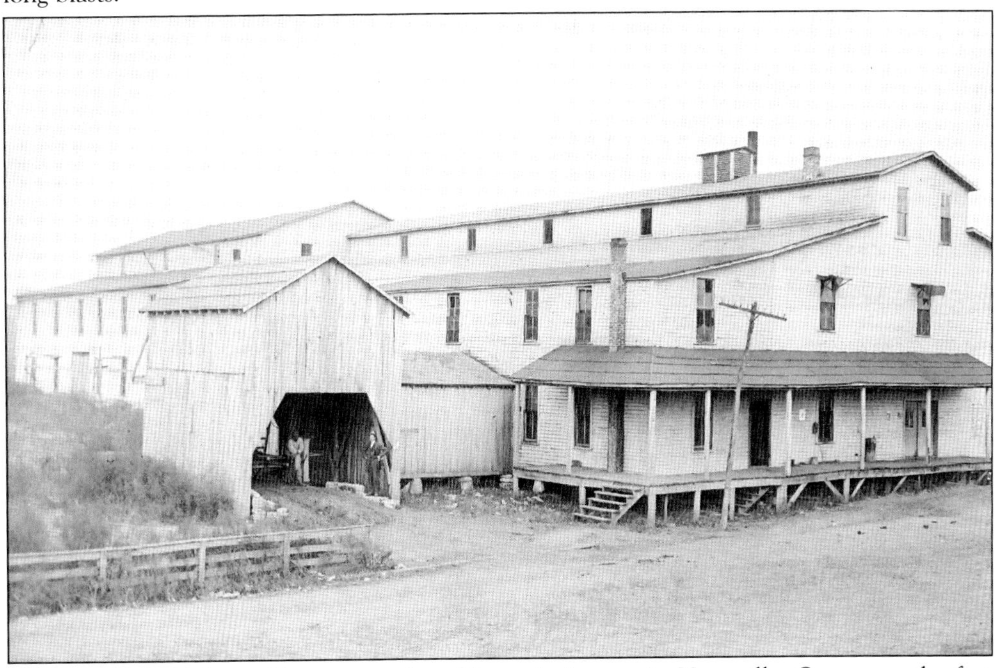

The R.C. Own Tobacco Factory stood on Planter's Avenue in Hartsville. Owen was the first maker of twist tobacco, flavoring the tobacco with such things as honey or licorice. At one time the plant employed 200 people. It moved to Gallatin in 1931.

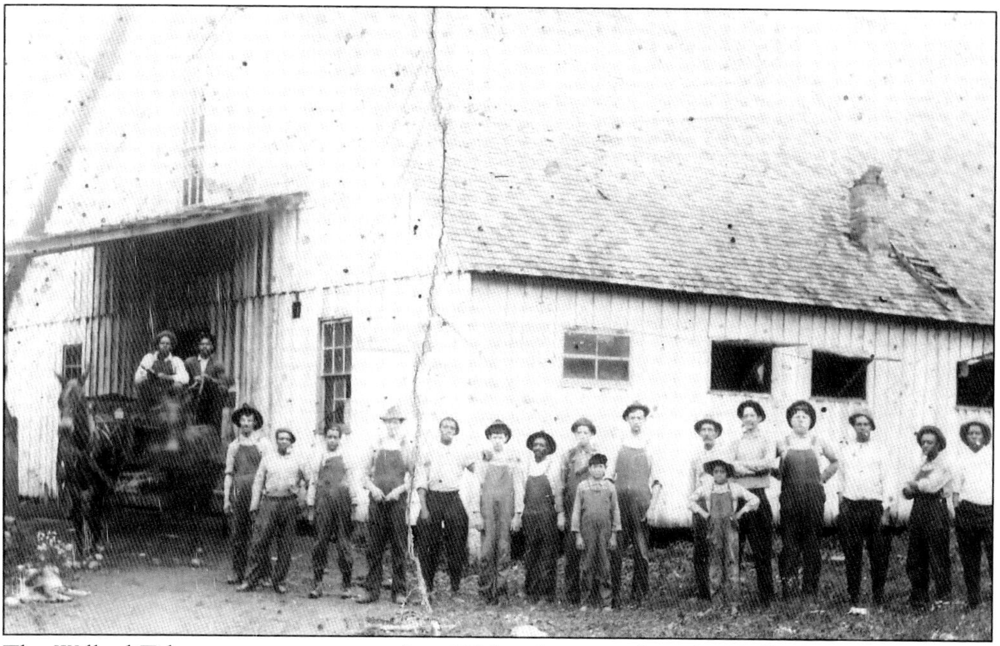

The Willard Tobacco company started in 1896 and operated in the Willard community until 1942. It produced the "Pat Burnley Twist," a nationally known twist tobacco. The building shown is no longer standing and this photograph of the once-prosperous plant is quite rare.

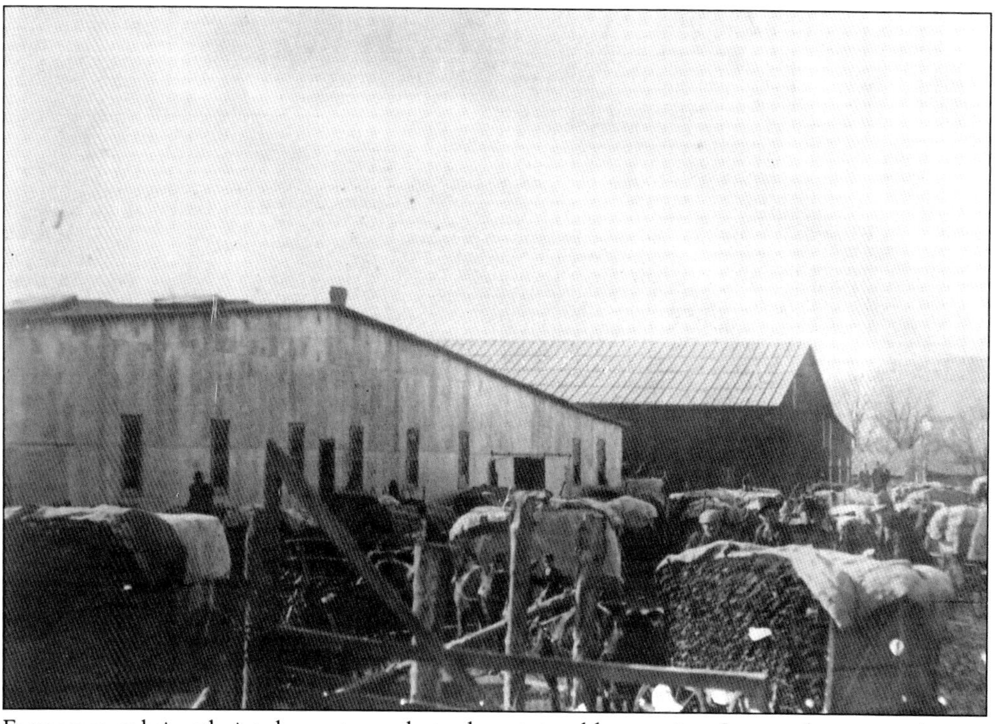

Farmers must bring their tobacco to market, where it is sold at auction. Large tobacco warehouses store the cured tobacco and provide a place for the auctioneer to work. In this old photograph, horse-drawn wagons line up for opening day at the Hartsville Tobacco Warehouse.

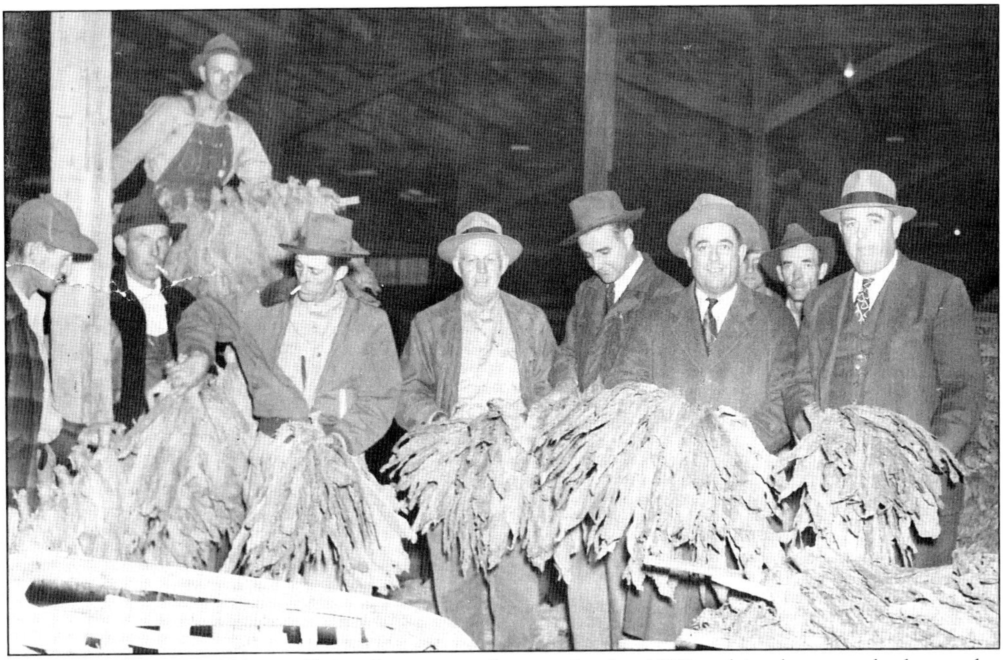

Taken inside one of Hartsville's tobacco warehouses in the 1950s, this photograph shows the tobacco being graded and stacked. Large flat baskets like the one on the left were used to hold huge stacks of tobacco. The last four men on the right are Ray Celsor, Mike Carey, C. M. Duncan, and Rom Wright.

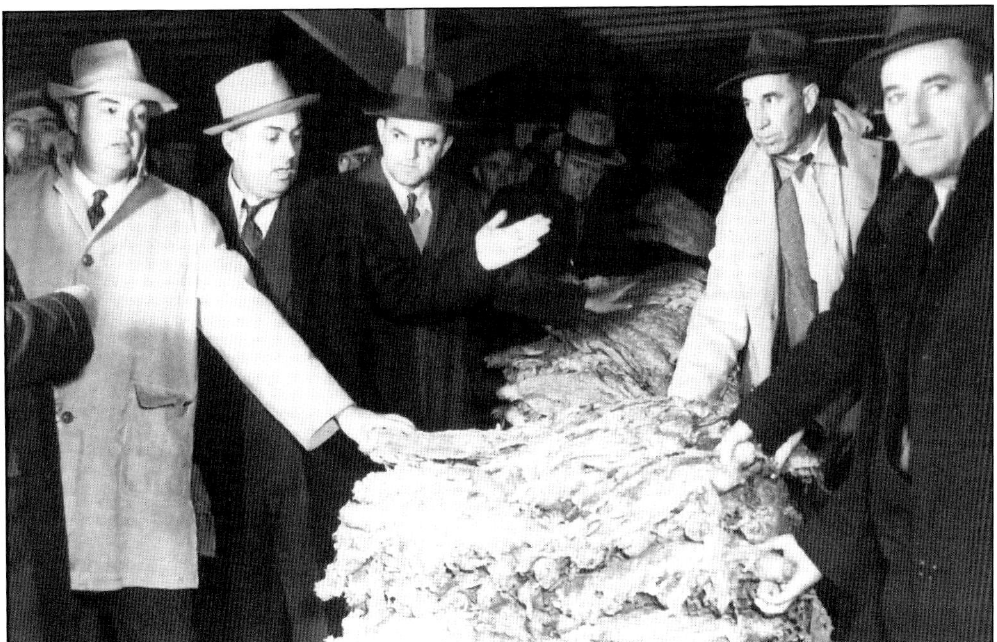

An auction is in progress in this photograph that shows buyers from several tobacco companies. From left to right are: Rom Wright (warehouse owner), an auctioneer, Bob Van Meter (a buyer for R.J. Reynolds), Joe DeBerry (a buyer for American Tobacco), and Cecil Wooten (an independent buyer).

ACKNOWLEDGMENTS

The purpose of this book is to preserve images of our county's past so that future generations will have a record of those who lived, worked, laughed, and loved before them.

The author would like to thank the Trousdale County Historical Society, whose impetus to create this book got him started. These individual members in particular worked diligently with the author to locate the old photographs and history necessary for the book: Margaret Rickman, Frances Ward Waller, Annie Farris Welch, the late Webb Ross, Walter Buckingham, Katherine McMurtry, and Janice Kyle Bassett. In addition, the hard work of Chamber of Commerce Executive Secretary Eleanor Ford was of crucial help. A special thanks goes to Lynn Hogin Oliver, my wife, for her help organizing and typing the copy. Many others took time to search attics, dresser drawers, and old trunks for precious photographs. Their help is appreciated.

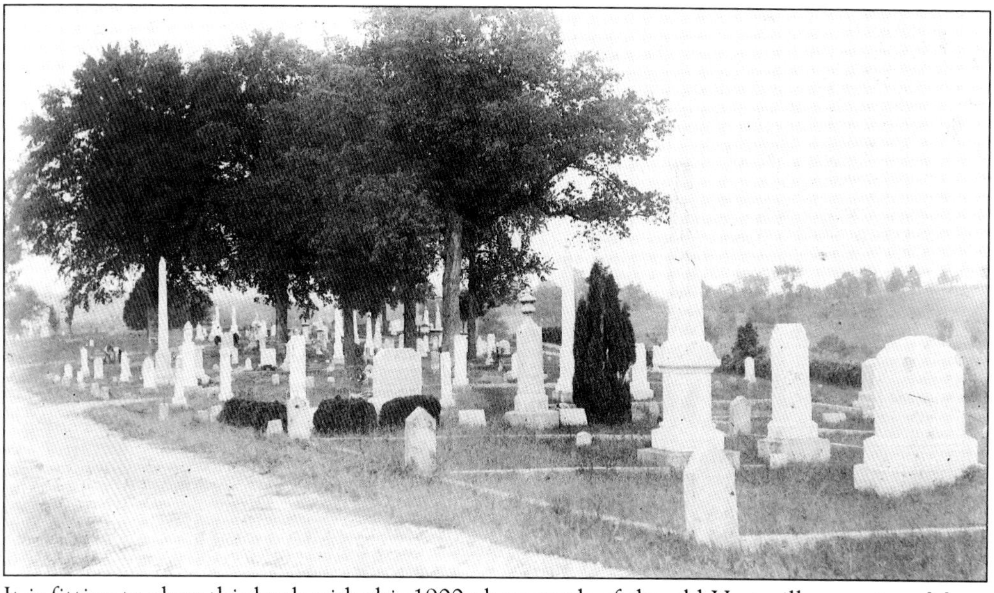

It is fitting to close this book with this 1900 photograph of the old Hartsville cemetery. Many of the people in this book are buried here. It is the final resting place of pioneers, farmers, and businessmen—the great and the small. Recently efforts have been made to repair damaged stones and to provide for perpetual care. Perhaps it, like Hartsville and Trousdale County, can look forward to another two hundred years.